A Fan's Guide to
WORLD CRICKET

ACKNOWLEDGEMENTS

Many thanks to everyone who has helped with information on this book, including… Matt Arnold at Glamorgan CCC, Rabib Imam of the Bangladesh Cricket Board, Dhiraj Jogani at Gujarat Cricket Association, Marvine D'Souza at the Board of Control for Cricket in India, Megan Dixon at Eden Park, Valerie Sisson at AMI Stadium, Keith Parker and Alayne Duthie at Seddon Park, Tracy Armstrong at Nashua Titans, Bev Weimann at Border Cricket Board, Ismail Minty at Senwes Park, Lindsay Stephen at Axxess DSL St George's, Natasha Stewart at the Bidwest Wanderers, Grace Modiselle at the South African Cricket Board, Jerome Chanmugam at the Tamil Union Cricket and Athletic Club, Saroja De Silva from www.islandcricket.lk, Derrick Nicholas at the West Indies Cricket Board, Bryan Calixte at Beausejour Cricket Ground, Jeffrey Murimbechi at Zimbabwe Cricket, Roland Toppin at the Barbados Cricket Association, Fiona Holmes at Bermuda Cricket Board, Samir Inamda on Kenyan cricket, Laurie Peters at Cricket Namibia, Dharmichand Mulewa at the Singapore Cricket Association, Naoki Alex Miyaji at the Japan Cricket Association, Stanley Perlman at the Israel Cricket Association, Ted Robinson, plus the following who gave information on the city guides… Trevor Clarke, Nicky Clarke (Sydney), Samantha Wilson (Brisbane), Grace Pundyk (Hobart), William Wood (Melbourne, Perth), Funky Punky (London), Lee White (Nottingham), Mike Bayliss, Annie Bayliss (Manchester), Mikey Leung, co-author of Bangladesh: the Bradt Travel Guide (Dhaka, Chittagong), Mahreen Ferdous (Dhaka), Adam Glover (Auckland, Wellington), Salim Karim (Karachi), Alexander Grosskord (Lahore), Ali Gulfaraz (Pakistan), Heather Carswell (Johannesburg, Pretoria), Shlomi Podgaetz (Johannesburg), Dustin Mills (Port Elizabeth), Lalin Jinasena (Sri Lanka), Heather Brand (Harare), Bhavesh Patel (Zimbabwe).

PICTURE CREDITS

Pg 8: Denise Hunter. Pg 9: Hai Linh Truong. Pg 10: Andrea Schaffer. Pg 11: Bruce Conolly, Adam JWC (1), Winterdove (2), Nev Stokes (3). Pg 12: Rae Allen. Pg 13 Paddynapper/Wikimedia (top), Robert Gyopos. Pg 14: Alan Levine. Pg 15: Syed Abdul Khaliq, Julius Rickett (1), Michael Johnson (2), Rennet Stowe (3). Pg 16: Wikimedia. Pg 17: Richard Woods (top and middle), Wikimedia. Pg 18: Endre Krossbakken. Pg 19: Alexander Rist, www.thenormanby.com.au (1), Allan Henderson (2), M Maddo (3). Pg 20: Wikimedia. Pg 21: Wikimedia (top), Wikimedia. Pg 22: Paddy Briggs (top), Wikimedia, Peter Whyte (1), Charlie McGregor(2), Jacob Kaplan Moss (3). Pg 23: Picasa 2.0. Pg 24: Wikimedia. Pg 25: Mandy Olszewski, Spearmint Rhino (1) Crown (2) Visual Density (3). Pg 26: Wikimedia. Pg 27: Chris Brown (top), Victor Iglesias (3). Pg 28: Tom Jackson. Pg 29: Vaughan James, Jeremiah Stuppy (1), Stewart Butterfield (2), Pascal Subtil (3). Pg 30: Wikimedia. Pg 31: Wikimedia (top), Summerly Noon. Pg 33: Wonderlane. Pg 34: Ashiful Haque. Pg 35: Denise Oldwhich, Wonderlane (1), Golam Kamal (2), Sharon Pruitt (3). Pg 36: M Tawsif Salam. Pg 37: Abir Anwar (top), US Geological Service. Pg 38: Nayeem Ayar (top), Wikimedia, Vivek Patankar (1), Azim Al Jabber (2), jaBinsi (3). Pg 39: Rayudu NVS. Pg 40: Wikimedia. Pg 41: Anthony Kelly. Pg 42: Stephen D Gibson. Pg 43: Lorenzo G, 10th Way (1), Amut Khan (2), Paul Duffett (3). Pg 44: Peter Meade. Pg 45: Paddy Briggs (top). Pg 46: Wikimedia. Pg 47: Wikimedia (top), Chris Chidsey. Pg 48: Stephen D Gibson. Pg 49: Stephen D Gibson, Mike Warren (1), Cadbury (2), Rolf van der Zwart (3). Pg 50: Pete Gates. Pg 51: Wikimedia (top), Ukexpat. Pg 52: Andrew Hazard (top), Andrew Hazard, Gordon Plant (1), Peter Morgan (2), Pete Birkinshaw (3). Pg 53: Alan Green. Pg 54: Graham Soult (top), GatoFrito, Laszlo Ilyes (1), Freephoto.com (2), Philip Edwards (3). Pg 55: Wikimedia. Pg 56: Fast Eddie 42. Pg 57: Paul Stevenson, Alpha (1), Cameron Cassan (2), Pinguino X (3). Pg 58: Oliver Brown. Pg 59: cricinfo.com (top), Amir Darafsheh. Pg 60: George M. Groutas. Pg 61: Jonathan Gill. Pg 62: Wikimedia. Pg 63: Cameron Spencer (top), Gustavo Buesto Padgett. Pg 64: Stephen D Gibson, Paul Gwyther (1), Eirik Refsdal (2), Comedy Store (3). Pg 65: Shining Darkness, Gabor Rozsa (1), David Lally (2), Henry Dodds (3). Pg 66: Craig Cameron. Pg 67: C Mitchell (top), Andy Gilmour. Pg 68: Matt Dawson. Pg 69: Sam Exeeson. Pg 70: Christopher Macsurak. Pg 71: Christian Schmidt,

Mike Matthews (1), Tom Thai (2), Christian Haugen (3). Pg 72: Wikimedia. Pg 73: Lensbug Chandru (top), Mohammad Jobaed Adnan. Pg 74: Emmanuel Dyan (top), Gloria Henderson , Wikimedia (1) Rolf2 (2), Gökçe (3). Pg 75: Hashir Milhan. Pg 76: Mélanie Molitor. Pg 77: Rajaram R, Wikimedia (1), Annie Mole (2), Wikimedia (3). Pg 78: Wikimedia. Pg 79: Wikimedia (top), Wikimedia. Pg 80: McKay Savage. Pg 81: Asif Akbar, Wikimedia (1), Michael Whays (2), Balamurugan Natarajan (3). Pg 82: Ian Tomlin. Pg 83: Wikimedia (top), www.a-middletonphotography.com (1). Pg 84: International Rice Research Institute (top), IRRI Images, Rita Mezzela (1), Hajime Nakano (2), Raveesh Vyas (3). Pg 85: Flying Cloud. Pg 86: Prakhar Amba (top), Meknits, Jeff Turner (1), Rob Lerner (2), Shiny Things (3). Pg 87: Faizhaider. Pg 88: McKay Savage. Pg 89: freerangestock. com, Roshan Rao (1), Lin Kristensen (2), Paul Kehrer (3). Pg 90: Hector Wright. Pg 91: Blnguyen (top), Hashir Milhan. Pg 92: freerangestock.com (top), Eduardo Guiot, GB Pandey (1), Iridhar Appaji Nag (2), Varun Bajar (3). Pg 93: Private Musings. Pg 94: Vyacheslav Argenberg. Pg 95: Meanest Indian, Chris Radzinski (1), Mikko Koponen (2), Meena Kadri (3). Pg 96: Wikimedia. Pg 97: B. Sandman (top), Blnguyen. Pg 98: Miles Holden. Pg 99: Picasa 2.6. Pg 100: Phillip Capper. Pg 101: Sefton Billington, Wikimedia (1), Khirol (2), Wikimedia (3). Pg 102: Wikimedia. Pg 103: Paul Burgess (top) Ben Oxbridge. Pg 104: Hsichen Hsieh. Pg 105: Margaret Young, Steve (1), Lesley duPont (2), Mark Carter (3). Pg 106: Sam Holliday. Pg 107: Yellow Monkey/Blnguyen (top), William Warby. Pg 108: Phillip Capper. Pg 109: Guidonz', Claudio Gennari (1), Conor Ogle (2), Corey Leopold (3). Pg 110: Keith Page. Pg 111: Andrew Lynch (top), Sam Photos8. Pg 112: Benjamin Earwicker (top), Benjamin Earwicker, Morgan (1), Phillie Casablanca (2), Ville Miettinen (3). Pg 113: James Dignan. Pg 114: Wikimedia (top), Wikimedia, "Justaddlight" (1), Basil Black (2), Sara K (3). Pg 115: Kieran Connellan. Pg 116: Sam Romilly. Pg 117: Colin Rose, Robyn Gallagher (1), Cianc (2), Josep M Rosell (3). Pg 118: Andrew Lynch. Pg 119: Paul Burgess (top), Graskopf. Pg 120: Wikimedia. Pg 121: Tayyab Mir. Pg 122: Kashif Mardani (top), Tayyab Nisar, Mir Muhammad Adnan Asim (1), Umair Mohsin (2), Marc Levin (3). Pg 123: Wikimedia. Pg 124: Atif Gulzar, Atif Gulzar, Besal (1), BrandontheMandon (2), Paolo Camera (3). Pg 125: 'The Junes'. Pg 126: David Dennis (top), Atif Gulzar, Miriam Kato (1), Kash If (2),

Mdid (3). Pg 127: Ben Luck. Pg 128: Lanz Von Hörsten/ SA Tourism. Pg 129: RogerT. Pg 130: Mark Skinner/SA Tourism. Pg 131: Beach Babez, Irene (1), Damien du Toit (2), Chris Willis (3). Pg 132: Wikimedia. Pg 133: Brent Good (top), Wikimedia. Pg 134: SA Tourism (top), Hein Von Hörsten/SATourism, Kevin King (1), Greenacre (2), Javier Lastras (3). Pg 135: Yellow Monkey/Blnguyen. Pg 136: SA Tourism (top), James Lourens, Brian Snelson (1), William Warby (2), Alberto Botton (3). Pg 137: Deon Maritz. Pg 138: Roger De la Harpe/SA Tourism. Pg 139: Media Club SA, Charles Edwin Fripp (1), Vividy (2), David Berkowitz (3). Pg 140: Deon Maritz. Pg 141: Stephen vd Merwe (top), Cedric Thompson. Pg 142: SahamJ (top), SA Tourism, Todd Huffman (1), NOAA (2), Wildebeest (3). Pg 143: Wikimedia. Pg 144: Chris Kirchhoff. Pg 145: Graeme Williams, Collin J (1), Cradle of Humankind (2), Robin (3). Pg 146: Mathew James. Pg 147: Yellow Monkey/Blnguyen (top), Gwashi. Pg 148: Rodger Bosch (top) Chris Kirchhoff, Steven Depolo (1), Greg Dunham (2), Linda Tanner (3). Pg 149: Wikimedia. Pg 150: MediaClubSA (top), Mary Alexander/ MediaClubSouthAfrica.com, Parry Bedi (1), Kevin McGee (2), Wikimedia (3). Pg 151: Yellow Monkey/Blnguyen. Pg 152: Rhythmic Diaspora Photography. Pg 153: Hash Milhan. Pg 154: Rhythmic Diaspora Photography. Pg 155: Graham and Sheila, Erich Ferdinand (1), Anne Oeldorfhirsch (2), Rada Giraya (3). Pg 156: Prem Halese. Pg 157: Hash Milhan (top), Alex Butler. Pg 158: Wikimedia. Pg 159: Tony Patterson. Pg 160: Augapfel/ Christopher. Pg 161: Rhythmic Diaspora Photography, 3Neus (1), Indi Samarajiva (2), Philippe Guglielmetti (3). Pg 162: Hash Milhan. Pg 163: Hash Milhan (top), Nicolas Pioch. Pg 164: Wikimedia (top), Himanga Mettananda, Chispita666/Lu (1), 3Neus (2), Diganta Talukdar (3). Pg 165: Tony Patterson. Pg 166: Roy Thomas Pg 167: Ray Bodden. Pg 168: Sigfus Sigmundsson. Pg 169: AntiguaBarbudaEvents, Ryan Kozie (1), Caitlin Regan (2), Greg Tee (3). Pg 170: The Junes'. Pg 171: Wikimedia. Pg 172: Mark Samuel. Pg 173: Alan Green, Gemteck 1 (1), Ben Ramirez (2), Wikimedia (3). Pg 174: Gareth George. Pg 175: Tomash Devenishek (top), Chris Chidsey. Pg 176: Peter D. Pg 177: Alex Barth, Soren Riise (1), George Mackenzie (2), Wikimedia (3). Pg 178: Graham Morris. Pg 179: BrooksLaTouche (top), www. kaieteurnewsonline.com. Pg 180: SunCat (top), Gailf548, Lauren (1), Peggy Reimchen (2), Rayda (3). Pg 181: Wikimedia. Pg 182: Ben Sutherland. Pg 183: Iri,

Wikimedia (1), Roger Barker (2), Hajime Nakano (3). Pg 184: © BrooksLaTouche. Pg 185: Jamaica Tourist Board (top), Sensormatic. Pg 186: Michael Gleave (top), Martin Versavsky, Curtis James (1), Hulivili (2), Francois Schnell (3). Pg 187: Brooks LaTouche. Pg 188: Simon (top), Jeremy Hetzel, Jeremy Hetzel (1), Jeremy Hetzel (2), Wikimedia (3). Pg 189: BrooksLaTouche. Pg 190: Jason Pratt (top), Lyn Gateley, Wikimedia (1), Wikimedia (2), Ctsnow (3). Pg 191: BrooksLaTouche. Pg 192: Bill Wood. Pg 193: Roza S, James Colin (1), Yun Huang Yong (2), Glenn Harper (3). Pg 194: BrooksLaTouche. Pg 195: Credence Williams (top), Goleo. Pg 196: Andreas Kollegger. Pg 197: Gary Bembridge. Pg 198: Ctsnow (top), Erich Ferdinand, Stephen Davies (1), Jessica Spengler (2), Adam Selwood (3). Pg 199: Rymaid. Pg 200: Whatleydude (top), Ctsnow, Cardamom (1), John Ramsy (2), Ctsnow (3). Pg 201: Wikimedia. Pg 202: Martin Hunter. Pg 203: Roger Shaddock. Pg 204: Rory Deegan. Pg 205: Gallo Images. Pg 206: William Wilson. Pg 207: Wikimedia.

A Fan's Guide to
WORLD CRICKET

by DANIEL FORD and ADAM HATHAWAY

NEW
HOLLAND

First published in 2010 by
New Holland Publishers (UK) Ltd
London • Cape Town • Sydney • Auckland
www.newhollandpublishers.com

Garfield House	80 McKenzie Street	Unit 1, 66 Gibbes Street,	218 Lake Road
86–88 Edgware Road	Cape Town 8001	Chatswood	Northcote
London W2 2EA	South Africa	NSW 2067	Auckland
United Kingdom		Australia	New Zealand

A catalogue record for this book is available from the British Library.

ISBN 978-1-84773-709-0

This book has been produced for New Holland Publishers by
SchreiberFord Publications Ltd
London • Cape Town

Project Manager: Daniel Ford
Art Director and Photo Editor: Grant Schreiber
Senior Editor: Louise Coe
Production: Marion Storz
Publishing Director: Rosemary Wilkinson

2 4 6 8 10 9 7 5 3 1

Reproduction by PDQ Digital Media Solutions Ltd, UK
Printed and bound by Tien Wah Press (Pte) Ltd, Singapore

The author and publishers have made every effort to ensure that all information given in this book is accurate, but they cannot accept liability for any
resulting injury or loss or damage to either property or person, whether direct or consequential and howsoever arising.

INTRODUCTION

For many years I spent the first few days of the New Year at Newlands in Cape Town. My friend Richard would book a block of tickets in the Railway Stand for the year's first Test match (whoever was playing) and we'd simply rustle up a few friends, sit in the sun, drink beer and talk cricket (among various other topics). It was a great place to meet up with friends from Johannesburg and Pretoria who'd be on holiday by the sea, or from England and Australia who'd be over catching South Africa's summer. There was never any need to organise a meeting, we'd simply bump into each other, whether it was on the walkway behind the seats as we sought shelter from the sun, or on the grass as we joined in the Mexican Wave, or the Members' Bar once a friend had signed us in. Oh look there's Geoffrey Boycott and Jonathan Agnew taking a break from their media duties. That's also one of the great things about cricket: the characters of the game often mingle at ease with the crowds and ex-players are always taking a stroll round the ground chatting to the spectators. My friend (he of the ticket booking) was tossing a ball up to his three-year-old son behind the seats at one Test match when West Indian fast bowler Ian Bishop strolled past

"Can you bowl at my son Bish?"

"Sure. You mean the little fella?"

"He's the one. He's too small to know what's going on but one day I'll tell him he faced a West Indian fast bowler."

The event even attracted a small crowd.

Great cricket venues and great cricket matches bring people together from all over the world. Cricket, perhaps of most sports, lends itself to quality travel. Other sporting fans travel, of course, but theirs is often a flying visit: fly in, see the event, fly out. Nothing wrong with that, but cricket fans do travel at their own pace, as you'd imagine from people who like a sport that allocates a full five days to find a winner of a contest. Cricket fans rarely travel to watch one match. For us, a trip is for weeks, sometimes even months, as we tour a country following our team, or simply enjoy good cricket in welcoming surroundings. Tales abound of people who have packed in their jobs to follow a Test tour around the balmy islands of the Caribbean, the historic regions of India, vibrant Australia, or welcoming South Africa – all wonderful trips that have been planned and dreamed about for years.

This book is for cricket fans who want to stop dreaming and start watching cricket around the world. So welcome to your guide to the ten major cricketing nations (plus details of many more should you want to try something a bit different), your snapshot to 55 cities that host international cricket (you'll need to know what to do when the cricketing day is over) and the rundown on 59 grounds that host the big events.

All that remains now is to read away, select your tour of choice, have a word with the boss about a long break, buy your ticket, and enjoy the cricket… Who knows, you might even bump into a West Indian fast bowler who'll test your batting skills.

Daniel Ford

Please note: Statistics correct to January 2010 for major cricket nations and to Dec 2009 for minor nations.

CONTENTS

ENGLAND & WALES
- Lord's   44
- The Oval   46
- Edgbaston   50
- Sophia Gardens   53
- The Riverside   55
- Headingley   58
- Old Trafford   62
- Trent Bridge   66

PAKISTAN
- National Stadium   123
- Gaddafi Stadium   125
- Iqbal Stadium   127

INDIA
- Kotla   72
- Sardar Patel Stadium   75
- M Chinnaswamy
Stadium   78
- MA Chidambaram
Stadium   82
- Barabati Stadium   85
- Green Park Stadium   87
- Eden Gardens   90
- Mohali Stadium   93
- Wankhede Stadium   96

NEW ZEALAND
- Basin Reserve   102
- Eden Park   106
- Lancaster Park   110
- University Oval   113
- Seddon Park   115
- McLean Park   118

ZIMBABWE
- Harare Sports Club   199
- Queen's Sports Club   201

BANGLADESH
- Sher-e-Bangla   36
- Zohur Ahmed
Chowdhury Stadium   39

SOUTH AFRICA
- Newlands   132
- Springbok Park   135
- Centurion Park   137
- Kingsmead   140
- Buffalo Park   143
- The Wanderers   146
- St George's Park   149
- North West Stadium   151

SRI LANKA
- R Premadasa Stadium   156
- Sinhalese Sports Club   158
- P Saravanamuttu
Stadium   159
- Galle International
Stadium   162
- Asgiriya Stadium   165

AUSTRALIA
- Sydney Cricket Ground   12
- Adelaide Oval   16
- The Gabba   20
- Bellerive Oval   23
- Melbourne Cricket
Ground   26
- The WACA   30

AUSTRALIA

<table>
<tr><td>

THE

3

MINUTE
GUIDE

</td><td>

</td><td>

Capital: *Canberra.* **Language:** *English.* **Beers:** *Tooheys (New South Wales), XXXX (Queensland), Swan (Western Australia), Victoria Bitter (Victoria).* **Food:** *Barbecues, Chiko roll, meat pie, Vegemite on toast.* **National Anthem:** *Advance Australia Fair.* **Population:** *22 million.* **Time zones:** *GMT +10 (Sydney, Melbourne, Brisbane, Hobart), GMT +9.30 (Adelaide), GMT +8 (Perth).* **Emergency number:** *000.* **Did you know?** *The Super Pit, Australia's biggest open cut gold mine is 3.5 km (2 miles) long, 1.5 km (1 mile) wide and 360 metres deep.* **Cricket body:** *60 Jolimont Street, Jolimont, Victoria, 3002, Australia. Tel: +61 3 9653 9999. E-mail: penquiries@cricket.com.au. Web: www.cricket.com.au.*

</td></tr>
</table>

Below: Keeping the sun out at a Test match in Sydney.

Home of the baggy greens

Ever since Charles Bannerman, ironically born in London, scored Test cricket's first century for Australia in the inaugural game against England in 1877, the Australians have had a big say in the world game. Eleven years earlier an Aboriginal team had toured England, playing 47 matches, and since then Australia has given cricket the Ashes, Kerry Packer's World Series, which revolutionized the game in the 1970s, Don Bradman, the master batsmen, and, more recently players such as Shane Warne, Steve Waugh and Glenn McGrath who formed the backbone of a virtually invincible team in the 1990s and early 2000s.

The Australians led the world rankings, from the day they were first published in 2001, until 2007 when South Africa went top. But their sides have been in six World Cup finals, winning four, in 1987, 1999, 2003 and 2007 and they won consecutive ICC Champions Trophy titles in 2006 and 2009.

Bradman, who died aged 92 in 2001, is the world's greatest batsman. Born in Cootamundra, New South Wales, he averaged 99.94 in Test cricket, and would have made that 100 if he had not been out for a duck in his final innings.

Warne is largely seen as the man who rescued leg spin by making it fashionable when it looked like it would die out altogether. He bowled 'the ball of the century' at Manchester in 1993, when he dismissed England's Mike Gatting with a huge leg-break. The Australian's famous baggy green caps are a source of great national pride.

Above: The world-famous Sydney Opera House.

TEST RECORD

Versus	First Test	Matches	Won	Lost	Drawn
Bangladesh	Jul 2003	4	4	0	0
England	Mar 1887	321	132	99	90
India*	Nov 1947	76	34	18	23
New Zealand	Mar 1946	48	24	7	17
Pakistan	Oct 1956	55	27	11	17
South Africa	Oct 1902	83	47	18	18
Sri Lanka	Apr 1983	20	13	1	6
West Indies*	Dec 1930	108	52	32	23
Zimbabwe	Oct 1999	3	3	0	0
ICC World XI	Oct 2005	1	1	0	0

* Includes one tied match v India (1986) and one tied match v West Indies (1960)
Most runs: RT Ponting (1995-) 11,859 runs, 142 Tests, average 55.68
Most wickets: SK Warne (1992-2007) 708 wickets, 145 Tests, average 25.42
Most catches: AC Gilchrist (1999-2008) 379 catches, 96 Tests

WORLD CUP RECORD

Year	Venue	Finished
1975	England	Runners-up
1979	England	Pool
1983	England	Pool
1987	India and Pakistan	Winners
1992	Australia and N Zealand	5th
1996	Ind, Pak and S Lanka	Runners-up
1999	England	Winners
2003	South Africa	Winners
2007	West Indies	Winners

Most ODI runs: RT Ponting (1995-) 12,311 runs, 330 matches, average 43.20
Most ODI wickets: GD McGrath (1993-2007) 381 wickets, 250 matches, average 22.02
Most ODI catches: AC Gilchrist (1996-2008) 417 catches, 287 matches

SYDNEY

Above: Surfers check out the waves at Sydney's legendary Bondi Beach.

The city of plenty

Sydney is one of the great modern cities in the world with a reputation for energy and beauty. Situated on the southeast coast of the country, it is the largest city in Australia with a population of about 4.5 million, and a hub for tourism, commerce and entertainment. The waterside central business district, dominated by the iconic Sydney Opera House and Harbour Bridge is one of the great urban backdrops.

The city is also famed for its many beaches – Bondi and Manly are well-known names among many – plus its many parks, rivers and attractive points jutting out into the inlet from the Tasman Sea on which the city is built.

Add to this a climate of warm summers and cool winters, an energetic multi-cultural population, plus a vibrant cultural and nightlife scene, and it is easy to see why Sydney is consistently ranked as one of the most livable cities according to various economic indicators. Head to the vibrant Rocks area for old pubs, tucked-away boutique shops and the weekend night market.

Like in all Australian cities, sport is integral to life and Sydney has hosted the 1938 Empire Games, the 2000 Olympic Games and the 2003 Rugby World Cup. It is home to top-level sides in various sports such as the NSW Waratahs (rugby union), Sydney Swans (Australian Rules), Sydney FC (football). The NSW Blues compete in cricket's Sheffield Shield. The city hosted the 1992 Cricket World Cup and will also host the 2015 competition.

Sydney Cricket Ground is situated about 3 km (2 miles) south of the central city area towards Centennial Park, while the ANZ Stadium, built for the Olympics in 2000 but sometimes used for cricket, is 16 km (10 miles) to the west.

3 THINGS YOU MUST DO...

1 ANZ STADIUM
Built to host the 2000 Olympic Games (Edwin Flack Avenue, Sydney Olympic Park, tel: + 61 2 8765 2000). When: weekdays 11.00, 12.30, 14.00, 15.30, weekends 11.00, 13.00, 15.00. Price: $28.50 adults, $18.50 concessions. To get there: trains to Sydney Olympic Park Station, buses 525, 401/404.

2 ROYAL RANDWICK
No-one enjoys a bet more than the Australians. Visit The Royal Randwick (Alison Road, Randwick, tel: +61 2 9663 8400) for horse racing action. When: race days usually Wed and Sat. Price: weekdays sometimes free, otherwise $15. To get there: bus from Central Station to Royal Randwick Racecourse.

3 MONORAIL
See the city as the monorail (tel: +61 2 8584 5288) winds through Chinatown, the Spanish Quarter and Darling Harbour. When: every three to five mins from Mon–Sat 07.00–22.00, Sun 08.00–22.00. Price: $4.90 per trip. To get there: Darling Park is a good place to start and finish your loop.

Above: Sydney Harbour Bridge.

WEATHER	LOW (°C)	HIGH (°C)	RAIN (MM)	SUNSET
January	18	26	95	20.09
February	18	26	104	20.01
March	18	24	129	19.36
April	14	22	135	18.53
May	12	18	128	17.17
June	9	17	122	16.56
July	8	16	122	16.59
August	9	17	79	17.20
September	11	20	77	17.37
October	12	22	75	17.57
November	16	23	79	19.22
December	17	25	79	19.50

SYDNEY CRICKET GROUND

Where heroes say goodbye

The Sydney Cricket Ground, known as the Garrison Ground until 1877, is one of the most famous arenas in world cricket. Situated 4 km (2.5 miles) from the city centre, the stadium opened in 1810 and cricket was first recorded as being played there in 1854.

It staged its first Test match in 1882, when England were the visitors and Australia won by five wickets. From George Lohmann's eight-wicket haul in 1887 to Brian Lara's brilliant 277 for the West Indies in 1993 and Darren Gough's hat-trick for England in 1998 the stadium has seen some of cricket's most historic feats. In 2006 Ricky Ponting made history at the ground by scoring two centuries in his 100th Test match, against South Africa and became the highest run scorer at the SCG in the process. Don Bradman made his mark on the ground when he scored 452 not out for New South Wales against Queensland in 1930, the highest score in Australian first class cricket.

Many of the great feats at the ground are commemorated in the museum which also features friendly 'ghosts' of past cricketing stars and visitors can take tours of the ground on non-match days and explore the dressing rooms and pavilion (www.scgt.nsw.gov.au).

Because the Sydney Test match is traditionally the last of the series it is often the scene of emotional farewells to retiring players. In recent times Mark Taylor, Steve Waugh, Shane Warne, Glenn McGrath and Justin Langer have all played their final Tests at the ground.

After a hot day in the sun many spectators drift off over the park to the nearby Captain Cook Hotel to talk through the day's play over a couple of cold beers.

The ground has also staged rugby league, rugby union, tennis, concerts and in 2009 was the venue for Sound Relief, a concert featuring Olivia Newton-John and Barry Gibb to raise money for victims of the Victorian bushfires and Queensland floods.

Below: *Two of the world's leading one-day players go head to head – Muttiah Muralitharan bowls to Adam Gilchrist.*

MATTER OF FACT

Ground: Sydney Cricket Ground
Capacity: 44,002
Located: Moore Park, Sydney, Australia
Address: Moore Park Road, Paddington, NSW 2021
Telephone: +61 2 9360 6601
E-mail: sales@scgt.nsw.gov.au, operations@scgt.nsw.gov.au
To get there: Central Station (train)
Stands: MA Noble, Bradman, Messenger, Victor Trumper, Bill O'Reilly, Clive Churchill, Brewongle, Members', Ladies'

PADDINGTON END

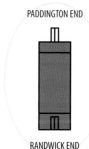

RANDWICK END

First Test: Australia v England 17-21 February 1882
First ODI: Australia v England 13 January 1979
First Twenty20: Australia v England 9 January 2007

Tests played: 98
Australia: Won 54, lost 27, drawn 17
Highest team total: 705-7 dec (Ind v Aus 2004)
Lowest team total: 42 (Aus v Eng 1888)
Highest individual total: 287 RE Foster (for Eng v Aus 1903)
Highest partnership: 405 (SG Barnes & DG Bradman, 5th wicket for Aus v Eng 1946)
Best bowling: 8-35 GA Lohmann (for Eng v Aus 1887)

ODIs played: 133
Australia: Won 73, lost 35, no result 4 (neutral games 21)
Highest team total: 368-5 (Aus v SL 2006)
Lowest team total: 63 (Ind v Aus 1981)
Highest individual total: 151 A Symonds (for Aus v SL 2006)
Highest partnership: 237 (MS Atapattu & ST Jayasuriya, 1st wicket for SL v Aus 2003 and RT Ponting & A Symonds, 5th wicket for Aus v SL 2006)
Best bowling: 5-15 GS Chappell (for Aus v Ind 1981)

Above: *Ricky Ponting, Australia's best batsman since Don Bradman.*

CRICKET NET

Stephen Harold Gascoigne, better known as 'Yabba' was an extrovert rabbit seller and regular at the SCG who shouted at the players from the old Hill in the days before the Second World War. There is a bronze statue of him in row 2 of Bay 15 of the Victor Trumper Stand.

ADELAIDE

Above: *The Art Gallery of South Australia.*

The food and wine capital

Situated on the south coast of the country, with a population of just over a million, Adelaide is Australia's food and wine capital. Central Adelaide is designed in a grid-like pattern and surrounded by parks and gardens and it is in this small area that you will find most of the best streets for food.

Take your pick from Rundle Street, to the northeast of the Victoria Square hub, where you can sit outside in one of many cafes or restaurants and watch the city pass you by, or Hutt Street, better known for its fine dining and upmarket gourmet shops.

But for varied sights and sounds it has to be Gouger Street with its range of cuisines, including Chinese, Japanese, Italian, Argentinian. It is off this street that you will also find the large red arch to Chinatown and Adelaide Central Market, both areas bustling with activity and looking to tempt you with their aromas.

South Australia is also renowned as a wine-producing region, and Adelaide is within easy striking distance of the main wine areas such as Barossa Valley, Clare Valley, Eden Valley and McClaren Vale, where you can sample till your wine heart's content.

The history of South Australian wine dates back to the early-mid 19th century and has steadily been building on its easy-drinking reputation as it seeks to establish itself as one of the leading wine-makers in the world.

Away from the table Adelaide also has great beaches, such as Henly Beach, West Beach and Glenelg Beach, plus other varied attractions such as Adelaide Botanic Gardens, the Adelaide Casino, the Migration Museum and the Art Gallery of South Australia.

The Adelaide Oval can be found in the North Adelaide area beside the Torrens River.

3 THINGS YOU MUST DO...

1 CHOCOLATE FACTORY

Haigh's Chocolates (154 Greenhill Road, Parkside, tel: +61 8 8372 7077 for bookings) offers a 20-minute tour of its factory and, of course, a tasting and a chance to shop for more... When: Mon-Sat, 11.00, 13.00, 14.00. Price: free. To get there: a five-minute taxi ride from the centre.

2 WINE

The National Wine Centre (Cnr Botanic and Hackney Rds, tel: +61 8 8303 3355) offers an exhibition, an interactive wine experience, wine-appreciation courses, food, and, of course, tastings of wine. When: daily 10.00–17.00 for tours and tastings. To get there: Adelaide Free Bus city loop (99C).

3 KOALA BEAR

See, photograph and hold a koala bear if that is your thing. Plus other Oz animals at Cleland Wildlife Park (Mount Lofty Summit Rd, Crafers, tel: +61 8 8339 2444). When: daily 09.30–17.00. Price: $16 adults, $9.50 child. To get there: a 20-minute drive, south along the South Eastern Freeway.

Above: *Adelaide is built along the River Torrens.*

WEATHER	LOW (°C)	HIGH (°C)	RAIN (MM)	SUNSET
January	16	30	20	20.33
February	18	30	18	20.25
March	15	26	25	19.54
April	12	23	46	19.11
May	10	19	71	17.35
June	8	16	76	17.12
July	7	16	68	17.17
August	9	17	66	17.34
September	9	19	52	17.56
October	11	23	43	18.18
November	13	26	28	19.45
December	15	29	25	20.14

ADELAIDE OVAL

Picture postcard ground

The Adelaide Oval is regarded as one of the most picturesque grounds in the world. Opened in 1871 it has St Peter's Cathedral, a French Gothic building similar to Notre Dame, as a back drop.

The stands include the Chappell Stand, which celebrates the achievements of the brothers Ian, Greg and Trevor and the nearest gates to the stand are named after the trio's grandfather, Vic Richardson, who was also an Australian Test player. The scoreboard is another striking feature. It was designed by the architect Kenneth Milne and started work in 1911.

The Oval has staged many sports, including Australian Rules, rugby league and hosted two games in the 2003 Rugby Union World Cup, including Australia's 142-0 win over Namibia, but it is for cricket that it is best known.

It staged its first Test in 1884 when England beat their hosts by five wickets and it was at the centre of the Bodyline storm on the infamous tour by Douglas Jardine's men in 1932-33. At Adelaide, Australia's Bill Woodfull and Bert Oldfield were hit by balls from Harold Larwood and mounted police had to be used to keep the angry crowd, of over 50,000, under control. In 1999 the Sri Lankan Muttiah Muralitharan was no-balled for throwing by umpire Ross Emerson in a one-day game against England. The Sri Lankans threatened to abandon the game but eventually played on after the Sri Lankan captain Arjuna Ranatunga had made his feelings known to Emerson.

In less controversial circumstances the late David Hookes hit a 34-ball century on the ground when playing for South Australia against Victoria in 1982 and Brian Lara surpassed Allan Border's aggregate of runs to become Test cricket's leading scorer, on his way to 226 in 2005.

The ground was subject to a major redevelopment that started in March 2009.

Below: The Adelaide Oval is a picturesque ground surrounded by parklands and situated beside the Torrens River.

MATTER OF FACT
Ground: Adelaide Oval
Capacity: 32,000
Located: North Adelaide, South Australia
Address: War Memorial Drive, North Adelaide, SA 5006
Telephone: +61 8 8300 3800
E-mail: sacareception@saca.com.au
To get there: Adelaide Station (train)
Stands: Sir Donald Bradman, Clem Hill, Chappell, Northern Mound

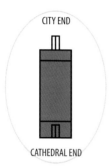

First Test: Australia v England 12-16 December 1884
First ODI: Australia v West Indies 20 December 1975
First Twenty20: N/A

Tests played: 68
Australia: Won 34, lost 16, drawn 18
Highest team total: 674 (Aus v Ind 1948)
Lowest team total: 82 (Aus v WI 1951)
Highest individual total: 299 not out DG Bradman (for Aus v SA 1932)
Highest partnership: 341 (EJ Barlow & RG Pollock, 3rd wicket for SA v Aus 1964)
Best bowling: 8-43 AE Trott (for Aus v Eng 1895)

ODIs played: 68
Australia: Won 28, lost 11, no result 1 (neutral games 28)
Highest team total: 339-4 (WI v Pak 2005)
Lowest team total: 70 (Aus v NZ 1986)
Highest individual total: 156 BC Lara (for WI v Pak 2005)
Highest partnership: 224 (DM Jones & AR Border, 3rd wicket for Aus v SL 1985)
Best bowling: 5-16 CG Rackeman (for Aus v Pak 1984)

Above: Brett Lee clocks 144 km/h in a Test v New Zealand. His best at Adelaide is 5-105 against the same side.

CRICKET NET
Don Bradman played for South Australia between 1934 and 1949. The career of the best-ever batsman is relived at the Bradman Collection Museum, which opened in 2008, at the Adelaide Oval. There is a statue of Bradman in Cresswell Gardens next to the ground.

BRISBANE

Above: *Brisbane city at night.*

Sun, sand and sport

Situated on the east coast of Australia, the two-million strong population of Brisbane has a worldwide reputation for being lovers of the sun and the sea.

And yet, the central part of the city, although close to the sea, is actually inland a few kilometers, the city development winding itself around the aptly named Brisbane River. In fact, the names best associated with sand and bronzed bodies in this area, the Gold Coast and Surfer's Paradise, are actually about 75 km (47 miles) to the south.

The Botanic Gardens, on the north bank and jutting out into the river, are centrally located with the streets off it forming the CBD. Across the river is the South Bank, a more cosmopolitan area with cafes and restaurants, featuring food from different ethnic backgrounds. Close by is the West End, an area of eclectic shops and cafes beloved by the art crowd.

The Gabba cricket ground is south of the river in the wonderfully named area of Woolloongabba. And this being Australia need we mention that this is a sport-loving city?

As well as cricket's legendary stadium, also used by the Australian Rules Football side the Brisbane Lions, there is the rugby stadium Suncorp, home to Rugby League's Brisbane Broncos, representative side Queensland Maroons, Rugby Union's Super 14 outfit Queensland Reds and football's Brisbane Roar. The city also boasts top-level national hockey, netball, and baseball teams. You certainly won't be short of your sporting fix when you've had enough of the sun and the sand.

3 THINGS YOU MUST DO...

1 NORMANBY HOTEL
Great setting, great fun. When: Sunday afternoon is the best time for drinks at the popular Normanby Hotel (1 Musgrave Road, Red Hill, tel: +61 7 3831 3353) where you could rub shoulders with players from the Lions (AFL) and the Broncos (Rugby League).

2 WEST END
This is an area thick on the ground with bars, restaurants and clubs. Try Über (100 Boundary Road, tel: +61 7 3846 6680). When: Tue–Sat, 19.00–late). To get there: South Brisbane Train Station is close or bus 190, 191.

3 THE WHEEL OF BRISBANE
Ride a gondola to a height of 60 metres (197 feet) and see a panoramic view of Brisbane. Situated in the South Bank (tel: South Bank Visitor Centre, +61 7 3867 2051). Price: $15 adult, $10 child aged 3–12. To get there: South Brisbane Train Station.

Above: Howzat!

WEATHER	LOW (°C)	HIGH (°C)	RAIN (MM)	SUNSET
January	22	30	166	18.47
February	20	29	160	18.43
March	19	28	148	18.20
April	17	27	94	17.48
May	13	23	72	17.17
June	12	21	66	17.01
July	9	20	58	17.06
August	10	22	48	17.19
September	14	25	48	17.34
October	16	27	68	17.49
November	18	28	94	18.05
December	19	29	127	18.29

THE GABBA

The modern Gabba

Established in 1895 the Brisbane Cricket Ground is better known as 'The Gabba' as it is situated in the suburb of Woolloongabba, and is a totally different ground nowadays after a comprehensive redevelopment that was started in 1993.

Gone are the old stands, the fig trees, the famous dog track and the grassy hill to be replaced by a modern-looking bowl that hosted soccer matches in the 2000 Olympics and staged a rugby union Test match against the British Lions in 2001.

The new structures may lack some of the character of their predecessors but the spectator facilities are as good as they get. The ground is also the home of the Brisbane Lions AFL team and the Queensland Bulls cricket team for whom England all-rounder Ian Botham had a spell in 1987-88.

Established in 1895 and built on swampland, the Gabba hosted its first Test in 1931, previously Brisbane Tests had been held at the city's Exhibition Ground, where Don Bradman made his debut in 1928. The switch did not affect Bradman as he made 226 in his first Test at the Gabba, against South Africa, a mark that endures as the highest Test innings at the ground.

About half an hour's walk from the centre of Brisbane, the ground was the venue for the first-ever tied Test match in history. Frank Worrell's 1960 West Indies were the visitors and with Australia chasing 233 to win they forced three run outs as the scores finished level. There was not another tie in Tests for 26 years.

In 1988, another West Indian, Courtney Walsh, became the first bowler to take a hat-trick at the ground and in 1994 Australia's Shane Warne opened the Ashes series by routing England with figures of 8-71.

For spectators there are around 50 bars and food areas in the ground, but if you take your own it has got to be in a container small enough to fit under your seat.

Below: The Gabba, where fans won't go thirsty or hungry: there are more than 50 bars and restaurants dotted around the stadium.

MATTER OF FACT

Ground: The Brisbane Cricket Ground
Capacity: 42,000
Located: Woolloongabba, Brisbane
Address: Brisbane Cricket Ground, Vulture Street, Woolloongabba, QLD 4151
Telephone: +61 7 3008 6166
E-mail: info@thegabba.org.au or reception@gabba.com.au
To get there: South Bank or Roma Street Stations (train) and shuttle bus
Stands: Western, Northern, Eastern, Southern

STANLEY STREET END

VULTURE STREET END

First Test: Australia v South Africa 27 November - 3 December 1931
First ODI: England v West Indies 23 December 1979
First Twenty20: Australia v South Africa 9 January 2006

Tests played: 52
Australia: Won 32, lost 8, drawn 11, tied 1
Highest team total: 645 (Aus v Eng 1946)
Lowest team total: 58 (Ind v Aus 1947 & Aus v Eng 1936)
Highest individual total: 226 DG Bradman (for Aus v SA 1931)
Highest partnership: 276 (DG Bradman & AL Hassett, 3rd wicket for Aus v Eng 1946)
Best bowling: 9-52 RJ Hadlee (for NZ v Aus 1985)

ODIs played: 63
Australia: Won 14, lost 13, no result 5 (neutral 31)
Highest team total: 303-4 (Ind v Aus 2004)
Lowest team total: 71 (Pak v WI 1993)
Highest individual total: 158 DI Gower (for Eng v NZ 1983)
Highest partnership: 206 (AC Gilchrist & ME Waugh, 1st wicket for Aus v WI 2001)
Best bowling: 5-25 IR Bishop (for WI v Pak 1993) & Shoaib Akhtar (for Pak v Aus 2002)

Above: Queensland-born fast bowler Mitchell Johnson.

CRICKET NET
The Gabba was not a happy place for Australian quick bowler Ian Meckiff. In 1963 against South Africa he was repeatedly called for throwing by umpire Colin Egar. Meckiff was chaired from the ground by furious fans but retired from first-class cricket the day after the match.

HOBART

A devil of a place

Although often jokingly maligned by other Australians, the intimate nature of Hobart (a population of around 215,000), the fine architecture, history (it's the second oldest city in the country dating back to 1804 after originally being established as a penal colony) and its picture-perfect location along the Derwent River, makes this a great place to visit. A number of bridges link the eastern and western banks of Hobart, the largest being the Tasman Bridge. It is this bridge you will probably cross to visit the Bellerive Oval, which sits on the east beside the river and is home to the Tasmanian Cricket Museum.

The city area is small and major city landmarks such as the Queen's Domain (where you will find the brightly coloured Eastern Rosella parrot and the Hobart Royal Botanical Gardens), Salamanca (famed for its Saturday markets) and Wrest Point Casino (the oldest casino in Australia) are all easily accessible.

Tasmania is probably best known for its famed Tasmanian Devil (now endangered) and (the extinct) Tasmanian Tiger, the mascot for the state cricket team, which are appropriately named the Tasmanian Tigers.

Above: Hobart. *Below:* A giant chess game in Franklin Square.

WEATHER	LOW (°C)	HIGH (°C)	RAIN (MM)	SUNSET
January	13	22	48	20.53
February	13	22	38	20.36
March	12	20	49	19.58
April	9	16	50	19.02
May	7	14	46	17.15
June	6	13	56	16.45
July	4	11	53	16.46
August	5	13	50	17.14
September	6	15	53	17.47
October	8	16	58	18.17
November	9	19	61	19.56
December	11	21	53	20.32

3 THINGS YOU MUST DO...

1 LARK DISTILLERY
Enjoy tours and tastings at Hobart's centrally located whisky distillery (14 Davey St, tel: +61 3 6231 9088). When: tours Mon–Sat 14.30. Price: $15.

2 PEPPERMINT BAY CRUISE
A leisurely cruise on a catamaran with great food while enjoying the sea views and local wildlife anyone? Hobart Cruise Centre (Brooke St Pier, tel: +61 3 6231 5113). When: daily. Price: from £88 for adults, $48 for under 14s, including lunch.

3 SALAMANCA PLACE
Stroll around this central area with its warehouses dating back to the whaling era of the 1830s, then enjoy a beer and a meal in one of the many cafes or restaurants for which the area in now popular. Saturday is the busy market day.

BELLERIVE OVAL

Cricket across the water

The Bellerive Oval, a five-minute walk from Bellerive Wharf on the shores of the Derwent River, houses the headquarters of Cricket Tasmania and after extensive redevelopment, which caused disquiet among some locals, is a thoroughly modern stadium although it can hold only around 16,000 spectators. Previously the foremost stadium in Tasmania was the Tasmanian Cricket Association Ground in Queens Domain.

The South Stand holds over 5,000 people but the most popular place on the ground, and the cheapest, is the Hill, where the replay screen and scoreboard are also located. There is also a cricket museum in the Members' Pavilion, that opened in 2003 and offers visitors the chance to test out their own cricket skills and showcases the history of the sport on the island, which hosted Australia's inaugural first class match in 1851.

In December 1989 Bellerive Oval became Australia's seventh Test ground, when Sri Lanka were the visitors, having hosted its first one-day international the year before. In 1999 Adam Gilchrist gave the world notice of talents when he got Australia home in a thrilling run chase against Pakistan. The wicket-keeper hit 149 not out, putting on 238 with Justin Langer, as Australia reached 369-6 to win by four wickets.

Although it is a relative newcomer on the international cricket stage the Oval staged a football match between Carlton and Bellerive back in 1884 but it was the Tasmanians' determination to secure and keep top-flight cricket at the ground that led to its modernization and subsequent promotion to the Test rota.

Below: *The Bellerive Oval. Tasmanian Ricky Ponting holds the top Test score at the ground with 209 in 2010.*

MATTER OF FACT
Ground: Bellerive Oval
Capacity: 16,200
Located: Bellerive, Hobart, Tasmania
Address: Derwent Street, Bellerive, TAS 7018
Telephone: +61 3 6211 4000
E-mail: info@crickettas.com.au
To get there: Bellerive Wharf (ferry),
Stands: Southern, North East, The Hill, Stuart Spencer

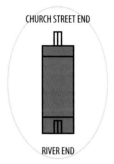

CHURCH STREET END

RIVER END

First Test: Australia v Sri Lanka 16-20 December 1989
First ODI: New Zealand v Sri Lanka 12 January 2007
First Twenty20: N/A

Tests played: 9
Australia: Won 7, lost 0, drawn 2
Highest team total: 558-8 dec (Aus v NZ 2001)
Lowest team total: 149 (WI v Aus 2005)
Highest individual total: 209 RT Ponting (for Aus v Pak 2010)
Highest partnership: 352 (RT Ponting & MJ Clarke, 4th wicket for Aus v Pak 2010)
Best bowling: 6-31 SK Warne (for Aus NZ 1993)

ODIs played: 27
Australia: Won 10, lost 3, tied 1, (neutral games 13)
Highest team total: 344-7 (Aus v Zim 2004)
Lowest team total: 120 (Aus v Pak 1997)
Highest individual total: 172 AC Gilchrist (for Aus v Zim 2004)
Highest partnership: 165 (NV Knight & ME Trescothick, 1st wicket for Eng v Aus 2003)
Best bowling: 5-42 OD Gibson (for WI v SL 1996)

MELBOURNE

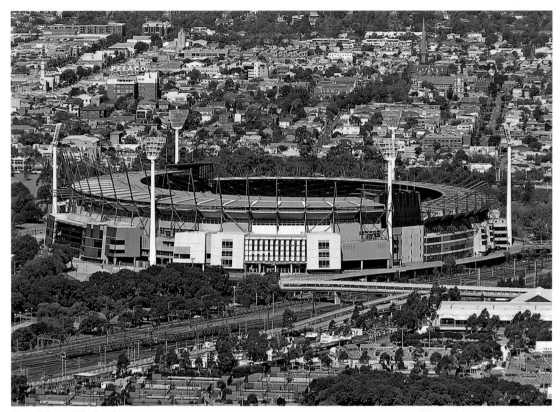

Above: *Melbourne Cricket Ground.*

Art on the Yarra

Melbourne is known as Australia's arts and cultural city. It's been the location for hundreds of films, including the first Mad Max (1979), the Baz Luhrmann-directed Strictly Ballroom (1992), the TV miniseries Salem's Lot (2004), Charlotte's Web (2006), and has a heritage stretching back to 1906 when The Story of Ned Kelly was filmed in the city, said to be the world's first feature-length film. The city also gave us Cate Blanchett, Eric Bana and Olivia Newton-John (born in England but grew up in Melbourne).

The earliest Australian television broadcast was from the city in 1929 and it has continued to play an important role in that industry in Australia. The city's station GTV-9 broadcast the moon landing in 1969 and later *Neighbours*, the soap in which Kylie Minogue started her climb to fame, was produced in the city.

Sports is also central to life in Melbourne; it was the host of the 1956 Summer Olympics and the 2006 Commonwealth Games and is considered the home of Australian Rules Football, with the rules drawn up by the Melbourne Football Club in 1859 and the bulk of the teams forming the national league from this area. The city is also an important centre for music, dance and education.

The city winds itself around the Yarra River on the south coast of the country and looks across the Bass Strait towards Tasmania, which is some 290 km (181 miles) away. The main street for nightlife is King Street, which runs from North Melbourne through the CBD and across the Yarra to the Southbank, while the St Kilda district is the area for beach life and the place to enjoy a laid-back beer or snack.

The MCG is on the north of the river in East Melbourne.

3 THINGS YOU MUST DO...

1 KING STREET

Nothing arty about King Street; this is where you will find clubs and strippers till your heart (and other body parts) are content. Try Spearmint Rhino (14 King Street, tel: +61 3 9629 2300). When: 19.00–late. Price: from free (to 20.30) to $20. Dances: $20–$100.

2 CROWN CASINO

Food, drink, dancing, shopping and gambling – all in one place (8 Whiteman Street, tel: +61 3 9292 8888). To get there: trams 96, 109, 112 to Casino Exhibition Centre or 55 to Casino East.

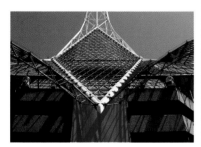

3 THE ARTS CENTRE

Art, opera, performance, exhibitions and shopping can be found at the Arts Centre (100 St Kilda Rd, tel: +61 03 9281 8350). For what's on: the artscentre.com.au. To get there: any tram (except 1) along the St Kilda Road to Arts Centre or the free Melbourne City Tourist Shuttle stops at the Arts Centre.

Above: *A mosaic sculpture along the Yarra River in Melbourne.*

WEATHER	LOW (°C)	HIGH (°C)	RAIN (MM)	SUNSET
January	13	26	50	20.45
February	13	26	49	20.35
March	13	24	56	20.00
April	11	19	58	19.14
May	8	17	53	17.35
June	6	14	53	17.09
July	6	14	49	17.11
August	6	15	48	17.33
September	9	18	58	18.00
October	9	19	66	18.24
November	11	22	58	19.54
December	12	24	58	20.26

MELBOURNE CRICKET GROUND

Where Test cricket began

Built in 1853 the massive Melbourne Cricket Ground is one of the world's finest stadiums and one of the most historic, having staged the first Test match, between Australia and England in 1877, and the first one-day international, between the same two sides in 1971. The inaugural one dayer was organized when the first three days of the third Ashes Test match were washed out and Australia won a game of 40 eight-ball overs by five wickets.

The MCG then staged the historic Centenary Test of 1977 when England were beaten by 45 runs, exactly the same result as a 100 years previously, with Dennis Lillee taking 6-26 to decimate the English in their first innings.

The stadium was the main arena for the 1956 Olympics, having been largely rebuilt for the games and Australian sprinter Betty Cuthbert christened it with three gold medals. Fifty years later it was the principal stadium as the city hosted the Commonwealth Games. In 1970, 121,696 people crammed into the ground for the VFL Grand Final between Carlton and Collingwood and in 1959, the American evangelist Billy Graham attracted 130,000 to the venue.

Outside the ground the Parade of Champions features statues of famous Australian sportsmen and women, including cricketers Dennis Lillee, Don Bradman, Bill Ponsford, athletes Cuthbert and Shirley Strickland and Australian Rules stars Ron Barassi, and Leigh Mathews. The National Sports Museum chronicles the Australian obsession with all things sporting and the Melbourne Cricket Club Museum houses a vast collection of cricketing artefacts.

Greg Baum once wrote in *The Melbourne Age*: "The MCG is a shrine, a citadel, a landmark, a totem. It is to this city what the Opera House is to Sydney, the Eiffel Tower to Paris and the Statue of Liberty is to New York; it symbolizes Melbourne to the world. It inspires reverence." It is a must-visit ground for anyone with even a passing interest in cricket.

Below: Melbourne Cricket Ground, scene of the first-ever Test match between Australia and England in 1877.

MATTER OF FACT

Ground: Melbourne Cricket Ground
Capacity: 100,000
Located: Jolimont, Melbourne, Australia
Address: Yarra Park, Jolimont, VIC 3002
Telephone: +61 3 9657 8867
E-mail communications@mcc.org.au
To get there: Jolimont or Richmond Stations (train), trams 48, 70, 75 or 246 bus
Stands: Ponsford, Southern, Olympic

MEMBERS' END

GREAT SOUTHERN STAND END

First Test: Australia v England 15-19 March 1877
First ODI: Australia v England 5 January 1971
First Twenty20: Australia v India 1 February 2008

Tests played: 102
Australia: Won 58, lost 29, drawn 15
Highest team total: 604 (Aus v Eng 1937)
Lowest team total: 36 (SA v Aus 1932)
Highest individual total: 307 RW Cowper (for Aus v Eng 1966)
Highest partnership: 346 (DG Bradman & JH Fingleton, 6th wicket for Aus v Eng 1937)
Best bowling: 9-86 Safraz Nawaz (for Pak v Aus 1979)

ODIs played: 128
Australia: Won 61, lost 41, tied 1, no result 3, (neutral games 22)
Highest team total: 344-8 (ICC World XI v ACC Asian XI 2005)
Lowest team total: 94 (Eng v Aus 1979)
Highest individual total: 173 ME Waugh (for Aus v WI 2001)
Highest partnership: 225 (AC Gilchrist & RT Ponting, 2nd wicket for Aus v Eng 2002)
Best bowling: 6-42 AB Agarkar (for Ind v Aus 2004)

Above: The maestro Shane Warne, voted one of Wisden's five cricketers of the last century.

CRICKET NET

Bay 13, in the Southern Stand of the MCG, housed some of the most raucous fans in world cricket with supporters mimicking local favourite, Merv Hughes, when he did his warm-ups and stretches. In 1999 Shane Warne came out with a helmet to placate fans throwing bottles in a one-day game.

PERTH

Above: Perth is pretty far from everywhere.

Far, far away

The capital of Western Australia is one the world's most remote cities, being more than 2,700 km (1,690 miles) away from Adelaide by road to the east and almost 4,000 km (2,500 miles) from Darwin to the north and the inland capital Canberra. Indonesia's capital Jakarta is only 3,000 km away (1,875 miles) albeit as 'the crow flies'. Thank goodness for planes then.

Yet, in many ways, the city of just around 1.5 million people can be said to be excellently located, being built around the Swan River as it winds its way to the Indian Ocean, and with Australia's Coral Coast and the legendary Outback both within close proximity. And if the residents can pull themselves away from the beautiful beaches come Ashes time they'll happily be in London drinking a beer a good few hours before Sydneysiders, thanks to their western location.

Although this laid-back city is spread out (no shortage of space here) if you don't fancy venturing far most of your entertainment needs can be found in the small area around Wellington Street, Hay Street and Barrack Street (where you will see the modern-looking Swan Bell Tower).

For shopping, King Street is well known for its range of international designer outlets and top-notch locally run boutiques, while nearby Northbridge offers a more eclectic range of shops. Northbridge also offers a good selection of restaurants and boasts the Perth Cultural Centre with its art gallery, museum and library. Other popular areas for food and drink are Subiaco a short distance to the west and Mount Lawley and Highgate to the north.

The WACA is centrally located in East Perth near to the Causeway, one of the main bridges linking the two sides of the Swan River.

3 THINGS YOU MUST DO...

1 COTTESLOE BEACH

Swim, surf, snorkel, or just relax by the Indian Ocean and take in the sights of the beach. Cottesloe Beach is one of the city's favourite sand and sea spots. To get there: a 15-minute drive southeast from the city centre on the Stirling Highway, Transperth bus to Cottesloe or train to Cottesloe Station.

2 OCEAN BEACH HOTEL

The hotel (Cnr Marine Parade and Eric St, Cottesloe, tel: +61 8 9384 2555) is the place to rub shoulders with AFL players (West Coast Eagles and Fremantle Dockers). When: Mon–Sat 10.00–midnight, Sun 10.00–22.00. To get there: a 15-minute drive southeast, bus to Cottesloe or train to Cottesloe Station.

3 FREMANTLE

Perth's port town. Head here for great architecture, markets, shops and the famed Cappuccino Strip with its many bars and cafes. To get there: trains runs regularly to Fremantle Station (30 mins). Night buses run back to Como and Bull Creek until 04.00.

Above: The modern Perth city. Who needs to be near other cities anyway?

WEATHER	LOW (°C)	HIGH (°C)	RAIN (MM)	SUNSET
January	17	29	8	19.26
February	17	29	10	19.20
March	16	27	22	18.52
April	15	24	48	18.13
May	13	22	126	17.40
June	10	19	180	17.20
July	9	17	169	17.24
August	10	19	145	17.40
September	10	19	86	18.00
October	12	20	56	18.19
November	14	24	20	18.41
December	16	27	13	19.08

THE WACA

Pitch doctored

The WACA, which lies close to the Swan River and is a pleasant walk from the centre of Perth, was opened in 1893, but Test cricket did not take place at the ground until Ray Illingworth's England drew with Australia in 1970, a game that marked Greg Chappell's international debut. Its name has punctuated the cricket history books ever since.

Australian fast bowler Merv Hughes took an unusual hat-trick at the ground in 1988 against the West Indies, his three victims being spread over two innings, three different overs and more than 24 hours. In 2000 Glenn McGrath completed a more conventional hat-trick, also against the West Indies, and passed 300 Test wickets in the process.

Three years later, Australian Matthew Hayden stuck up for the batsmen as he flayed the Zimbabwean bowlers to make 380, breaking Brian Lara's Test record of most runs in an innings, although Lara reclaimed the record shortly afterwards.

The WACA has a reputation for being a hard, fast wicket as the former England batsman David Lloyd can testify. On his Ashes debut in 1974 Lloyd had his protective box smashed by the Australian quick bowler Jeff Thomson and has used the story as part of his after-dinner speaking routine ever since.

The pitch is hard and bouncy because of the intense Western Australian heat that can get up to 40 degrees, which is only eased, for the players and fans, by the 'Fremantle Doctor' a cooling breeze which rises up in the mid-afternoon.

The museum is open on match days featuring the great names of Western Australian cricket with entrance costing just $5.

The ground has been used for Australian Rules football, rugby league and concerts but many of these activities have since moved to the larger Subiaco Oval which is 3 km (2 miles) to the west of the centre of Perth.

Below: The WACA, where the Western Australian heat ensures a hard and bouncy wicket.

MATTER OF FACT

Ground: Western Australia Cricket Association Ground
Capacity: 22,000 (24,000 with temporary stands)
Located: East Perth, Australia
Address: Nelson Crescent, East Perth, WA 6004
Telephone: +61 8 9265 7222
E-mail: reception@waca.com.au
To get there: Red CAT (bus) from Murray Street to stop 6 or Yellow CAT from Wellington Street to stop 7
Stands: Lillee Marsh, Inverarity, Prindiville

MEMBERS' END

PRINDIVILLE STAND END

First Test: Australia v England 11-16 December 1970
First ODI: India v New Zealand 9 December 1980
First Twenty20: Australia v New Zealand 11 December 2007

Tests played: 37
Australia: Won 21, lost 9, drawn 7
Highest team total: 735-6 dec (Aus v Zim 2003)
Lowest team total: 62 (Pak v Aus 1981)
Highest individual total: 380 ML Hayden (for Aus v Zim 2003)
Highest partnership: 327 (JL Langer & RT Ponting, 5th wicket for Aus v Pak 1999)
Best bowling: 8-24 GD McGrath (for Aus v Pak 2004)

ODIs played: 63
Australia: Won 18, lost 15, tied 1, (neutral 29)
Highest team total: 343-5 (Aus v NZ 2007)
Lowest team total: 91 (Aus v WI 1987)
Highest individual total: 144 not out DR Martyn (for Aus v Zim 2001)
Highest partnership: 200 (ML Hayden & RT Ponting, 2nd wicket for Aus v NZ 2007)
Best bowling: 5-15 RJ Shastri (for Ind v Aus 1991)

Above: *Marcus North, Australian middle-order batsman and spin bowler who captained Western Australia.*

CRICKET NET
Quick bowler Dennis Lillee and wicketkeeper Rodney Marsh have a stand at the WACA named after them for their exploits in the 1970s and early 1980s. The entry 'caught Marsh bowled Lillee' appeared 95 times in Test score books and, coincidentally, these sons of Western Australia both finished with 355 career Test dismissals.

BANGLADESH

Capital: *Dhaka.* **Language:** *Bengali.* **Drinks:** *Chai (sweet tea), lassi (yoghurt drink).* **Food:** *Biryani, fish and rice or fish and daal.* **National Anthem:** *Amar Shonar Bangla (My Golden Bengal).* **Population:** *162 million.* **Time zone:** *GMT +6.* **Emergency number:** *999.* **Did you know?** *Bangladesh means Land of the Bengalis.* **Cricket body:** *Sher-e-Bangla National Cricket Stadium, Mirpur, Dhaka, 1216, Bangladesh. Tel: +880 2 803 1001/2/3/4.*

Below: A colourful rickshaw has been found a nice, tight parking space.

New kids on the block

Bangladesh became the tenth Test nation when they played their first five-day match against India in 2000 at Dhaka and their elevation was a reward for the fanaticism that cricket is followed with in the country. Known as the Tigers, the national side famously beat Pakistan in the 1999 World Cup, Australia in 2005 and India in the 2007 World Cup but at Test level they struggled through their first decade.

They might be comparative newcomers to the international stage but cricket has a long history in the country, having been introduced to the region by British rulers in the 1800s. Following independence in 1971 cricket grew thanks to tours by the MCC and 40,000 people turned up to watch the tourists play in Dhaka in January 1977.

Bangladesh rose to become the best of the second-tier nations, becoming associate members of the ICC in the same year, played its first one-day international against Pakistan in 1986 and in 1997 won the ICC Trophy in Malaysia to gain entrance to the 1999 World Cup and signal another rise in the game's popularity. Also in 1999 a new first class league was established in the country with divisional teams taking part from Dhaka, Chittagong, Sylhet, Khulna, Barisal and Rajshahi.

In 2009 the Bangladeshi all-rounder Shakib Al Hasan was named the World Test Player of the Year by the British magazine, *Wisden Cricketer*, beating the likes of Mitchell Johnson, Ricky Ponting and Andrew Strauss to the title.

Above: A traditional geometric-painted boat in Dhaka.

TEST RECORD

Versus	First Test	Matches	Won	Lost	Drawn
Australia	Jul 2003	4	0	4	0
England	Oct 2003	4	0	0	0
India	Nov 2000	5	0	4	1
New Zealand	Dec 2001	8	0	7	1
Pakistan	Aug 2001	6	0	6	0
South Africa	Oct 2002	8	0	8	0
Sri Lanka	Sept 2001	12	0	12	0
West Indies	Dec 2002	6	2	3	1
Zimbabwe	Apr 2001	8	1	4	3

Most runs: Habibul Bashar (2000-) 3,026 runs, 50 matches, average 30.88
Most wickets: Mohammad Rafique (2000-08) 100 wickets, 33 matches, average 40.79
Most catches: Khaled Mashud (2000-07) 78 catches, 44 matches

WORLD CUP RECORD

Year	Venue	Finished
1975	England	Not eligible
1979	England	Not eligible
1983	England	Not eligible
1987	India and Pakistan	Not eligible
1992	Australia and N Zealand	Not eligible
1996	Ind, Pak and S Lanka	Not eligible
1999	England	Pool
2003	South Africa	Pool
2007	West Indies	7th

Most ODI runs: Mohammad Ashraful (2001-) 3,260 runs, 156 matches, average 23.97
Most ODI wickets: Mashrafe Mortaza (2001-) 103 wickets, 135 matches, average 29.81
Most ODI catches: Khaled Mashud (1995-2006) 126 matches, 91 catches

DHAKA

Above: *A driver touts for business in the City of Rickshaws.*

Rickshaws, muslin and mosques

The capital of Bangladesh is one of the largest cities in the world with a population of around 13 million in the megacity, and it is one of the most densely populated. Like many cities in developing countries it continues to attract people from other parts of the country so the growth can be expected to continue.

With so many people, just getting around the city can be an experience, so it's no surprise to hear that Dhaka is dubbed the rickshaw capital of the world – with hundreds of thousands of them taking to the streets every day. That's a lot of leg power.

The rickshaws are beautifully decorated as the pullers compete for trade and prestige – and you'll have plenty of opportunity to see their decorative work up close as you're likely to get snarled up in a rickshaw jam at some stage.

Dhaka is also famed for its two Ms – muslin and mosques. The muslin produced in the city is renowned as among the best in the world (the textile industry employs around 800,000 people). Worldwide exports continue, a trade that has a proud history from this region, dating back hundreds of years. The city is also home to many hundreds of mosques, including the national mosque Baitul Mukarrum Mosque, a large modern white building with a main prayer hall of nearly 2,500 square metres (26,900 square feet). Other well-known mosques are Satgumbad, which means seven domed and is believed to date back to the start of the 18th century, and the Sitara Mosque with its beautiful, ornate details.

Sher-e-Bangla, the 2011 Cricket World Cup opening ceremony stadium, is north of the Buriganga River in the Mirpur district.

3 THINGS YOU MUST DO...

1 RICKSHAW

The most popular vehicles to get stuck in the traffic jam that is known as Dhaka. Pick one of the brightest and most elaborately decorated rickshaws and take a ride round the city (once you get moving). Price: locals pay about Tk40 per trip but work on a rule of thumb of Tk1 per minute.

2 BAKOR KHANI

Locally loved, this is a flaky pastry about the size of a cookie, and is cooked using ghee in the tandoor oven. Eat it freshly cooked with your favourite kebab.

3 BLAZE ENTERTAINMENT LOUNGE AND BAR

If you're looking for respite from the whirlwind of Dhaka then try the chilled Blaze Bar in the Radisson Water Garden Hotel (Airport Road, tel: +880 2 875 4555). When: Sat–Thur, 06.30–00.30. Closed Fri. Big Blue Entertainment on Facebook is another way to get linked into the local party scene.

Above: Another quiet afternoon in the capital of Bangladesh.

WEATHER	LOW (°C)	HIGH (°C)	RAIN (MM)	SUNSET
January	12	25	18	17.23
February	13	28	31	17.46
March	18	34	58	18.01
April	23	36	110	19.14
May	25	34	196	19.28
June	27	33	321	19.42
July	26	32	429	19.53
August	25	31	305	19.42
September	24	31	254	19.16
October	24	32	167	18.46
November	18	28	28	17.20
December	13	26	3	17.11

SHER-E-BANGLA

The new home of Bangladeshi cricket

Otherwise known as 'The New Home of Bangladesh Cricket', the Sher-e-Bangla National Stadium became Bangladesh's sixth Test ground in 2007, when India were the visitors. Holding 47,000 spectators the ground was built in 1970, when it was known as the Mirpur Stadium but is now named after Abul Kashem Fazlul Huq, a Bengali statesman and freedom fighter from the early 20th century.

The first international match – a 50-over game between Bangladesh and Zimbabwe – was held at the ground in December 2006 with the hosts winning by eight wickets and it is now the centre of cricket in the country.

Built as a football stadium the ground now houses the offices of the Bangladesh Cricket Board, as well as Dhaka's largest furniture market, which is only shut when there are international matches being staged.

Found around 10 km (6 miles) from the centre of Dhaka, the move from the Bangabandhu National Stadium was controversial but the BCB wanted a dedicated cricket stadium to help develop the game, and they did not own the Bangabandhu, which has since been given over to soccer.

The fact that it is now the spiritual home of Bangladeshi cricket is emphasized by the number of informal cricket games that take place on a grassless ground next to the stadium. Popular all over the sub-continent the game is played without stumps, pads or protective equipment and participants use a tape ball – a tennis ball wrapped in electrical tape.

The ground was renovated to stage games at the 2011 World Cup with Richard Winter, the curator at the WACA in Perth, Australia, giving advice on the preparation of the wickets.

In the first Test played at Sher-e-Bangla the hosts were beaten in three days with the Indians scoring 610-3 declared, all of the top four batsmen, including Sachin Tendulkar, making centuries, and bowling out Bangladesh twice.

Below: The Bangladesh team at Sher-e-Bangla Cricket Stadium.

MATTER OF FACT

Ground: Sher-e-Bangla National Stadium
Capacity: 42,000
Located: Mirpur, Dhaka
Address: Mirpur, Dhaka 1216, Bangladesh
Telephone: +880 2 803 1001/2/3/4
E-mail: info@bcb-cricket.com or
zaki@bcb-cricket.com
To get there: 10 km (6 miles) north of the centre in
Section 6 of the Mirpur district

ISPAHANI END

AQUA PAINTS END

First Test: Bangladesh v India 25-27 May 2007
First ODI: Bangladesh v Zimbabwe 8 Dec 2006
First Twenty20: N/A

Tests played: 4
Bangladesh: Won 0, lost 3, drawn 1
Highest team total: 610-3 dec Ind v Ban 2007
Lowest team total: 118 (Ban v Ind 2007)
Highest individual total: 166 DPM Jayawardene (for
SL v Ban, 2008)
Highest partnership: 175 (KKD Karthik & W Jaffer, 1st
wicket for Ind v Ban 2007)
Best bowling: 6-27 Shahadat Hossain (for Ban v SA
2008)

ODIs played: 32
Bangladesh: Won 12, lost 14 (neutral games 6)
Highest team total: 330-8 (Pak v Ind 2008)
Lowest team total: 80 (Zim v SL 2009)
Highest individual total: 129 Salman Butt (Pak v Ind
2008) & Tamim Iqbal (Ban v Ire 2008)
Highest partnership: 215 (WU Tharanga & DPM
Jayawardene, 1st wicket for SL v Ban 2010)
Best bowling: 5-29 Abdur Razzak (for Ban v Zim
2010)

Above: Bangladesh fans remain cheerful despite their country's lack of cricketing success.

CRICKET NET
Bangladesh authorities claim the
ground will be fit to play within half
an hour of a sub-continental shower
thanks to a new drainage system.
There is a slope of nearly a metre
from the wicket to the boundary to
aid the process.

CHITTAGONG

On the Bay of Bengal

Chittagong is Bangladesh's import-export city, located on the Bay of Bengal. It is not only the country's second biggest city with a population of around 2.5 million but it is also its main port. Chittagong is also, according to the *The Economist*, one of the world's fastest growing cities as it sucks in people from surrounding areas looking for opportunities.

If it's throngs of people, rickshaws bustling for fares, traders and even more people you are after then head downtown to the area around the train station. For a bit of recreation head to Foy's Lake to the north of here, where you will find Foy's Lake Amusement Park and Sea World or, to the west towards the airport you will find the popular and sandy Patenga Beach.

Zohur Ahmed Chowdhury Stadium is up the coast about 8 km (5 miles) northwest of the railway station.

Above: Chittagong beaches are lined with ship breaking yards. *Below:* Chittagong.

WEATHER	LOW (°C)	HIGH (°C)	RAIN (MM)	SUNSET
January	13	26	5	17.00
February	16	28	28	17.24
March	19	31	64	17.39
April	24	32	150	17.51
May	24	32	264	18.01
June	25	31	533	18.16
July	26	31	599	18.24
August	24	30	518	18.18
September	24	31	318	17.54
October	23	30	178	17.23
November	18	29	52	16.59
December	14	26	15	16.51

3 THINGS YOU MUST DO...

1 A BEER

The Peninsula Hotel (Bulbub Centre, 468B, OR Nizam Rd, tel: +880 31 285 0860) is one of the few hotels in the city licensed to sell alcohol. It seems like a good reason to visit, don't you think? Sip a Heineken or Tiger on the rooftop Club 21 or head to Isles Bar or the restaurant or cafe.

2 WORLD WAR II CEMETERY

Pay tribute at this well-cared-for cemetery (Badshah Mia Chowdhury Road) where more than 700 Commonwealth and Japanese soldiers are buried. To get there: centrally located by the Chittagong Medical College and Hospital.

3 CHITTAGONG CLUB

A dining room, bar and sports facilities as you rub shoulders with the city's high-fliers. The club (Empress Rd, tel: +880 31 635 747) is membership only but you might get in as a 'temporary member'. When: 08.00-midnight. To get there: centrally located, it's a short taxi ride from the rail station.

ZOHUR AHMED CHOWDHURY STADIUM

The stadium of milestones

Formerly officially known Bir Sreshtha Shaheed Ruhul Amin Stadium and, more commonly, as the Chittagong Divisional Stadium, the ground was re-christened the Zohur Ahmed Chowdhury Stadium after a former leader of the Awami League, the country's biggest political party, in 2009 following a government directive. Situated around 8 km (5 miles) from the centre of Chittagong by the shore of the Bay of Bengal, it was one of five purpose-built grounds for the Under-19 World Cup in 2004, staging its first one-day international against Sri Lanka in February 2006 and its first Test match, against the same opponents, a few days later.

The stadium hit the headlines in the wrong way in April 2006 when several journalists were injured by police as they covered a Test match against Australia. The press decided not to report on the match itself and the trouble delayed play. Jason Gillespie, coming in as a nightwatchman for Australia, scored 201 not out in what turned out to be his final Test match.

Prior to this, Test matches in Chittagong were played at the multi-purpose MA Aziz Stadium but the Zohur Ahmed Chowdhury Stadium is dedicated to cricket. To mark its inaugural Test the Sri Lankan spinner Muttiah Muralitharan celebrated his 100th Test match by taking his 1,000th wicket in international cricket, including one-day games, and his nine victims in the match helped the tourists to an eight-wicket win.

The stadium itself is a concrete bowl, found in agricultural land, with a three-tier pavilion being the main attraction.

Below: Muttiah Muralitharan celebrated his 100th Test match at the Zohur Ahmed Chowdhury Stadium.

MATTER OF FACT
Ground: Zohur Ahmed Chowdhury Stadium
Capacity: 15,000
Located: Chittagong, Bangladesh
Address: Sagorika Road, Pahartoli, Chittagong
Telephone: +880 31 751150
E-mail: rubelcricket@yahoo.com
To get there: 8 km (5 miles) northwest of the centre

ISPHANI END

UCB END

First Test: Bangladesh v Sri Lanka 28 Feb-3 Mar 2006
First ODI: Bangladesh v Sri Lanka 25 Feb 2006
First Twenty20: N/A

Tests played: 6
Bangladesh: Won 0, lost 5, drawn 1
Highest team total: 583-7 (SA v Ban 2008)
Lowest team total: 119 (Ban v SA 2008)
Highest individual total: 232 GC Smith (for SA v Ban 2008)
Highest partnership: 415 (GC Smith & ND McKenzie, for 1st wicket SA v Ban 2008)
Best bowling: 7-36 Shakib Al Hasan (for Ban v NZ 2008)

ODIs played: 7
Bangladesh: Won 3, lost 4
Highest team total: 309-7 (SL v Ban 2006)
Lowest team total: 44 (Zim v Ban 2009)
Highest individual total: 118 not out BRM Taylor (for Zim v Ban 2009)
Highest partnership: 143 (HH Gibbs & GC Smith, for 1st wicket SA v Ban 2008)
Best bowling: 3-8 Shakib Al Hasan (for Ban v Zim 2009)

ENGLAND & WALES

THE **3** **MINUTE** **GUIDE**		**Capitals:** *London (England), Cardiff (Wales).* **Language:** *English.* **Beers:** *Spitfire, Newcastle Brown Ale (England), Brains SA (Wales).* **Food:** *Pork pie, bangers (sausages) and mash, bacon and egg sandwich.* **National Anthem:** *God Save the Queen.* **Population:** *62 million.* **Time zone:** *GMT.* **Emergency number:** *999.* **Did you know?** *There is a Welsh whisky (called Penderyn).* **Cricket body:** *Lord's Cricket Ground, London, NW8 8QZ, UK. Tel: +44 207 432 1200. Web: www.ecb.co.uk*

Below: Kevin Pietersen warms up before a match at Lord's, the ground where he made his Test debut.

England expects

There is a saying that the three hardest jobs in England are Prime Minister, manager of the England football team and captain of the England cricket team. Every captain from James Lillywhite Jnr, who captained England in their first Test in 1877, to Kevin Pietersen, who was sacked in 2009 knows how true this is.

Historians are unsure exactly how long cricket has been played in England but there is a reference to it in Edward I's accounts of 1300. In 1739 an all-England side played the mighty Kent and another England team went to North America under the captaincy of George Parr in 1859. Over the years the game was nurtured in the public schools system although in the professional era they do not have such a big influence as they once did.

England played Australia in the first Test match in Melbourne in 1877 and since then have had many ups and downs. Douglas Jardine's team of 1932-33 caused outrage with their Bodyline tactics in Australia, captain Tony Greig was a leading figure in setting up the Packer circus in the late 1970s and England's power in the world game has diminished politically in recent times with Asian countries becoming more influential.

The English also introduced the world to Twenty20 cricket, as a means to increase revenues in country cricket with the first domestic competition being held in 2003. The brainchild of the ECB's marketing manager, Stuart Robinson, the shortened game became instantly popular worldwide.

Above: An eye over the capital city.

TEST RECORD

Versus	First Test	Matches	Won	Lost	Drawn
Australia	May 1877	321	99	132	90
Bangladesh	Oct 2003	4	4	0	0
India	Jun 1932	99	34	19	46
New Zealand	Jan 1930	94	45	8	41
Pakistan	Jun 1954	67	19	12	36
South Africa	Mar 1889	138	56	29	53
Sri Lanka	Feb 1982	21	8	6	7
West Indies	Jun 1928	145	43	53	49
Zimbabwe	Dec 1996	6	3	0	3

Most runs: GA Gooch (1975-1995) 8,900 runs, 118 Tests, average 42.58
Most wickets: IT Botham (1977-1992) 383 wickets, 102 Tests, average 28.40
Most catches: APE Knott (1967-1981) 250 catches, 95 Tests

WORLD CUP RECORD

Year	Venue	Finished
1975	England	Semi-final
1979	England	Runners-up
1983	England	Semi-final
1987	India and Pakistan	Runners-up
1992	Australia and N Zealand	Runners-up
1996	Ind, Pak and S Lanka	Quarter-final
1999	England	Pool
2003	South Africa	Pool
2007	West Indies	5th

Most ODI runs: AJ Stewart (1989-2003) 4,677 runs, 170 matches, average 31.60
Most ODI wickets: D Gough (1994-2006) 235 wickets, 159 matches, average 26.42
Most ODI catches: AJ Stewart (1989-2003) 148 catches, 170 matches

LONDON

Above: *Big Ben, a magnet for tourists. Check your watch now.*

Choices, choices

With more tourist books on London than other cities have attractions, if you struggle for something to do while you are here then you are probably walking about with your eyes closed. Pubs? On every street corner. History? Buckingham Palace, the Houses of Parliament, the whole city. Theatre? Head to the West End for some of the world's best shows. Museums to match any city's, clubs, fashion, royalty, parks and sport, this is a city that can offer it all. You want a chat with a Londoner? Get in a taxi. Drivers are paid to take you where you are going and give you their views on everything from politics to the national obsession, the weather.

For a bit of sun (yes, it does come out sometimes) head to one of London's famous Royal Parks such as Hyde Park, Regent's Park, St James's Park and Greenwich Park. These and other green areas have an important part to play in the city and in the summer in particular this is where Londoners blossom. Watch for the famous moment when the sun appears for the first time of the year and people start shedding clothes to get a bit of colour.

People have lived along this part of the River Thames, where London is situated, for thousands of years, and today more than 7.5 million people call it home. Famously the city grew as a collection of villages that simply merged together, which is why you will find pockets of neighbourhood life like other great old cities such as New York and Paris.

Lord's is about 4 km (2.5 miles) northwest of the West End, while the Oval is a similar distance south of the Thames.

3 THINGS YOU MUST DO...

1 WEMBLEY STADIUM

The new 90,000 seater Wembley Stadium (No 1 Olympic Way, Wembley, tel: +44 844 800 2755) is England's football home. When: tours daily 09.30–16.30. Price: adults £15, children £8. To get there: tube to Wembley Park Station or Wembley Central, or rail to Wembley Stadium or Wembley Central.

2 INDIAN FOOD

Hot, spicy, mild, expensive, cheap, smart, down-at-heel – the country's favourite food comes in all guises, with over 2,000 Indian restaurants in the city. Try Brick Lane, which has a concentration of them that will astound. To get there: tube to Aldgate East.

3 GREYHOUND RACING

Not as glorious as it was in its heyday, but dog racing is still a great night out. Wimbledon Greyhound Stadium (Plough Lane, tel: +44 870 840 8905). When: Tues, Fri, Sat, racing from 19.30. Price: adults £5, child 12–17 £2.50. To get there: rail to Haydons Road or tube to Wimbledon or Tooting Broadway.

Above: The London skyline, with the distinctive Swiss Re Building, nicknamed the Gherkin, to the right.

LOW (°C)	HIGH (°C)	LOW (°C)	RAIN (MM)	SUNSET
January	2	6	54	16.02
February	3	7	40	16.50
March	3	9	37	17.39
April	6	13	37	19.33
May	8	17	48	20.22
June	12	20	45	21.08
July	15	23	57	21.21
August	13	21	60	20.50
September	11	20	49	19.47
October	9	14	57	18.39
November	5	10	64	16.33
December	4	7	48	15.55

LORD'S

The home of cricket

Lord's is the most famous ground in the world, home to the Marylebone Cricket Club (MCC), the guardians of the Laws and Spirit of Cricket, Middlesex County Cricket Club and the offices of the England and Wales Cricket Board. It was also headquarters of the International Cricket Council until its move to Dubai in 2005.

The stadium is named after Thomas Lord, a bowler with White Conduit CC, who leased a ground in Marylebone on what is now the site of Dorset Square. Lord's moved to the current site in St John's Wood in 1814. In 1825 Lord sold the ground to William Ward, a director of the Bank of England but his name is still synonymous with the 'Home of Cricket'.

The pavilion, for MCC members mainly, although they can sign in a guest on some match days, is a Victorian structure that contrasts starkly with the modern media centre directly opposite it at the Nursery End that was opened in 1999 and looks like a spaceship. MCC members can be identified by their red and yellow, or 'egg and bacon', ties that add to the colour of the ground as well as causing amusement to visitors.

Ticket holders can visit the museum, behind the pavilion, on match days and will find memorabilia from the likes of Don Bradman, Shane Warne, Geoff Boycott and WG Grace plus the sparrow killed by Jahangir Khan of Cambridge University in 1936. But the most important exhibit is the Ashes, contained in a tiny urn.

The ground first staged Test cricket in 1884 and has staged many epic games. Famous for its slope from the Grandstand to the Mound the pitch is hard for visiting bowlers to get used to first time although that did not stop Bob Massie of Australia taking 16 wickets on his debut, against England there in 1972.

Lord's also staged the World Cup final in 1975, 1979, 1983 and 1999.

Below: Lord's futuristic Media Centre was built for the 1999 World Cup.

MATTER OF FACT

Ground: Lord's Cricket Ground
Capacity: 30,000
Located: St John's Wood, London
Address: St John's Wood, London NW8 8QN
Telephone: +44 207 616 8500
E-mail: ticketing@mcc.org.uk, cricket@mcc.org.uk
To get there: St John's Wood station (tube), Baker Street station (tube)
Stands: Compton, Edrich, Allen, Mound, Grandstand, Warner, Tavern

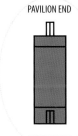

PAVILION END

NURSERY END

First Test: England v Australia 21-23 July 1884
First ODI: England v Australia 26 August 1972
First Twenty20: England v Netherlands 5 June 2009

Tests played: 118
England: Won 44, lost 27, drawn 46 (neutral games 1)
Highest team total: 729-6 dec (Aus v Eng 1930)
Lowest team total: 42 (Ind v Eng 1974)
Highest individual total: 333 GA Gooch (for Eng v Ind 1990)
Highest partnership: 370 (WJ Edrich & DCS Compton, 3rd wicket for Eng v SA 1947)
Best bowling: 8-34 IT Botham (for Eng v Pak 1978)

ODIs played: 48
England: Won 19, lost 19, tied 1, no result 1 (neutral games 8)
Highest team total: 334-4 (Eng v Ind 1975)
Lowest team total: 107 (SA v Eng 2003)
Highest individual total: 138 not out IVA Richards (for WI v Eng 1979)
Highest partnership: 226 (AJ Strauss and A Flintoff, 4th wicket for Eng v WI 2004)
Best bowling: 5-30 DL Vettori (for NZ v Eng 2004)

Above: An MCC member takes a nap in his 'egg-and-bacon' blazer.

CRICKET NET

Nancy Doyle, who died in 2005, aged 76, ran the players' dining room for many years at Lord's where she cooked legendary lunches. Middlesex captain Mike Brearley once asked her, without success, to limit the number of courses to five. She received an honorary MBE in 1994.

THE OVAL

England's first Test venue

Lord's might be the most famous ground in England but it is the Oval, sometimes called the Kennington Oval, and home to Surrey County Cricket Club, in the south of London, that staged England's first home Test, a five-wicket win against Australia, in 1880. The Oval opened in 1845 but in 1848 Prince Albert had to step in to save the ground from building works that would have seen it close and the same year the first of the world famous gas holders, which identify the Oval, was built.

In 1872 the first soccer FA Cup final was played at the ground, between Wanderers and Royal Engineers, and it has also held rugby internationals and Australian Rules Football.

But it is cricket that dominates, from Len Hutton's 364 in 1938, Don Bradman's last Test innings, through Michael Holding and the West Indies in 1976, to England's Ashes wins in 1953, 2005 and 2009. In 1998 Muttiah Muralitharan took 16 wickets to bowl Sri Lanka to a victory that seemed highly unlikely once England had scored 445 in their first innings. But

a double century from Sanath Jayasuriya and Murali's genius got the tourists home comfortably.

The ground, owned by the Duchy of Cornwall, hence the Prince of Wales feathers on the Surrey badge, has undergone extensive renovation in recent years, (and more is planned) with the impressive OCS stand at the Vauxhall End dominating the skyline.

This stand, opened in 2005, has an open-air bar and dining area on the fourth floor, numerous boxes, bars and restaurants and is also home to the media centre. The nearest entrance to the OCS Stand is via the Alec Stewart Gates, named in honour of the former England and Surrey wicket-keeper-batsman who played 133 Tests.

For spectators there are plenty of pubs, such as the Hanover Arms, the Greyhound and the Beehive, and restaurants in the local area to retire to at close of play.

Below: The Oval has been the scene of many emotional Ashes finales.

MATTER OF FACT

Ground: The Brit Oval
Capacity: 23,500
Located: Kennington, London
Address: Kennington, London, SE11 5SS
Telephone: 08712 461100/ +44 207 582 6660
E-mail: enquiries@surreycricketclub.com
To get there: Oval Station (tube), Vauxhall Station (tube, train)
Stands: Bedser, OCS

PAVILION END

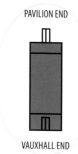

VAUXHALL END

First Test: England v Australia 6-8 September 1880
First ODI: England v West Indies 7 September 1973
First Twenty20: England v West Indies 28 June 2007

Tests played: 92
England: Won 38, lost 18, drawn 36
Highest team total: 903-7 dec (Eng v Aus 1938)
Lowest team total: 44 (Aus v Eng 1896)
Highest individual total: 364 L Hutton (for Eng v Aus 1938)
Highest partnership: 451 (WH Ponsford & DG Bradman, 2nd wicket for Aus v Eng 1934)
Best bowling: 9-57 DE Malcolm (for Eng v SA 1994)

ODIs played: 44
England: Won 17, lost 13, no result 1 (neutral games 13)
Highest team total: 347-4 (NZ v USA 2004)
Lowest team total: 103 (Eng v SA 1999)
Highest individual total: 145 not out NJ Astle (for NZ v USA 2004)
Highest partnership: 200 (ME Trescothick & VS Solanki, 1st wicket for Eng v SA 2003)
Best bowling: 5-26 RC Irani (for Eng v Ind 2002)

BOBBY ABEL, TO W. G.:—"LOOK HERE, WE PLAYERS INTEND TO BE SUFFICIENTLY PAID, AS WELL AS THE SO-CALLED GENTLEMEN!"

Above: England's WG Grace and Bobby Abel. Grace scored 504 runs and took four wickets in eight Oval Tests.

CRICKET NET

In 1994 England fast bowler Devon Malcolm uttered the words 'You guys are history' when he was hit on the helmet, whilst batting, by South Africa's Fanie de Villiers. A fired-up Malcolm then took 9-57, the third best figures ever for England, to help his side to an eight-wicket win.

BIRMINGHAM

Above: Birmingham is known for its maze of roads and its shopping centres.

Where balti beats spaghetti

The country's second city certainly won't win any aesthetic awards and has often been the butt of jokes, especially about its famous Spaghetti Junction – the hugely messy interchange of the M6, A38(M), A38 and A5127 roads, which is known officially as the Gravelly Hill Interchange.

Yet this West Midlands city has slowly built itself a reputation for shopping, good food (particularly as the home of the south Asian dish, the balti) and vibrant nightlife, all of this with the backdrop of a canal network that is its legacy of its industrial history.

At the heart of the shopping district is the famous Bullring, which originally opened in 1964, with its offering of more than 160 shops. If that's not enough for you retail lovers, there are a number of smaller shopping centres nearby as well as the ever-busy New Street and

Corporation Street near Birmingham New Street Rail Station.

For an endless choice of clubs and bars head to Broad Street and Digbeth High Street in the city and, to the south, the areas of Selly Oak and Moseley.

The city has a range of food options but no visit to Birmingham would be complete without an aromatic, spicy balti mopped up with a giant naan bread. The balti, named after the pan in which it is cooked, first appeared in the city in the 1970s (it's originally from north Pakistan) and is now one of the nation's most popular dishes. The highest concentration of balti houses (restaurants) can be found in the Sparkbrook area.

Edgbaston is about 4 km (2.5 miles) south of the city centre.

3 THINGS YOU MUST DO...

1 BROAD STREET

Birmingham takes nightlife seriously and Broad Street does it better than most with a huge choice of bars and clubs. Try the massive Gatecrasher (187 Broad St, tel: +44 121 633 1520 for guest list) with its four clubs and nine bars.

2 CADBURY'S WORLD

Everything you ever wanted to know about chocolate, including the world's biggest Cadbury's shop (Linden Road, Bournville, tel: 0845 450 3599 from UK). When: varies but usually daily 09.00/10.00–16.00/17.00. Price: £13.45 adult, £10.10 child. To get there: train to Bournville Rail Station.

3 SPEEDWAY

The one-gear, no brake sport. Birmingham Brummies (Perry Barr Stadium, Aldridge Rd, Perry Barr tel: +44 1691 774 321) are in the Premier League. When: Mar–Oct, Weds 19.30, sometimes Sun 18.00. Price: £15 adult, £5 child 11–15. To get there: train to Perry Barr Station, buses 33, 46, 90, 91, 107, 113.

Above: Birmingham Library.

WEATHER	LOW (°C)	HIGH (°C)	RAIN (MM)	SUNSET
January	2	5	74	16.03
February	2	6	58	16.51
March	3	9	50	17.40
April	6	12	56	19.34
May	7	16	64	20.23
June	10	19	50	21.09
July	13	21	72	21.21
August	12	20	69	20.50
September	10	17	61	19.49
October	7	14	70	18.39
November	5	9	84	16.34
December	3	6	67	15.57

EDGBASTON

The Midlands' party piece

Edgbaston, found about 1.5 km (1 mile) from New Street Station, in the south of Birmingham is probably the most atmospheric ground in the country when England are playing a Test match, and is home to Warwickshire County Cricket Club.

The Eric Hollies Stand, named after the man who dismissed Don Bradman is his final innings, is the most lively in the ground with fans supplying an endless run of songs and banter which increases as the day goes on and the beer flows. If you do not want to be in amongst this raucous area then there are plenty of quieter areas to watch the cricket.

Edgbaston became England's fifth Test ground in 1902, with Australia, the visitors, salvaging a draw after being bowled out for 36, in a three-day match. However only three more Tests were held at the ground before the 1957 West Indians arrived to draw a match that featured a stand of 411 between England's Peter May and Colin Cowdrey against the spin of Sonny Ramadhin.

In 1981 Ian Botham's spell of 5-1 drove England onto a second improbable win against Australia that season and, in 2005, a nail-biting match ended with Michael Vaughan's England beating the same tourists by two runs to level the series and set up another memorable summer. Less happily for England, Graeme Smith's 154 not out in 2008 sealed the series for South Africa and led to Vaughan's tearful resignation as captain the next day.

The Eric Hollies Stand and the Edgbaston Cricket Centre arrived in the 1990s as the result of a refurbishment aided by lottery funding and, in 1999, the ground hosted possibly the greatest one-day game in history. Australia and South Africa tied the World Cup semi-final, with Australia seemingly out of the contest in the last over, putting Steve Waugh's men through to the final as they finished higher in the Super Sixes. The irony was that it was fast bowler Allan Donald, who served Warwickshire with distinction on the ground for many years, who was last man out to seal South Africa's fate.

Below: Edgbaston was the scene of Michael Vaughan's final Test in 2008 and led to his emotional resignation as captain of England the next day.

MATTER OF FACT

Ground: The County Ground
Capacity: 21,000
Located: Edgbaston, Birmingham
Address: Edgbaston, Birmingham B5 7QU
Telephone: +44 121 446 4422
E-mail: tickets@edgbaston.com, annabutler@
edgbaston.com
To get there: Birmingham New Street Station (train),
45 & 47 (bus)
Stands: Eric Hollies, RES Wyatt, RV Ryder, Raglan,
Stanley Barnes, William Ansell, Leslie Deakin

PAVILION END

CITY END

First Test: England v Australia 29-31 May 1902
First ODI: England v Australia 28 August 1972
First Twenty20: N/A

Tests played: 44
England: Won 22, lost 8, drawn 14
Highest team total: 633-5 (Eng v Ind 1979)
Lowest team total: 30 (SA v Eng 1924)
Highest individual total: 285 not out PBH May (for
Eng v WI 1957)
Highest partnership: 411 (PBH May & MC Cowdrey,
4th wicket for Eng v WI 1957)
Best bowling: 7-17 WH Rhodes (for Eng v Aus 1902)

ODIs played: 42
England: Won 17, lost 10, no result 2, (neutral won 11,
tied 1, no result 1)
Highest team total: 328-7 (Eng v WI 2009)
Lowest team total: 70 (Aus v Eng 1977)
Highest individual total: 171 not out GM Turner (for
NZ v East Africa 1975)
Highest partnership: 176 (GH Kirsten & HH Gibbs, 1st
wicket for SA v NZ 1999)
Best bowling: 5-11 Shahid Afridi (for Pak v Ken 2004)

Above: Steve Harmison, who rounded off England's dramatic two-run win over Australia at Edgbaston in 2005.

CRICKET NET
Away from international cricket
West Indian Brian Lara hit 501 not
out whilst playing for Warwickshire
against Durham at Edgbaston in
1994, breaking the record for the
highest first class score. Lara hit 62
fours and 10 sixes in nearly eight
hours at the crease.

CARDIFF

When horizons sing

S ituated in the south of the country, Cardiff is the capital of Wales, with a city population of about 350,000. Known as a tough port and industrial city, Cardiff grew on the back of its coal exporting and was made the country's capital only in 1955. It has also been the seat of the Welsh Assembly Government since devolution in 1999. Parliament meets at the hi-tech, glass-dominated Senedd building that is situated at Cardiff Bay.

The Bay area is the regenerated former dockland area to the south and includes many other impressive buildings including the tube-like Visitor Centre, the Wales Millennium Centre with its giant inscription spelling out the words 'In These Stones Horizons Sing' in both English and Welsh, as well as the older Pierhead Building and Norwegian Church (which author Roald Dahl used to attend as a child).

Sophia Gardens is centrally located on the western bank of the River Taff.

Above: Water has played an important role in the history of Cardiff. *Below:* The castle seen from Bute Park.

WEATHER	LOW (°C)	HIGH (°C)	RAIN (MM)	SUNSET
January	2	7	108	16.16
February	2	7	72	17.02
March	3	10	63	17.54
April	6	13	65	19.46
May	8	16	76	20.36
June	12	19	63	21.20
July	13	20	92	21.33
August	13	21	99	21.02
September	11	19	99	19.59
October	8	15	109	18.51
November	5	10	118	16.46
December	3	8	108	16.07

3 THINGS YOU MUST DO...

1 MILLENNIUM STADIUM

Home of the Welsh rugby team and scene of the 1999 Rugby World Cup final. Stadium tours (Westgate St, tel: +44 29 2082 2228) last one hour. When: Mon-Sat 10.00–17.00, Sun 10.00–16.00. Price: £6.50 adult, £4 child. To get there: train to Cardiff Central Rail Station, bus to Cardiff Central Bus Station.

2 ST MARY STREET

One of the busiest streets for nightlife with a host of bars, restaurants and clubs. Try the stylish 411 (3–6 St Mary St, tel: +44 29 2066 7996). When: Thur 09.00–03.00, Fri–Sat 10.00–04.00. Price: free until midnight, £10 after.

3 CARDIFF CASTLE

The castle (Castle St, tel: +44 29 2087 810) has over 2,000 years of history and beautiful grounds. Try to allow three hours. When: Mar–Oct 09.00–18.00, Nov-Feb 09.00–17.00. Price: £8.95 adult, £6.35 child 5–16. To get there: near Cardiff Central Rail Station and Cardiff Central Bus Station.

SOPHIA GARDENS

Pride of Wales

Better known to cricket fans as Sophia Gardens, the SWALEC Stadium, is a short walk from Cardiff city centre, past the Millennium Stadium, on the banks of the River Taff. It hosted its first Test in 2009, becoming the 100th Test match venue in the world in the process. That opening match of the Ashes series ended in a tense draw with England tailenders Monty Panesar and James Anderson holding out with one wicket left. The first game at the newly revamped ground was felt to be a huge success with the whole of Wales throwing their weight behind the occasion and showing visitors a warm welcome.

Prior to the match, former England captain Mike Atherton had said the ground, with a 16,000 capacity, was too small for an Ashes Test and other observers felt grounds such as Durham, Old Trafford and Trent Bridge had better claims to put on a five-day game against Australia.

That draw was not the first moment of international drama the ground had seen as Bangladesh defeated the world number one Australians at the ground in a one-day game in 2005. Three years earlier and to much local delight, a Wales team, with nine Glamorgan players in the side and led by Steve James, beat England in a 50-over match at the ground.

It is the home of Glamorgan County Cricket Club, who have played matches on the ground since 1967, although they did not acquire the lease until 1995.

During the renovations, Michael Powell, the Glamorgan all-rounder who had had a rib removed in a life-saving operation, persuaded the authorities to let him bury the bone on the ground in 2007.

Below: Tailender James Anderson held out with Monty Panesar to salvage a draw against Australia in 2009.

MATTER OF FACT
Ground: The SWALEC Stadium
Capacity: 16,000
Located: Cardiff, Wales
Address: Cathedral Road, Cardiff CF11 9XR
Telephone: +44 29 2040 9380
E-mail: info@glamorgancricket.co.uk
To get there: Cardiff Central Station (train), 24, 25 & 62 (bus)
Stands: The Really Welsh Pavilion, Pro-Copy, Morgan Signs Riverside, Castell Howell, Grandstand, Spar, Biffa, The Regent Cleaning Members'

RIVER TAFF END

CATHEDRAL ROAD END

First Test: England v Australia 8-12 July 2009
First ODI: Australia v New Zealand 20 May 1999
First Twenty20: N/A

Tests played: 1
England: Won 0, drawn 1, lost 0
Highest team total: 674-6 (Aus v Eng 2009)
Lowest team total: 435 (Eng v Aus 2009)
Highest individual total: 150 RT Ponting (for Aus v Eng 2009)
Highest partnership: 239 (RT Ponting & SM Katich, 2nd wicket for Aus v Eng 2009)
Best bowling: 3-47 BW Hilfenhaus (for Aus v Eng 2009)

ODIs played: 7
England: Won 0, lost 0, no result 2 (neutral games 5)
Highest team total: 258-3 (Aus v Pak 2001)
Lowest team total: 202 (Eng v Pak 2006)
Highest individual total: 100 Mohammad Ashraful (Ban v Aus 2005)
Highest partnership: 154 (GC Smith & HH Gibbs, 1st wicket for SA v Zim 2003)
Best bowling: 4-37 GI Allott (for NZ v Aus 1999)

DURHAM

A city of history

L ocated in the North East of England, this small city of just over 40,000 people is well known for its beautiful architecture and medieval history. Durham traces its roots back to the 10th century and its heart is dominated by its cathedral and castle (which is now part of Durham University) both of which were built in the Norman era. But this hilly city, built around the River Wear, has many other interesting buildings dotted around it, notably the Elvert Bridge and St Giles Church.

Being so small, Durham is never going to be England's nightlife central, but there are many cosy old pubs (or at least cosy pubs in old buildings) to while away a warm summer evening. And being a university town there is plenty of youthful energy and enthusiasm around.

The Riverside Ground is 15 km (9 miles) to the north of Durham near the small town of Chester-le-Street.

*Above: A 12th century Durham door knocker. **Below:** Durham Cathedral is a popular tourist attraction.*

WEATHER	LOW (°C)	HIGH (°C)	RAIN (MM)	SUNSET
January	2	6	63	15.53
February	2	7	42	16.50
March	3	9	52	17.50
April	4	11	47	19.53
May	7	14	53	20.54
June	11	17	52	21.48
July	13	19	56	22.03
August	12	19	71	21.21
September	10	17	59	20.10
October	8	13	54	18.51
November	4	8	65	16.35
December	3	7	56	15.46

3 THINGS YOU MUST DO...

1 DURHAM CATHEDRAL

One of the finest pieces of Norman architecture in the country, this building was founded back in the early 11th century. When: Mon–Sat 07.30–9.30, Sun 07.45–12.30 (for prayer), closes Mon–Sat 18.00, Sun 17.30. Price: free, but a donation requested. How to get there: you can't miss it!

2 PUB CRAWL

There are dozens of decent pubs within walking distance of the cathedral – perfect for a meandering pub crawl. Include the Shakespeare Tavern (63 Saddler St, tel: +44 191 3843 261) which claims to be the smallest pub in Durham.

3 NEWCASTLE

The bright lights and celebrated nightlife scene of Newcastle lie just 27 km (17 miles) to the north. To get there: train to Newcastle (about 15 mins). The N21 night bus runs from Newcastle to Chester-le-Street hourly from 23.45–04.15 (continues to Durham Sat-Sun 23.45–03.15).

THE RIVERSIDE

Coming of age

Durham staged its first Test match in 2003 after a long fight for recognition. Successive County Championships, in 2008 and 2009, for its home side and the award of an Ashes Test for the 2013 series meant that top-flight cricket in the area had finally come of age.

Prior to the award of the Ashes Test, Riverside, overlooked for the 2009 series, had hosted Tests against Zimbabwe, Bangladesh and the West Indies in 2007 and 2009 with local boy Paul Collingwood scoring a century in 2007.

The 1992 season was the county's inaugural campaign in first class cricket and the signing of players such as Ian Botham sparked interest in cricket in the area and one of the conditions of their promotion was to build an international arena.

Previously a nomadic club, Durham's first first-class match at The Riverside, about a 1.5 km (1 mile) walk from Chester-le-Street Station, was held in 1995 against Warwickshire. Steady development saw it host two matches in the 1999 World Cup and a year later its first England one-day international against the West Indies.

In 1999 Austin's Bar & Bistro was added and by the time the Australians visited in 2005 a new media centre was fully operational.

Lumley Castle, formerly the home of 14th-century military hero Sir Ralph Lumley, provides a spectacular backdrop to the ground. The ghost of his wife Lily, who was murdered by priests, is said to walk the corridors of her former home with the spirits of her murderers. In 2005 the Australian cricket team were spooked, when staying at the hotel, with Shane Watson moving to sleep on Brett Lee's floor and in 2000 several of Jimmy Adams' West Indies side checked out after feeling uneasy.

Below: The Riverside was awarded an Ashes Test match in 2013.

MATTER OF FACT
Ground: The County Ground
Capacity: 15,000 (for internationals), increasing to 20,000 by 2013
Located: Chester-le-Street, Durham
Address: Chester-le-Street, County Durham DH3 3QR
Telephone: +44 191 387 1717
E-mail reception@durhamccc.co.uk, box.office@durhamccc.co.uk
To get there: Chester-le-Street Station (train), shuttle buses available for big matches, 21 (bus) from Durham
Stands: North Terrace, South Terrace, Don Robson, South West Terrace, North East Terrace, North West Terrace, County Durham,

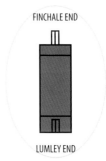

FINCHALE END

LUMLEY END

First Test: England v Zimbabwe 5-7 June 2003
First ODI: Pakistan v Scotland 20 May 1999
First Twenty20: England v South Africa 20 Aug 2008

Tests played: 4
England: Won 4, lost 0, drawn 0
Highest team total: 569-6 dec (Eng v WI 2009)
Lowest team total: 94 (Zim v Eng 2003)
Highest individual total: 162 not out IR Bell (for Eng v Ban 2005)
Highest partnership: 213 (AN Cook & RS Bopara, 2nd wicket for Eng v WI 2009)
Best bowling: 6-33 RL Johnson (for Eng v Zim 2003)

ODIs played: 10
England: Won 3, lost 3, no result 1 (neutral games 3)
Highest team total: 307-5 (Eng v NZ 2008)
Lowest team total: 101 (Eng v NZ 2004)
Highest individual total: 126 not out DPM Jayawardene (for SL v Eng 2006)
Highest partnership: 186 (MW Goodwin & GW Flower, 5th wicket for Zim v WI 2000)
Best bowling: 5-28 GP Swann (for Eng v Aus 2009)

LEEDS

Above: *The former industrial city of Leeds has reinvented itself as a lively centre for shopping.*

Grand city arcades

A focal point in Leeds for locals and visitors alike thanks to its many shops, restaurants (and pubs off the alleyways) is the commercial area called Briggate, a pedestrianized street. More in the way of entertainment and shopping can be found in the northern part (New Briggate) and the southern end (Lower Briggate). Many of the city's arcades for which it is well known run off Briggate, including Queen Victoria Street and County Arcade, which form the impressive Victoria Quarter, the Grand Arcade and the upmarket Queens Arcade.

The dominant building in the city is the high-rise office and residential building called Bridgewater Place, known locally as the Dalek. It is the tallest building in the city at 110 metres (361 feet). Another focal point is the Millennium Square where you will find many of the city's important landmarks including the town hall, the civic hall and the Leeds City Museum among others. The square has hosted many events including concerts by Meat Loaf, Kaiser Chiefs and Snow Patrol.

Leeds was originally built on the strength of the wool industry and lies at the heart of the north of England in West Yorkshire. It has a city population of nearly 450,000 and today is a modern, vibrant city.

With two universities and a university college there are plenty of students to stoke the nightlife fires of the city, a scene that has been growing in reputation in recent years. As well as the Briggate attractions, people also flock to the area around Millennium Square, the Clarence Dock, Exchange Quarter, and to the north Chapel Allerton.

Headingley is about 3 km (2 miles) northwest of the city centre.

3 THINGS YOU MUST DO...

1 CURRY

Leeds has excellent south Asian food. Try Aagrah (St Peter's Square, Quarry Hill, tel: +44 113 245 5667). When: Mon–Sat 17.30–midnight for last orders, Sun 05.30–23.00 last orders. Price: £11.95 buffet on Sun and Mon till 21.30. To get there: near Leeds City Bus Station.

2 XSCAPE CASTLEFORD

Snow slope, rock climbing walls, aerial assault course, and other energetic activities (Colarado Way, Glasshoughton, Castleford, tel: 0871 222 5671 in UK for snow slope). When: 09.00–23.00 (snow slope). To get there: Junction 32 off M62, train to Glasshoughton Station, buses 410, 411, X62.

3 THE EXCHANGE QUARTER

Take your pick from a range of bars and clubs in this area around the Corn Exchange Centre. Try The Hifi Club (2 Central Rd, tel: +44 113 242 7353). When: every night except some Mon and Thur, usually 21.00/22.00–03.00 (Wed 19.00–22.00). Price: from £2–£6. To get there: centrally located.

Above: *The Corn Exchange shopping centre in Leeds.*

WEATHER	LOW (°C)	HIGH (°C)	RAIN (MM)	SUNSET
January	0	6	61	15.53
February	0	6	45	16.50
March	2	9	52	17.50
April	4	11	50	19.52
May	6	15	54	20.54
June	9	18	54	21.47
July	10	20	51	22.02
August	12	21	67	21.20
September	9	17	59	20.10
October	6	14	56	18.50
November	2	9	57	16.35
December	1	7	61	15.45

HEADINGLEY

Yorkshire's rose

Headingley, about 3 km (2 miles) from the centre of Leeds, is home to Yorkshire County Cricket Club, although they did not buy it until 2005, and has staged rugby and cricket since 1890. There is a separate rugby ground lying immediately next to the cricket ground and the sports share a stand. Rugby hosts the Leeds Carnegie rugby union team and the Leeds Rhinos rugby league side.

England played Australia in the first Headingley Test in 1899 and since then the ground has seen some of the most dramatic games in cricketing history. It was the scene of local hero Geoff Boycott's 100th first class hundred, made in 1977 against Australia, and the heroics of Ian Botham (50 and 149 not out) and Bob Willis (8-43) in 1981 inspired England to the unlikeliest of Ashes wins. In 2001 Mark Butcher's 173 not out helped England chase 315 to beat Australia but the Ashes had already been lost that summer and the tourists declaration, under stand-in captain Adam Gilchrist, was over generous.

Headingley has a reputation for suiting seam bowlers, especially if there is a bit of cloud cover, but no-one seems to have told Australia's Don Bradman. In four Tests at the ground he made 963 runs, at an average of 192, including two triple centuries and his 29th and final Test hundred, 173 not out in 1948. In 1930 he made 309 not out in a day.

There are several landmarks named after the greats of Yorkshire cricket. The Len Hutton Gates, commemorating the career of the former England and Yorkshire captain, were unveiled in 2001 and the Dickie Bird clock, on the West Stand, was revealed by the eccentric former umpire himself in the same year.

The West Stand, better known as the Western Terrace, has a reputation for raucous behaviour and has seen several unseemly episodes over the years. Yorkshire have successfully clamped down on this without losing any of the atmosphere. Many fans wear fancy dress at Headingley, so do not be surprised to sit next to Superman or Fred Flintstone.

Below: County Championship cricket has been played at Headingley since 1891. The first Test was held here in 1899.

MATTER OF FACT

Ground: Headingley Carnegie Cricket Ground
Capacity: 17,000
Located: Headingley, Leeds
Address: St Michael's Lane, Leeds, West Yorkshire LS6 3BR
Telephone: +44 113 278 7394
E-mail: cricket@yorkshireccc.com
To get there: Burley Park Station (train), Headingley Station (train), various buses including 18, 18A, 38, 56, 91 or 74,75,76,77 from Leeds Central Station
Stands: West, North, East, North East and Family, Carnegie Lower

KIRKSTALL LANE END

FOOTBALL STAND END

First Test: England v Australia 29 June-1 July 1899
First ODI: England v West Indies 5 September 1973
First Twenty20: N/A

Tests played: 69
England: Won 30, lost 22, drawn 17
Highest team total: 653-4 dec (Aus v Eng 1993)
Lowest team total: 61 (WI v Eng 2000)
Highest individual total: 334 DG Bradman (for Aus v Eng 1930)
Highest partnership: 388 (WH Ponsford & DG Bradman, 4th wicket for Aus v Eng 1934)
Best bowling: 8-43 RGD Willis (for Eng v Aus 1981)

ODIs played: 33
England: Won 14, lost 9, no result 1, (neutral games 8, no result 1)
Highest team total: 324-2 (SL v Eng 2006) & 324-6 (Ind v Eng 2007)
Lowest team total: 93 (Eng v Aus 1975)
Highest individual total: 152 ST Jayasuriya (for SL v Eng 2006)
Highest partnership: 286 (ST Jayasuriya & WU Tharanga, 1st wicket for SL v Eng 2006)
Best bowling: 7-36 Waqar Younis (for Pak v Eng 2001)

Above: Andrew Strauss rebuilt the reputation of English cricket after Kevin Petersen's reign.

CRICKET NET

'George Davis is Innocent'. The 1975 Ashes Test match at Headingley was abandoned, after protestors broke in at night and dug up the pitch whilst pouring oil on one end, to highlight the imprisonment of robber George Davis. Davis was released in 1976 but imprisoned again for further offences.

MANCHESTER

Above: *Manchester has a rich music history and attracts top bands such as Coldplay.*

Let the music play

Today, sport and music run deep in the veins of this city, which originally built itself on the industrial strength of cotton and textiles. Manchester United and Manchester City are the city's football clubs, and there are many more within just a few kilometres. The 2002 Commonwealth Games were held here and helped boost the city's already impressive sporting facilities, with the National Squash Centre, Manchester Velodrome, Manchester Aquatics Centre and, most significantly, the City of Manchester Stadium, now the home of City.

But it is music that has given Manchester its verve. The Stone Roses, Inspiral Carpets, Simply Red, The Happy Mondays, and the less happy The Smiths were just some of the bands that formed the backbone of the city's line-up as Manchester stamped its mark on the UK's indie music scene in the 1980s. Before them was the punk of Buzzcocks, Joy Division (and New Order) and in the 1960s Herman's Hermits and The Hollies. Take That and Oasis emerged in the 1990s. Legendary music venue the Haçienda was central to all this (it also drove the acid house and rave scene), and today venues like the huge Manchester Arena, Academy and Apollo continue the proud music tradition.

In the city centre near Victoria railway station is the Arndale Centre, Europe's biggest shopping centre with more than 220 shops. Originally built in the 1970s, it has been redeveloped extensively after 1996 when the city centre was the target of a bombing by the IRA.

Old Trafford, is about 5 km (3 miles) southwest of the centre.

3 THINGS YOU MUST DO...

1 URBIS
Urbis (Cathedral Gardens, tel: +44 161 605 8200) is a centrally locally venue that has constantly changing exhibitions, events and tours that celebrate city life. When: daily 10.00–18.00. Price: vary. To get there: it's next to Victoria railway station

2 OLD TRAFFORD
Tour the stadium and museum at one of the world's greatest football clubs (Sir Matt Busby, Old Trafford, tel: +44 161 868 8000). When: Mon–Sun 09.40–16.30, museum 09.30–17.00. Price: £12.50 adult, £8.50 child, museum only £9/£7. To get there: metrolink tram to Old Trafford, train to Man Utd FC Halt.

3 COMEDY STORE
It's a nightclub, theatre, bar and restaurant, but go to the Comedy Store (1a-3a Deansgate Locks, tel: +44 161 839 9595) for the laughs. When: Wed–Sun, comedy starts at 20.00. Prices: from £9.50. To get there: metrolink to Gmex.

Above: Manchester city centre.

WEATHER	LOW (°C)	HIGH (°C)	RAIN (MM)	SUNSET
January	1	6	69	15.53
February	2	7	53	16.50
March	3	9	62	17.50
April	4	12	52	19.52
May	7	16	61	20.54
June	11	17	68	21.47
July	12	19	65	22.02
August	12	20	79	21.20
September	10	17	76	20.10
October	8	14	77	18.50
November	4	9	78	16.35
December	2	7	78	15.45

OLD TRAFFORD

Take an umbrella

Old Trafford, found south of the centre of Manchester, has been the home of cricket in the city since 1857. It is the headquarters of Lancashire County Cricket Club and hosted its first Test match in 1884 when England and Australia drew.

In the shadows of another Old Trafford, the home of Manchester United and so-called 'Theatre of Dreams', the ground has seen plenty of drama itself. In 1902 Australia's Victor Trumper scored 103 not out against England before lunch, in 1993 Shane Warne announced himself by bowling Mike Gatting with the 'Ball of the Century' – his first delivery in Ashes cricket – and in 1995 Dominic Cork took a hat-trick against the West Indies. In 1964 Australia's Bobby Simpson made 311, and in 1976 Gordon Greenidge's twin centuries for the West Indies helped them to a 425-run win over England. That match saw some of the most brutal fast bowling ever with 45-year-old Brian Close and 39-year-old John Edrich being hit relentlessly by the West Indian fast bowlers.

But the greatest feat seen at Old Trafford was accomplished by the Surrey and England spinner, and later commentator, Jim Laker, who had match figures of 19-90 against Australia in 1956. He took nine wickets in the first innings and ten in the second, whilst his spinning partner Tony Lock toiled for 69 overs in total, to claim just one victim.

Cricket fans joke that if you go to Old Trafford, make sure to take an umbrella (it rains a lot if you haven't already guessed) but a trip round the museum will fill the time and gives an insight into cricket in the area. Alternatively, frustrated fans can wander around the Manchester United museum over the road.

Rebuilding work started in 2009 to increase the capacity of the ground to 25,000 by 2012 and the ground has regularly been used for musical events, including the Move concerts in 2002 where the likes of Paul Weller, David Bowie and New Order appeared.

Below: The Barmy Army, always ready for a cheer. England's fans have become the most vociferous in the world.

MATTER OF FACT

Ground: Old Trafford Cricket Ground
Capacity: 19,000
Located: Stretford, Manchester
Address: Talbot Road, Manchester M16 0PX
Telephone: +44 161 282 4000
E-mail: enquiries@lccc.co.uk
To get there: Old Trafford Station (Metrolink) via Manchester Piccadilly or Manchester Victoria Stations
Stands: Washbrook and Statham, Eddie Paynter, AN Hornby

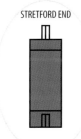

STRETFORD END

BRIAN STATHAM END

First Test: England v Australia 10-12 July 1884
First ODI: England v Australia 24 August 1972
First Twenty20: England v New Zealand 13 June 2008

Tests played: 73
England: Won 24, lost 14, drawn 34 (neutral game 1)
Highest team total: 656-8 dec (Aus v Eng 1964)
Lowest team total: 58 (Ind v Eng 1952)
Highest individual total: 311 RB Simpson (for Aus v Eng 1964)
Highest partnership: 267 (GP Thorpe & MP Vaughan, 3rd wicket for Eng v Pak 2001)
Best bowling: 10-53 JC Laker (for Eng v Aus 1956)

ODIs played: 37
England: Won 17, lost 10, no result 1 (neutral games 9)
Highest team total: 318-7 (SL v Eng 2006)
Lowest team total: 45 (Can v Eng 1979)
Highest individual total: 189 not out IVA Richards (for WI v Eng 1984)
Highest partnership: 194 (Saeed Anwar & Wajahatullah Wasti, 1st wicket for Pak v NZ 1999)
Best bowling: 5-14 GD McGrath (for Aus v WI 1999)

Above: Sachin Tendulkar hit 119 at Old Trafford, becoming the second youngest player to score a Test century.

CRICKET NET

On his way home after taking 19 Australian wickets, in 1956, Jim Laker stopped at a pub for a pint and a sandwich. Highlights of his exploits were on the television in the bar but he managed to finish his drink and leave without a single customer recognizing him. It would not happen today.

NOTTINGHAM

Above: The Council Hall is located just off the Old Market Square in Nottingham city centre.

Ye olde party town

Nottingham is another of England's old industrial cities that has slowly re-invented itself as a town which parties. Growing initially on the back of the lace industry, then later on the production of bicycles (Raleigh and Sturmer-Archer in particular), the city quickly became an important centre in the East Midlands. Today the city of just under 300,000 people has much more diverse employment with Alliance Chemists (Boots), HM Revenue & Customs, and Paul Smith (fashion) headquartered here plus others from the pharmaceutical, finance, and energy industries.

But the lace industry has left its legacy and today the Lace Market, an area within the city centre, boasts some fine architecture as well as being the heart of the busy nightlife scene. The area of tightly packed red-bricked buildings, which used to be the warehouses and salesrooms serving the world's lace market, includes the large and renovated Adams Building, and the Galleries of Justice, a museum of crime and punishment.

But if it's lights, shooters and action you are after instead of Victorian splendour you won't be disappointed here. The Lace Market, and the adjoining Hockley Village is home to an array of stylish, cool bars such as Browns, Bluu, Brass Monkey, Muse and Pitcher & Piano, as well as a selection of restaurants. Another good place to head for a night (or day) out is the Corner House which has venues such as Saltwater, Wagamamas and Strada.

Nottingham, of course, has long been the country's greenest city thanks to the legend of Robin Hood, the outlaw famed for 'robbing the rich to give to the poor', so check out famous sites related to the story such as Sherwood Forest (where he was said to live) and Nottingham Castle (which stood for Prince John against King Richard).

Trent Bridge is just to the north of the Lace Market.

3 THINGS YOU MUST DO...

1 YE OLDE TRIP TO JERUSALEM
This pub (Brewhouse Yard, tel: +44 115 947 3171), cut into the rock, claims to date back to 1189 and to be the oldest pub in England. When: Sun–Thur 10.00–23.00, Fri–Sat 10.00–midnight. To get there: centrally located near Nottingham Rail Station.

2 NOTTINGHAM CASTLE
Located on the site of the old medieval castle, 17th century Ducal Mansion is now a museum and art gallery (tel: +44 115 915 3700). When: Tues–Sun, Mar–Sept 10.00–17.00, Oct–Feb 10.00–16.00. Price: £3.50 adult, £2 concessions. To get there: centrally located near Nottingham Rail Station.

3 NOTTINGHAM CAVES
Wander underground in the ancient caves (tel: +44 115 988 1955) that spread under Nottingham city centre. Main entrance to caves in Broadmarsh Shopping Centre. When: daily 10.30–17.00. Price: £5.75 adults, £4.25 concessions. To get there: centrally located by Broadmarsh Bus Station.

Above: The legend of Robin Hood is alive and well in Nottingham.

WEATHER	LOW (°C)	HIGH (°C)	RAIN (MM)	SUNSET
January	2	5	74	16.03
February	2	6	54	16.51
March	3	10	50	17.40
April	5	12	53	19.34
May	7	17	64	20.23
June	10	19	50	21.09
July	13	20	69	21.21
August	12	20	69	20.50
September	10	17	61	19.49
October	7	13	69	18.39
November	6	10	84	16.34
December	3	6	67	15.57

TRENT BRIDGE

Larwood's lair

Trent Bridge, around 1.5 km (1 mile) over the River Trent, from Nottingham Station, is considered to be one of the best grounds in England to watch cricket and has hosted Test matches since the Ashes Test of 1899, which marked WG Grace's last England appearance. It is home to Nottinghamshire County Cricket Club for whom the likes of Harold Larwood, Gary Sobers and Richard Hadlee have starred.

The pleasant surroundings seemed to inspire Australia who were unbeaten at the ground between 1934 and 1977. The match in 1977 saw Ian Botham take 5-74, on debut, and England opener Geoff Boycott, returning to Test cricket after a self-imposed exile, run out the local hero Derek Randall, to the crowd's disgust. England won by seven wickets, Boycott scored a hundred and was forgiven by the spectators.

Australia resumed their love affair with the ground, winning four and drawing two of the next six Tests there before England's dramatic victory in 2005. In 1989 Mark Taylor and Geoff Marsh put on 329 for Australia's first wicket and in 1998 Trent Bridge was the scene of a memorable duel between England opener Mike Atherton and South African fast bowler Allan Donald.

Neville Cardus, the famous English cricket writer described Trent Bridge as 'a place where it is always afternoon and 360 for two'. That was a reference to the normally batsman-friendly conditions, which saw Denis Compton score 173 between lunch and tea, for England against Pakistan, in 1954. But the nature of the pitch has changed dramatically since Cardus's day making it a much more even contest between bat and ball. The ball swings more now at the ground and players have put this down to the micro-climate created by the impressive New Stand, on the Bridgford Road side, that was opened in 2008.

No visit to the ground would be complete without a drink in the Trent Bridge Inn. The founder of the ground, William Clarke, spying a patch of meadow at the back of the inn, in 1938, married the landlady, Mary Chapman, and was soon hosting matches there.

Below: Trent Bridge. Andrew Flintoff has just completed his century in the fourth Ashes Test against Australia in 2005.

MATTER OF FACT

Ground: Trent Bridge Cricket Ground
Capacity: 17,500
Located: West Bridgford, Nottinghamshire
Address: Trent Bridge, Nottingham, Nottinghamshire, NG2 6AG
Telephone: + 44 115 982 3000 or 0844 811 8711 (ticket office)
E-mail: administration@nottsccc.co.uk
To get there: Nottingham Station (train)
Stands: Larwood and Voce, William Clarke, Hound Road, Fox Road, Radcliffe Road, New

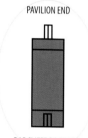

PAVILION END

RADCLIFFE ROAD END

First Test: England v Australia 1-3 June 1899
First ODI: England v Pakistan 31 August 1974
First Twenty20: Bangladesh v India 6 June 2009

Tests played: 55
England: Won 17, lost 16, drawn 22
Highest team total: 658-8 dec (Eng v Aus 1938)
Lowest team total: 88 (SA v Eng 1960)
Highest individual total: 278 DCS Compton (for Eng v Pak 1954)
Highest partnership: 329 (GR Marsh & MA Taylor, 1st wicket for Aus v Eng 1989)
Best bowling: 8-70 M Muralitharan (for SL v Eng 2006)

ODIs played: 33
England: Won 10, lost 11, tied 1 (neutral games 11)
Highest team total: 391-4 (Eng v Ban 2005)
Lowest team total: 83 (SA v Eng 2008)
Highest individual total: 152 AJ Strauss (for Eng v Ban 2005)
Highest partnership: 210 (AJ Strauss & PD Collingwood, 4th wicket for Eng v Ban 2005)
Best bowling: 6-31 PD Collingwood (for Eng v Ban 2005)

Above: Paul Collingwood might be known as 'Brigadier Block' to his colleagues but can hit out when needed.

CRICKET NET

Harold Larwood and Bill Voce, two Nottinghamshire quick bowlers have a stand named after them and spearheaded England's Bodyline attack in 1932-33. They both attended Kirkby Woodhouse Primary School, just outside of Nottingham, and there is a statue of Larwood in full flow in Kirkby-in-Ashfield.

INDIA

Capital: *New Delhi.* **Languages:** *Hindi, English.* **Beer:** *Kingfisher.* **Food:** *Korma, Pasanda, Rogan Josh Gosht, Vindaloo.* **National Anthem:** *Jana Gana Mana (Thou Art the Ruler of the Minds of All People).* **Population:** *1.17 billion.* **Time zone:** *GMT +5.30.*
Emergency numbers: *100 (police), 102,108,104 (medical), 101 (fire).* **Did you know?** *Indian State Railways is one of the world's biggest employers with about 1.5 million staff.*
Cricket body: *Cricket Centre, 2nd Floor, Wankhede Stadium, D Road, Churchgate, Mumbai, 400 020, India. Tel: +91 22 2289 8800. E-mail: bcci@vsni.com or cricketboard@gmail.com. Web: www.bcci.tv.*

Below: Indian fans get their 15 nanoseconds of fame as they play to TV cameras.

Powerbase of modern cricket

Tourists are amazed by the fanaticism for cricket the first time they visit India. Here cricketers are god-like figures – every move of stars like Sachin Tendulkar is scrutinized and the faces of the top players look down on you from virtually every advertising hoarding you see.

The Calcutta Cricket Club was formed in 1792, although all its members were European, but it was in Bombay (now Mumbai) that Indians started to fall in love with the game.

Since then it has become the powerbase of the world sport, with the Indian Premier League attracting the world's top names in return for millions of dollars. Attendances at Test cricket have suffered in comparison with the limited-overs versions of cricket, which attracts massive crowds and television audiences.

India was the sixth side given Test status, playing its first five-day match against England at Lord's in 1932 and hosting its first, also against England, at the Bombay Gymkhana Ground, in December 1933.

It took them until their 25th Test, against England, in Madras (now Chennai), to record their first Test win, but in the 1970s they emerged as one of the powers of world cricket with the legendary quartet of spinners, Erapalli Prasanna, Srinivas Venkataraghavan, Bhagwat Chandrasekhar and Bishan Bedi leading the way with batting superstar Sunil Gavaskar. Later, the emergence of all-rounder Kapil Dev, and Rahul Dravid and Sachin Tendulkar saw India become one of the world's leading cricket nations.

Above: Impromptu games of cricket spring up in India anywhere there is a space and willing players.

TEST RECORD

Versus	First Test	Matches	Won	Lost	Drawn
Australia*	Oct 1956	76	18	34	23
Bangladesh	Nov 2000	5	4	0	1
England	Jun 1932	99	19	34	46
New Zealand	Nov 1955	47	15	9	23
Pakistan	Oct 1952	59	9	12	38
South Africa	Nov 1992	22	5	10	7
Sri Lanka	Sep 1982	32	13	5	14
West Indies	Nov 1948	82	11	30	41
Zimbabwe	Oct 1992	11	7	2	2

* Includes one tied match v Australia (1986)
Most runs: Sachin Tendulkar (1989-) 13,075 runs, 163 Tests, average 55.17
Most wickets: Anil Kumble (1990-2008) 619 wickets, 132 Tests, average 29.65
Most catches: Syed Kirmani (1976-1986) 160 catches, 88 Tests

WORLD CUP RECORD

Year	Venue	Finished
1975	England	Pool
1979	England	Pool
1983	England	Winners
1987	India and Pakistan	Semi-final
1992	Australia and N Zealand	Pool
1996	Ind, Pak and S Lanka	Semi-final
1999	England	6th
2003	South Africa	Runners-up
2007	West Indies	Pool

Most ODI runs: Sachin Tendulkar (1989-) 17,394 runs, 440 matches, average 44.27
Most ODI wickets: Anil Kumble (1990-2007) 337 wickets, 271 games, average 30.90
Most ODI catches: Mohammad Azharuddin (1985-2000) 156 catches, 334 matches

DELHI

Above: The Bahá'í House of Worship in Delhi, inspired by the lotus flower, was completed in 1986 and holds 2,500 people.

Of old and new

Steeped in history, Delhi is the capital of India and the second largest city in this huge country, with a population of more than 12 million. People have lived on the site of this city for over 3,000 years and it has been an important city for Hindus, Muslims and later the British Raj. Following the Hindu dynasties, it was the capital of the influential Mughal Empire for two hundred years from the mid 17th century. It was this great Islamic power that built the walled city of Delhi (by Emperor Shahjahan in 1639) and who contributed greatly to the architecture and food (chicken tikka or biriyani, anyone?) of the country. When the British arrived the centre of influence originally moved to Calcutta but Delhi was declared the capital again early in the 20th century, and it was this decision that led to the creation of New Delhi to the south of the old centre.

New Delhi and Old Delhi can virtually be considered completely separate cities such are their differences. Old Delhi is bustling and lively, full of architectural and historical gems including the Red Fort, numerous mosques and the many gates that provided the entrances to the walled city, the most famous of which is Kashmiri Gate, which was scene of a famous mutiny in 1857 by Indian pro-Independence fighters against the British.

New Delhi, created by the British architect Edward Lutyens, is more serene, its huge, wide avenues creating a feeling of more time and space. It is here that you will find Connaught Place, the busy commercial centre, India Gate, the national monument which commemorates Indian soldiers who died in World War I and Anglo-Afghan Wars, and Akshardham, the important, elaborate Hindu temple complex.

Feroz Shah Kotla cricket stadium is located about 3 km (2 miles) east of Connaught Square.

3 THINGS YOU MUST DO...

1 RED FORT
Built between 1638-1648 the red sandstone Lal Qila (Chandni Chowk, tel: tourist office, +91 11 332 0005) as it is also known locally, is at the heart of Old Delhi. Tickets from the kiosk near Lahore Gate. When: Sun–Sat sunrise–sunset. Price Rs100. To get there: metro to Chawri Bazaar.

2 OLD DELHI
Chandni Chowk is the main street in Old Delhi. Simply stroll along and become part of the seething mass of people, rickshaws, traders and life of the city. To get there: metro to Chandni Chowk.

3 NEW DELHI
If Chandni Chowk gives you a taste of Old Delhi then Connaught Place lets you know just what the New Delhi is all about. This is the centre of the busy, modern Delhi. To get there: metro to Rajiv Chowk.

Above: *A beauty parlour sign in Delhi's Old City.*

WEATHER	LOW (°C)	HIGH (°C)	RAIN (MM)	SUNSET
January	7	21	23	17.36
February	9	24	18	18.00
March	14	31	13	18.21
April	21	37	10	18.40
May	26	41	13	18.56
June	28	39	74	19.14
July	27	36	182	19.24
August	26	34	180	19.12
September	24	34	117	18.43
October	19	34	10	18.09
November	12	29	3	17.38
December	8	23	10	17.24

KOTLA

Where the Devils dare to play

The Feroz Shah Kotla Stadium, named after Feroz Shah Tughlaq, the Emperor of Delhi from 1351 to 1388, became India's fourth Test venue in 1948 when India hosted the West Indies and is now the home of the Delhi Daredevils Indian Premier League franchise.

Established as a cricket ground in 1883, it is found close to India Gate in the city centre and has undergone huge renovations in recent years to make it one of the best stadiums on the subcontinent. The reconstruction began in 2002 although delays in the building work nearly caused the cancellation of the one-day international against Pakistan in 2005.

The Feroz Shah Kotla has seen some of the finest moments in Indian cricket history notably when Anil Kumble became the second bowler in Test history to take all ten wickets in an innings when he spun out Pakistan in 1999 and in 1952 India gained its first win on the ground, also against Pakistan. In 1981 England's Geoffrey Boycott overtook Gary Sobers's aggregate number of runs to become Test cricket's highest scorer in 1981 and Sunil Gavaskar scored his 29th Test hundred on the ground to equal Don Bradman's record in 1983. Both batting marks have long since been eclipsed thanks to the increased amount of cricket being played in the modern era.

Despite all the modernization, the stadium retains one old relic of the past: Feroz Shah Kotla still has an old-style board. Players' names are painted on metal strips that are slotted into place – with cricketers who have fewer letters in their names given more prominence than those with more, leaving spectators straining with binoculars to read them. The main stand has been described as resembling a multi-storey car park. In January 2010, the ICC banned the ground from hosting internationals for one year after the previous month's ODI against Sri Lanka was abandoned because of a poor pitch.

Below: Indian fans use a giant flag to cheer on their heroes and escape from the blistering sun.

MATTER OF FACT
Ground: Feroz Shah Kotla Stadium
Capacity: 48,000
Located: New Delhi, India
Address: Bahadur Shah Zafar Marg, New Delhi, 110002
Telephone: +91 11 2331 9323
E-mail: ddcastadium@yahoo.co.in
To get there: Old Delhi Station (train), New Delhi Stadium (metro)
Stands: North, West, East Hill, Old Clubhouse

STADIUM END

PAVILION END

First Test: India v West Indies 10-14 Nov 1948
First ODI: India v Sri Lanka 15 Sep 1982
First Twenty20: N/A

Tests played: 30
India: Won 10, lost 6, draw 14
Highest team total: 644-8 dec (WI v Ind 1959)
Lowest team total: 75 (Ind v WI 1987)
Highest individual total: 230 B Sutcliffe (for NZ v Ind 1955)
Highest partnership: 278 (G Gambhir & VVS Laxman for 4th wicket, Ind v Aus 2008)
Best bowling: 10-74 A Kumble (for Ind v Pak 1999)

ODIs played: 16
India: Won 8, lost 5, no result 1 (neutral games 2)
Highest team total: 303-8 (Pak v Ind 2005)
Lowest team total: 144 (Ind v Pak 2005)
Highest individual total: 145 RT Ponting (for Aus v Zim 1998)
Highest partnership: 219 (ME Waugh and RT Ponting for 2nd wicket, Aus v Zim 1998)
Best bowling: 6-45 IVA Richards (for WI v Ind 1989)

Above: Anil Kumble took 619 Test wickets with his leg spin in his 18-year international career.

CRICKET NET
Local boy Virender Sehwag scored India's first triple hundred, against Pakistan in 2004, and is known as the Nawab of Najafgarh – the region he hails from in the city. He can be seen coaching youngsters on the outskirts of New Delhi and handing out pocket money.

AHMEDABAD

No spice for me thanks

Those who love cricket in India but are not so keen on spicy food will be glad to hear that Gujarat, the state in which the city of Ahmedabad is situated, has among the least spicy food in the country. Meat-lovers won't be so pleased to discover this is a vegetarian-loving state. The Parsee influence (the Persians lived in Gujarat for hundreds of years from the 12th century) means sugar is a commonly used ingredient as well as yoghurt and gram flour. Pakoras, bhajis, and the popular snack known as Bombay Mix (crunchy nibbles) originate from this area.

Built around the River Sabarmati, the city of about 4.5 million, is one of India's growth cities in the IT and science industries, although it originally prospered on the back of the textile industries.

The city has deep roots in the Indian Independence movement as Mahatma Gandhi set up base here in 1915, and the city was the centre for many protests against British Rule. His former home, Gandhi Ashram is now a national monument.

Sardar Patel Stadium is centrally located on the western bank of the river.

Above: Cows have right of way. **Below:** A water house on the River Sabarmati.

WEATHER	LOW (°C)	HIGH (°C)	RAIN (MM)	SUNSET
January	12	29	3	18.17
February	14	31	1	18.35
March	20	36	1	18.47
April	23	40	1	18.57
May	26	42	6	19.04
June	27	38	113	19.15
July	26	33	270	19.20
August	26	32	223	19.18
September	24	33	171	18.56
October	21	36	11	18.30
November	16	33	9	18.07
December	14	30	3	18.03

3 THINGS YOU MUST DO...

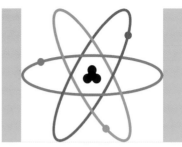

1 GUJARAT SCIENCE CITY

Bringing science and technology to the people, with exhibits, models and demonstrations plus an Imax cinema, and musical fountain (Science City Road, off Sarkhej Gandhinagar Highway, tel: +91 79 6522 0111). When: daily noon–21.00. To get there: 9 km (6 miles) northwest of the city.

2 GANDHI ASHRAM

One of the homes of one of the great men of history, you will see many personal items in the museum (Ashram Rd, tel: +91 79 2755 7277). When: daily 08.30–18.30. Price: free. To get there: near Vadaj by the river. Buses 81, 83/1, 84/1.

3 JHULTA MINARA

The swaying minarets (near Sarangpur Gate) are part of the Siddir Bashir Mosque, and are famous because, er, they sway back and forth when the arch is pushed. To get there: near Ahmedabad Railway Station and Sarangpur Bus Depot.

SARDAR PATEL

It's dry but not for runs

Situated 4 km (2.5 miles) to the west of Ahmedabad, the Sardar Patel Stadium is the home of the Gujarat Cricket Association and became India's 14th Test venue when staging the match, famous for Kapil Dev taking 9-83, against the West Indies in 1983. Despite the all-rounder's efforts to set up a home victory, the Indians were bowled out for 103, with six of their batsman managing just a single run.

Sunil Gavaskar passed 10,000 Test runs here in 1987 and in 1994 Dev became, for a while, the leading wicket taker in Test history when he claimed his 432nd victim, Hashan Tillakaratne, in the Test against Sri Lanka.

The first one-day international on the ground was played when India hosted Allan Border's Australian tourists in 1986, with Dev's side winning by 52 runs, thanks largely to three run outs.

In 2002 Chris Gayle's 140 for the West Indies was not enough to stave off defeat as India, thanks to 109 not out from Rahul Dravid, got home by five wickets.

Gujarat is dry, so tourists seeking an alcoholic drink will be out of luck, however there are a plenty of stalls selling local Indian food and water around the stadium.

Now named after Sardar Vallabhbhai Patel, who was known as the 'Iron Man' and played a leading role in the struggle for Indian independence, it was formerly known as Gujarat Stadium. Built in 1982 on the banks of the Sabarmati River, the ground is also termed Motera by the locals, after the area where it is located.

Below: Mahela Jayawardene holds the ground's highest Test score with his mammoth 275 against India in 2009.

MATTER OF FACT
Ground: Sardar Patel Gujarat Stadium
Capacity: 48,000
Located: Ahmedabad, India
Address: Motera, Sabarmati, Ahmedabad 380 005
Telephone: +91 79 2644 3787 or +91 79 2656 5391
E-mail: gcaaso@vsnl.net/gcaahd@yahoo.co.in
To get there: Rickshaw or taxi 8 km (5 miles) from Ahmedabad Railway Station or 5 km (3 miles) from Ahmedabad Airport
Stands: Presidents Gallery, North, East, West Pavilion, Club Pavilion, Adani Pavilion, GMDC Pavilion

ADANI PAVILION END

GMDC END

First Test: India v West Indies 12-16 Nov 1983
First ODI: India v Australia 5 October 1984
First Twenty20: N/A

Tests played: 10
India: Won 3, lost 2, drawn 5
Highest team total: 760-7 dec (SL v Ind 2009)
Lowest team total: 76 (Ind v SA 2008)
Highest individual total: 275 DPM Jayawardene (for SL v Ind 2009)
Highest partnership: 351 (DPM Jayawardene & HAP Jayawardene, 6th wicket for SL v Ind 2009)
Best bowling: 9-83 Kapil Dev (for Ind v WI 1983)

ODIs played: 16
India: Won 5, lost 5 (neutral games 6)
Highest team total: 325-5 (Ind v WI 2002)
Lowest team total: 85 (Zim v WI 2006)
Highest individual total: 144 SC Ganguly (for Ind v Zim 2000)
Highest partnership: 175 (SC Ganguly & R Dravid, 2nd wicket for Ind v Zim 2000)
Best bowling: 4-20 MF Maharoof (for SL v Ind 2005)

BANGALORE

Above: Flower sellers and other traders can be found in Old Bangalore, away from the bright lights of India's Silicon Valley.

Hello, this is India calling

There can be few people in the world who haven't talked to someone in Bangalore at some stage. Or had some business transaction conducted by someone in Bangalore. It's not because some great exchange programme means we all have friends in this city; it's quite simply because Bangalore is the leading business outsourcing centre in India. You want to do some banking? Speak to India. Problem with your internet connection? India will get you back online. Need a software solution? Let India sort it out. And this city of over five million leads the way to such a degree in information technology that it has earned itself the reputation as the Silicon Valley of India.

With so much high-flying business around it's no surprise to learn that there are quite a few wealthy people around, as well as a strong middle-class, which has helped grow the retail attractions of the city as well as the bar and restaurant options when the sun sets on the world of IT each night.

A lot of the action can be found to the east of Cubbon Park along Mahatma Gandhi Road and the roads leading off it, specifically Brigade Road and Church Road. This is where you will find food, drink and Bangalore's young and hip enjoying a night away from work. This is also the area where you will find designer shops should you need a new Tommy Hilfiger T-shirt.

But in what is probably India's most Westernized city, how about this... Bangalore is the city of baked beans. Well, that at least is the story. The name of the city means this because, according to the story, a travelling king (King Veeraballa of Vijayanagara) got lost and was offered a meal of boiled beans from an old lady. He was so impressed that is what he named the place. Where modern meets baked beans.

And if the modern gets a bit too much and you want a taste of the 'real' India, you'll still be able to find it in Bangalore with a little bit of searching. Head to the area around the city market to the south of Cubbon Park where you will find lively streets, flower and spice traders and bustling activity that seems another world from the modern city of outsourcing centres. See it while you can before the silicon part of the city spreads its tentacles ever further.

3 THINGS YOU MUST DO...

1 BANGALORE TURF CLUB
Go horse racing (Racecourse Rd, tel: +91 80 2226 2391).
When: Fri, Sat or Sun, May–Jul and Nov–Mar. To get there:
2 km (1 mile) northwest of Cubbon Park

2 PUB WORLD
Bangalore is the pub capital of India. Try Pub World (65
Laxmi Plaza, Residency Rd, tel: +91 80 2558 5206) for theme
overload and fun. When: noon–23.00. To get there: 2 km
(1 mile) east of Cubbon Park, nearest bus station is Mayo Hall.

3 BANGALORE PALACE
For some Tudor-style architecture, including towers, in India's
Silicon Valley take a look at Bangalore Palace (Jayamahal
Ext, Armane Nagar). To get there: 3 km (2 miles) north of
Cubbon Park

Above: Indians expect. Flying the flag for the country.

WEATHER	LOW (°C)	HIGH (°C)	RAIN (MM)	SUNSET
January	15	27	3	18.05
February	17	30	7	18.21
March	19	32	4	18.29
April	22	34	46	18.31
May	21	33	120	18.35
June	21	29	85	18.43
July	20	28	115	18.50
August	19	27	137	18.47
September	19	28	195	18.31
October	19	28	178	18.10
November	18	26	64	17.53
December	15	26	22	17.51

M CHINNASWAMY STADIUM

Miss World comes to Mahatma Gandhi Road

Known as the Karnataka State Cricket Association Stadium, when building commenced in 1970, the ground was renamed after Mangalan Chinnaswamy, a prominent cricket administrator, who served as president of the Indian board for 13 years from 1977.

Found on Mahatma Gandhi Road, home to some of the best restaurants in Bangalore, the stadium is close to Cubbon Park in the heart of the city and easily reachable by foot from most of the tourist hotels.

Home to the Royal Challengers Bangalore Twenty20 franchise, the ground is dominated by the huge three-tiered President's Stand with the rest of the ground surrounded by a two-level stand. Vendors under the stands offer a variety of Indian food and drinks.

The M Chinnaswamy Stadium became India's 11th Test ground when the West Indies were the visitors in 1974 as Clive Lloyd's 163 helped the tourists to a 267-run victory. It did not take India long to register their first win at the ground though. In the next Test staged there in 1977 Bhagwat

Chandrasekhar took nine wickets to bowl India to victory against England.

The ground was renovated prior to the 1996 World Cup when India and Pakistan met in an epic quarter-final, under the newly installed floodlights, with the hosts getting home by 39 runs. Since then the ground has seen some notable feats such as Australia's Michael Clarke scoring a century on his Test debut in 2004, England's Michael Vaughan becoming only the seventh player in Test history to be given out handled ball and Pakistan's Inzamam-ul-Haq reaching three figures in his 100th Test match.

In 1996 the stadium was at the centre of a controversy, but it had nothing to do with cricket. Used as the venue for the Miss World pageant, over 1,000 people were arrested in the surrounding area for protesting against the competition being demeaning to women.

Below: Bangalore's cricketing arena was renovated prior to the 1996 World Cup and holds 55,000 fans.

MATTER OF FACT

Ground: M.Chinnaswamy Stadium
Capacity: 55,000
Located: Bangalore, India
Address: Karnataka State Cricket Association, Mahatma Gandhi Road, Bangalore, 560001
Telephone: +91 80 4015 4015 or +91 80 2286 9970
E-mail: ksca@cricketkarnataka.com
To get there: 8 km (5 miles) from Bangalore Railway Station
Stands: President's

PAVILION END

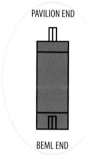

BEML END

First Test: India v West Indies 22-27 November 1974
First ODI: India v Sri Lanka 26 September 1982
First Twenty20: N/A

Tests played: 18
India: Won 4, lost 6, drawn 8
Highest team total: 626 (India v Pak 2007)
Lowest team total: 116 (Pak v Ind 1987)
Highest individual total: 267 Younis Khan (for Pak v India 2005)
Highest partnership: 324(Younis Khan & Inzamam-ul-Haq 3rd wicket, for Pak v Ind 2005)
Best bowling: 7-27 Maninder Singh (for Ind v Pak 1987)

ODIs played: 17
India: Won 10, lost 4, no result 2 (neutral games 1)
Highest team total: 347-2 (Aus v Ind 2003)
Lowest team total: 168 (Ind v Pak 1999)
Highest individual total: 130 SM Pollock (for ACA Africa XI v ACC Asian XI 2007) & MJ Clarke (for Aus v Ind 2007)
Highest partnership: 169 (SC Ganguly & SR Tendulkar 1st wicket for Ind v NZ 1997)
Best bowling: 5-35 PW Jarvis (for Eng v Ind 1993)

Above: Kapil Dev, India's great all-rounder. In 1990 he hit four sixes in a row to avoid the follow-on (at Lord's).

CRICKET NET
Anil Kumble, India's most successful bowler, learnt his cricket on the streets of Bangalore and his family name is derived from the Kumble Village near the Karnataka Border. He retired with 619 Test wickets to his name and took his 400th, on his home ground when bowling Australia's Simon Katich in 2004.

CHENNAI (MADRAS)

Above: All Indian boys dream of emulating their cricket heroes and swapping the beach for a Test ground.

History and art

The start of British Rule in India has strong links to Chennai (Madras) as the first British fortress, Fort St George, was established here in 1639 to secure trade for the British East India Company. Interestingly Fort St George is now the seat of the modern Tamil Nadu government and houses Indian troops. Just to the north of the fort, the settlement of George Town developed and today the streets of this old area, which gradually gave birth to the city, are still vibrant and bustling with shops, offices and bazaars. The modern part of the city lies just to the south, just follow the main thoroughfare, Anna Salai Road

For a taste of shopping Indian-style, head to the Ranganathan Street, where you won't find any shortage of retail outlets, formal and informal, or fellow shoppers after a bargain. Busy, busy.

Chennai has a healthy arts and cultural scene with dance, theatre, music, and this being India, film flourishes in the city. The renowned Madras Music Season, which celebrates Carnatic music, a form of Indian classical music, features established and up-and-coming artists in hundreds of performances taking place over a six-week period in December and January. The graceful classical dance form Bharatanatyam – which originated in this area – also thrives. Impress the locals by mentioning Hastas (the elaborate hand movements), Karanas (the main movements) and Adavus (the steps). Bharatanatyam is usually accompanied by Carnatic music. The city's film industry has a long history dating back to the early 20th century, and today produces more than 150 Tamil films every year, in an industry that is known as 'Kollywood'.

MA Chidambaram Stadium is centrally located near the Bay of Bengal.

3 THINGS YOU MUST DO...

1 FORT MUSEUM
Memories of the British Raj and the British East India Company abound in this museum (tel: +91 44 2567 1127) with its collection of items from that era. Note the 46-metre-high flag post outside, which was taken from a shipwreck. When: Sat–Thurs 10.00–17.00. Price: Rs100.

2 ROYAL ENFIELD
This famous bike has been produced in India since 1955. You can visit the factory (Tiruvottiyur High Rd, Tiruvottiyur, tel: +91 44 4204 3300) that still produces the Classic Bullet. When: tours every Saturday. Price: Rs600. To get there: the factory is 17 km (11 miles) from Chennai.

3 MARINA BEACH
Said to be one of the longest beaches in the world (or the longest if you talk to a local), the sandy Marina Beach is some 13 km (8 miles) long. This is a beach for strolling, jogging and people watching, not swimming.

Above: *A Chennai temple brings colour to the city.*

WEATHER	LOW (°C)	HIGH (°C)	RAIN (MM)	SUNSET
January	19	29	36	17.53
February	20	31	10	18.11
March	22	34	8	18.18
April	25	35	15	18.22
May	27	38	28	18.24
June	27	38	51	18.31
July	26	36	91	18.39
August	27	36	123	18.35
September	25	34	119	18.20
October	24	32	305	17.58
November	22	29	359	17.42
December	21	29	141	17.40

MA CHIDAMBARAM STADIUM

The stadium of knowledge

The MA Chidambaram Stadium, formerly Chepauk and the Madras Cricket Club Ground, is found 3 km (1.86 miles) to the south of the city near the Buckingham Canal. As well as lying next to this historic waterway the ground, the spiritual home of cricket in the state of Tamil Nadu, has seen its fair of history with cricket having been played here since 1865.

Named after a famous industrialist, who was also head of India's Board of Control and the Tamil Nadu Cricket Association, the stadium was the scene of Test cricket's second tie in history – between India and Australia in 1986. It also hosted the final match of the epic series between the same two countries in 2001 when Harbhajan Singh took 15 wickets in the game to give the Indians a historic win.

After hosting, and losing heavily to, Douglas Jardine's England tourists in 1934, India only played three more games at the ground before 1952 after which it was not used for Test cricket until 1967. During that time all matches in Madras were played at the Nehru Corporation Stadium.

The ground itself is a mass of knowledgeable cricket fans, although during breaks in play they do allow their concentration to wander from the cricket as they dance to music on the stands creating a memorable atmosphere.

In 2008 the Chennai Super Kings, the local Twenty20 franchise, made it to the final of the first Indian Premier League with captain Mahendra Singh Dhoni saying the atmosphere at the ground had spurred them to their success. A year later the team's owners bid a record US$1.5million to secure the services of English all-rounder Andrew Flintoff for the tournament.

The locals here appreciate their cricket. In 1999 after winning a Test by two runs the Pakistani team, India's biggest rivals, were given a standing ovation by the home crowd.

Below: *A first day cover celebrates the 75th anniversary of the first England team to play at the ground. Douglas Jardine led his touring side here in 1934.*

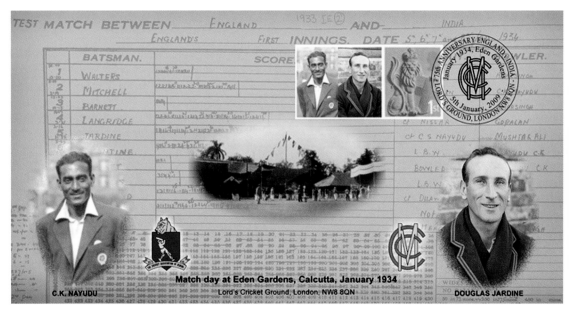

NNA PAVILION END

V PATTABHIRAMAN GATE END

First Test: India v England 10-13 Feb 1934
First ODI: India v Australia 9 Oct 1987
First Twenty20: N/A

Tests played: 30
India: Won 12, lost 6, drawn 11, tied 1
Highest team total: 652-7 (Eng v Ind 1985)
Lowest team total: 83 (Ind v Eng 1977)
Highest individual total: 319 V Sehwag (for Ind v SA 2008)
Highest partnership: 316 (GR Viswanath & Yashpal Sharma 3rd wicket, for Ind v Eng 1982)
Best bowling: 8-55 MH Mankad (for Ind v Eng 1952)

ODIs played: 12
India: Won 2, lost 3, no result 1, (neutral 6)
Highest team total: 337-7 (ACA Asia XI v ACA Africa XI 2007)
Lowest team total: 139 (Zim v Aus 1987)
Highest individual total: 194 Saeed Anwar (for Pak v Ind 1997)
Highest partnership: 218 (DPM Jayawardene & MS Dhoni 6th wicket, for ACC Asia XI v ACA Africa XI)
Best bowling: 5-61 Aaqib Javed (for Pak v Ind 1997)

Above: *Mahendra Singh Dhoni, the pin-up boy of Indian cricket, attempts a sharp stumping v South Africa.*

CRICKET NET

Sport is huge in Chennai. The tennis player Vijay Armitraj hails from the city and Australian Dennis Lillee helped to set up the MRF Pace Academy to nurture fast bowlers in the town in 1987. Graduates include Zaheer Khan and Javagal Srinath. Australians Brett Lee and Mitchell Johnson have also trained there.

CUTTACK

Pure gold on the delta

The relatively small city (in Indian terms) of Cuttack is built on a delta of the Mahanadi River as it splits and winds its way east towards to Bay of Bengal. Despite its position on the delta, the population of over half a million (repeat, small by Indian terms) are well connected not only off the delta to the east but also by road and rail bridges to both the north and the south. To the south lies Cuttack's 'twin' city, Bhubaneswar, which is where the Orissa state capital was moved in 1948 due to the space constraints on the delta city.

As well as textiles – cotton and silk – Cuttack is best known for its delicate and pure silver and gold filigree and there is no shortage of shops and traders displaying the Silver City's work for sale.

Barabati Stadium is situated towards the north shore of the delta.

Above: Cycling through a rice field. Below: Temples in Cuttack.

WEATHER	LOW (°C)	HIGH (°C)	RAIN (MM)	SUNSET
January	15	29	5	16.58
February	19	31	28	17.21
March	22	35	26	17.35
April	25	37	24	17.47
May	26	37	60	18.00
June	26	35	203	18.13
July	25	32	330	18.21
August	25	32	327	18.13
September	25	32	251	17.50
October	23	31	129	17.20
November	19	30	49	16.55
December	16	27	8	16.50

3 THINGS YOU MUST DO...

1 BARABATI FORT
The fort (Cantonment Rd) dates back to the 14th century, and its ruins, including the gate and moat, can still be seen. To get there: towards the north shore near the Barabati Stadium.

2 DAHIBARA WITH ALOO DUM
A Cuttack favourite, this is essentially a combinations of three dishes – Dahibara (fritters soaked in yoghurt), Aloo dum (potatoes in spicy sauce) and ghugni (curried chickpeas). This is a street food snack.

3 SUN TEMPLE
This celebrated religious site (Konark) dates back to the 13th century and was built as a chariot (there are seven huge carved stone horses and 12 pairs of wheels) for Surya, the sun god. To get there: Konark is 95 km (59 miles) south of Cuttack.

BARABATI STADIUM

Forgotten Test ground of India

The Barabati Stadium in Cuttack was the host for the third one-day international in India, when the touring English were beaten, but has had only a few chances to stage Test cricket, putting just two five-day games on between 1987 and 1995 and no more up to 2009. Many visiting teams have been reluctant to travel from Bhubaneshwar, an hour away by car, where most of the good hotels in the area are situated.

Home of the Orissa Cricket Association the ground put on its first Test match when the Sri Lankans were the visitors on an under-prepared wicket. Here, with no other batsman passing 60, Dilip Vengsarkar scored his Test best of 166 and won by an innings. The match was also notable for Kapil Dev taking his 300th Test wicket.

In one-day cricket the Barabati Stadium staged games in the 1987 and 1996 World Cups but in 2007 the future of cricket at the ground was put into doubt when the Indian coach Greg Chappell was attacked by an angry fan at the nearby Bhubaneshwar airport.

However that threat was staved off in 2008 when England were the visitors again. Kevin Pietersen, England's new captain, made a century, even though it was not enough for his side to avoid defeat.

The ground was severely damaged in the cyclone of 1999 with the scoreboard, press box and boundary walls all suffering, However 13 months later after extensive work it was back in operation to host the one-day match between India and Zimbabwe in December 2000.

Below: Sachin Tendulkar limbers up for yet another one-day match. Barabati Stadium is a popular ODI venue.

MATTER OF FACT
Ground: Barabati Stadium
Capacity: 45,000
Located: Cuttack, Orissa, India
Address: Cuttack, 753005
Telephone: +91 671 2302 742
E-mail: orissacricket@yahoo.co.in
To get there: Cuttack Railway Station
Stands: Five galleries, two pavilions, one special enclosure

MAHANADI RIVER END

PAVILION END

First Test: India v Sri Lanka 4-7 January 1987
First ODI: India v England 27 January 1982
First Twenty20: N/A

Tests played: 2
India: Won 1, drawn 1
Highest team total: 400 Ind v SL 1987
Lowest team total: 142 SL v Ind 1987
Highest individual total: 166 DB Vengsarkar (for Ind v SL 1987)
Highest partnership: 111 (DB Vengsarkar & Kapil Dev, 6th wicket for Ind v SL 1987)
Best bowling: 6-59 N Hirwani (for Ind v NZ 1995)

ODIs played: 15
India: Won 9, lost 4 (neutral games 2)
Highest team total: 301-3 (Ind v Zim 1998)
Lowest team total: 169 (WI v Ind 2007)
Highest individual total: 153 not out M Azharuddin (for Ind v Zim 1998)
Highest partnership: 275 (M Azharuddin & AD Jadeja, 4th wicket for Ind v Zim 1998)
Best bowling: 4-27 DB Powell (for WI v Ind 2007)

KANPUR

Where the Moghuls roamed

Poor old Kanpur. Uttar Pradesh is a state that's embarrassed with historical and cultural riches – Agra and its Taj Mahal, Varanasi and its Ganges ghats, Lucknow's city-of-culture reputation. Kanpur, meanwhile, gets to be the biggest city in the state (ok, it is on the Ganges as well). Thank goodness it gets to share the great traditions of Moghul cuisine. It was the Moghuls who knew the art of blending spices and together with cream and butter created what most people in the rest of the world today refer to as 'curry' – creating such classic dishes as the aromatic Roghan Josh Gosht and the rich, creamy Chicken Korma.

Kanpur, with a population of nearly five million, is one of the largest in the country, and is an important industrial centre, particularly for leather, textiles, engineering and chemicals.

Green Park Stadium is northeast of the centre by the Ganges River.

Above: The holy river Ganges. *Below:* Kanpur silk and local flowers are used to adorn headgear.

WEATHER	LOW (°C)	HIGH (°C)	RAIN (MM)	SUNSET
January	7	22	24	17.19
February	9	27	15	17.40
March	14	32	8	18.00
April	20	39	3	18.12
May	25	42	18	18.28
June	28	39	110	18.43
July	26	34	301	18.53
August	24	32	321	18.43
September	24	34	180	18.17
October	19	32	43	17.44
November	12	29	3	17.15
December	8	24	10	17.07

3 THINGS YOU MUST DO...

1 NANA RAO PARK

The park (where you will see peacocks) is the site of the 1857 Indian Mutiny where over 100 women and children were held, then killed. Many Indians were massacred when the English relief arrived. The ridge of the well can still be seen, and there is a statue. To get there: east by the river.

2 JAIN GLASS TEMPLE

This Jain temple is elaborately decorated with carvings, with marble floors and ornamental arches. To get there: near Kamla Tower, Birhani Road.

3 KANPUR ZOO

As well as the expected animals (including tigers) there are parklands and a lake at the zoo (Allen Park). When: Tues–Sun. To get there: near Allen Park Bus Terminal.

GREEN PARK

In and out of favour

Established in 1945, and initially known as Modi Stadium, Green Park Stadium is set a short walk from the centre of Kanpur close to the river Ganges. It became India's sixth Test ground when hosting the 1952 English tourists who won the inaugural match by eight wickets. Seven years later India recorded its first win at the ground when Richie Benaud's Australians were bowled out for 105 with Jasubhai Patel and Pahlan Umrigar sharing nine second innings wickets between them. Patel also took a remarkable 9-69 in the first innings. In 1985 it was the scene of Mohammad Azharuddin's third century in his third Test and Kapil Dev hit a hundred off just 74 balls against Sri Lanka a year later. In 2005 Pakistan all-rounder Shahid Afridi hit 102 from 45 balls in a one-day international.

The ground did not host any Test cricket for ten years from 1986 and for five years from 1999 after the Indian authorities stated it was not 'in proper shape to conduct an international match'. But improvements by the Uttar Pradesh Cricket Association saw it put back on rota as it hosted the first Test between India and South Africa in 2004. More trouble followed in 2006 when the ICC ordered the stadium to be removed from the list of international venues. The problems included poor visibility, due to local pollution, a lifeless pitch and poor floodlights. However, after more improvements one-day international cricket returned in 2007 and Test cricket the next year when South Africa were beaten by eight wickets.

Below: Green Park hosting of Test matches had been interrupted by poor facilities before its renovation.

MATTER OF FACT
Ground: Green Park Stadium
Capacity: 45,000
Located: Civil Lines, Kanpur, India
Address: E/23, Ashram Building, PO HN Shastri Nagar, Kamla Nagar, Township, Kanpur, 208 005
Telephone: +91 512 2240 933 or +91 512 2218 076
E-mail: upcaknp@gmail.com
To get there: 6 km (4 miles) northeast of the centre by the Ganges River

MILL PAVILION END

HOSTEL END

First Test: India v England 12-14 Jan 1952
First ODI: India v Sri Lanka 24 Dec 1986
First Twenty20: N/A

Tests played: 21
India: Won 6, lost 3, drawn 12
Highest team total: 676-7 (Ind v SL 1986)
Lowest team total: 105 (Aus v Ind 1959)
Highest individual total: 250 SFA Bacchus (for WI v Ind 1979)
Highest partnership: 272 (M Azharuddin & Kapil Dev, 6th wicket for Ind v SL 1986)
Best bowling: 9-69 JM Patel (for Ind v Aus 1959)

ODIs played: 12
India: Won 8, lost 3 (neutral game 1)
Highest team total: 294-6 (Ind v Pak 2007)
Lowest team total: 78 (Ind v SL 1986)
Highest individual total: 129 Salman Butt (for Pak v Ind 2007)
Highest partnership: 175 (SC Ganguly & SR Tendulkar, 1st wicket for Ind v Aus 1998)
Best bowling: 5-24 J Srinath (for Ind v SL 1993)

KOLKATA (CALCUTTA)

Above: *The yellow taxis of Kolkata.*

Impoverished but grand

Close to the border of Pakistan, and with high levels of poverty, sprawling Kolkata (Calcutta) is one of the largest urban areas in the world, with nearly 15 million people living in the greater urban area and surrounds.

Once the capital of the British Raj, the city boasts an eclectic range of architectural styles such as the Indo-Gothic Victoria Memorial, a memorial to Queen Victoria that was built using European and Mughal influences. The Victorian Gothic St Paul's Cathedral, with its stained-glass windows and frescoes would not look out of place in an English city, while the building of the Calcutta High Court is a copy of a structure in Ypres, Belgium. There are two significant bridges, the cantilevered Howrah Bridge, and the cable-stayed Vidyasagar Setu and many religious sites, including the nine-spired Dakshinewar Kali Temple. Downtown Kolkata has many modern high-rise commercial buildings.

Sadly it is poverty that most people instantly associate with Kolkata and it is a town of huge slum areas that can spring up and grow at an unprecedented rate. The city was, of course, renowned as the home of Nobel Peace Prize winner Mother Teresa, who dedicated her life to helping the poor before her death in 1997.

Ultimately the city will bombard your senses, with the energy of its street traders and its business life constantly rubbing shoulders with the in-your-face poverty. From its simple street food and humble flower sellers to its workers in the modern, growing IT industry, it's impossible not to be carried along in the vibrancy of the seething mass of people in this city.

Eden Gardens is centrally located near the Hooghly River.

3 THINGS YOU MUST DO...

1 VICTORIA MEMORIAL

The memorial (built in 1921) is now a museum (Hospital Rd, tel: +91 33 2223 1889) where you can discover everything about British Rule in India. When: Tues–Sun, Mar–Oct 10.00–17.00, Nov–Feb 10.00–16.00. Light show 19.15–20.00 Price: Rs150. To get there: nearest metro is Maidan.

2 NATIONAL LIBRARY

The largest library in India with well over 2.4 million books, this is the country's library of public record (Belvedere Estate, tel: +91 33 2479 1381/2/3/4. When: Mon–Fri 09.00–20.00, Sat–Sun and holidays 09.30–18.00.

3 ROYAL CALCUTTA TURF CLUB

A day at the races, Indian style (Hastings, tel: +91 33 2248 7170) the course dates back to 1820. When: Jul–Sept, Nov–Mar, mostly Sat and Weds but varies. To get there: near Victoria Memorial, the nearest metro is Maidan.

Above: An elephant puts in a day's work in India.

WEATHER	LOW (°C)	HIGH (°C)	RAIN (MM)	SUNSET
January	13	27	10	17.03
February	15	29	31	17.24
March	20	34	40	17.41
April	24	36	47	17.52
May	25	36	140	18.03
June	25	33	297	18.18
July	26	33	325	18.25
August	27	32	333	18.20
September	26	32	252	17.54
October	24	32	114	17.25
November	17	28	20	16.59
December	13	26	5	16.51

EDEN GARDENS

The Lord's of Asia

Eden Gardens, found in the massive park Kolkata Maidan, a ten-minute walk from the centre of the city in the Dalhousie area, is one of the largest grounds in the world and hosts one of the game's most enthusiastic and knowledgeable crowds. It is known as 'The Lord's of Asia'.

This enthusiasm has gone too far on a few occasions when riots have interrupted matches. In 1966 the crowd disrupted the Test match against the West Indies and in 1969 the game against Australia was also affected. In the 1996 World Cup semi-final, unruly fans caused the abandonment of the game between India and the eventual winners of the tournament, Sri Lanka.

On a happier note, the ground became the second Test venue in India when Douglas Jardine's India visited in 1934 but the tourists were frustrated by rain when needing just 82 to win. It also hosted the 1987 World Cup final, won by Australia and one of the most epic Test matches of all time in March 2001 when VVS Laxman and Rahul Dravid set up a memorable win for India, who had been forced to follow on, against the Australians. In the same game Harbhajan Singh became the first Indian to take a Test hat-trick which helped him to 13 wickets in the match.

Established in 1864 the ground is home to the Kolkata Knight Riders Indian Premier League franchise and the Bengal cricket team. Its capacity has been reduced from 120,000 in recent times but it is still the second largest stadium of any kind in India behind the Salt Lake Stadium.

The ground is dominated by the DR BC Roy Clubhouse, a three-tier structure to the south of the ground that is named after the former Chief Minister of the State of West Bengal. It is said a cricketer's education is not complete until he has played at Eden Gardens. The same can be said of spectators.

Below: Sachin Tendulkar (right) practises his hand bumping. Hardly a run can be scored in modern cricket without the batsmen congratulating each other.

MATTER OF FACT

Ground: Eden Gardens
Capacity: 90,000
Located: Kolkata, India
Address: Eden Garden Rd, Kolkata, West Bengal 700021
Telephone: +91 33 2248 0411 or +91 33 22482447
E-mail: thecab@vsnl.net
To get there: Esplanade Station (metro)
Stands: Dr BC Roy Clubhouse, Blocks B-L

HIGH COURT END

PAVILION END

First Test: India v England 5-8 Jan 1934
First ODI: India v Pakistan 18 Feb 1987
First Twenty20: N/A

Tests played: 35
India: Won 8, lost 8, drawn 19
Highest team total: 657-7 dec (Ind v Aus 2001)
Lowest team total: 90 (Ind v WI 1983)
Highest individual total: 281 VVS Laxman (for Ind v Aus 2001)
Highest partnership: 376 (VVS Laxman & R Dravid, 5th wicket for Ind v Aus 2001)
Best bowling: 8-64 L Klusener (for SA v Ind 1996)

ODIs played: 22
India: won 9, lost 6, no result 1 (neutral games 6)
Highest team total: 317-3 (Ind v SL 2009)
Lowest team total: 123 (WI v Ind 1993)
Highest individual total: 150 not out G Gambhir (for Ind v SL 2009)
Highest partnership: 224 (G Gambhir & V Kohli, 3rd wicket for Ind v SL 2009)
Best bowling: 6-12 A Kumble (for Ind v WI 1993)

Above: Virender Sehwag became the third batsman in Test history to score two treble hundreds.

CRICKET NET

Sourav Ganguly, known as the Prince of Kolkata, is the highest profile player to come out of the city. He became a hero to the locals by becoming the first Indian captain to win a Test series in Pakistan, in 2004.

CHANDIGARH

A little plan goes a long way

People who love planned cities will love Chandigarh (together with Mohali, where you'll find the cricket stadium and Panchkula it forms the Chandigarh Tricity). Built from a plan from American Albert Mayer and later French architect Le Corbusier, the city grew up after the partition of India in 1947. With the Punjab split and its capital Lahore going to Pakistan, the Indian authorities decided it needed a new capital and the city was born. Today the city is the joint capital of Punjab and Haryana states.

With a lake and forested areas to the northeast, the city is built on a classic grid-pattern, with wide avenues, making orientation easy. The logical naming of areas (Sector 1, Sector 2 etc) makes the job of getting around this city of around 900,000 people even easier for visitors, if a little soulless.

Mohali Stadium is centrally located in Mohali, in Sector 63.

*Above: A Buddha statue. **Below:** Le Corbusier's Open Hand Monument in Chandigarh.*

WEATHER	LOW (°C)	HIGH (°C)	RAIN (MM)	SUNSET
January	6	20	33	17.38
February	9	24	39	18.03
March	13	28	30	18.23
April	18	34	15	18.40
May	22	38	28	18.58
June	25	38	149	19.16
July	23	34	280	19.25
August	23	33	307	19.15
September	22	33	133	18.45
October	17	31	28	18.10
November	10	26	12	17.38
December	6	21	22	17.26

3 THINGS YOU MUST DO...

1 THE PLANNED CITY
Stroll around this planned city and witness what man will create when given an empty slate. Le Corbusier (Le Corbusier Centre, Sector 19-B, tel: +91 171 277 7077) had immense influence across the world in the fields of architecture and urban design and here is a chance to see it first hand.

2 NEK CHAND'S ROCK GARDEN
This fun garden (Sector 1, tel: +91 172 740 645) was started by one man (Nek Chand) who cleared a patch of ground and started building back in the 1970s. When: Apr–Sept 09.00–19.00, Oct–Mar 09.00–18.00. Price: Rs5 adult, Rs3 child. To get there: hop-on-hop-off coach (Tel: +91 172 270 3839).

3 SUKNA LAKE
For some energetic jogging or just some peace and quiet, Sukna Lake (Sector 1) is a popular place for chilling out. To get there: hop-on-hop-off coach (tel: +91 172 270 3839) visits all tourist attractions.

MOHALI STADIUM

Jewel of Chandigarh

The Punjab Cricket Association Stadium, commonly referred to as Mohali Stadium is one of the most modern grounds in India and is found about 10 km (6.2 miles) from the centre of Chandigarh. Built on the site of a swamp the stadium was opened in 1993, when it was inaugurated with a one-day game against South Africa during the Hero Cup, and has some of the best spectator facilities in the country.

It staged its first Test in 1994, when the West Indies toured and beat India by 243 runs, and was the scene of a nail-biting World Cup semi-final in 1996 when Australia squeezed home against the West Indies by five runs thanks to four wickets from Shane Warne.

Home to the Kings XI Indian Premier League franchise, Mohali was also where Sachin Tendulkar overtook Brian Lara's aggregate of 11,953 runs to become Test cricket's leading scorer in the 2008 Test match against Australia.

Unusually for India, the ground had a reputation for a lively seamer-friendly pitch and, in 1999 the New Zealand fast bowler Dion Nash took 6-27 as India were bowled out for 83.

In 2005 members of the hardline Hindu Shiv Sena movement tried to damage the pitch at the ground ahead of the first Test against Pakistan leading to increased security at the ground.

The ground has had problems with falling attendances in recent years. Cars, apart from those carrying VIPs, are not allowed near to the stadium leaving fans a walk of around 1,000 metres to get in.

Below: Sachin Tendulkar. The Little Master became the first player to reach 12,000 Test runs in 2008.

MATTER OF FACT
Ground: Punjab Cricket Association Stadium
Capacity: 45,000
Located: Mohali, Chandigarh
Address: Sector 63, SAS Nagar, Mohali, 160059
Telephone: +91 172 223 2300/1/2
E-mail: pcastadium@yahoo.com
To get there: Chandigarh Railway Station
Stands: Terrace Block, North Pavilion, Chair Block

PAVILION END

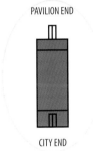

CITY END

First Test: India v West Indies 10-14 Dec 1994
First ODI: India v South Africa 22 Nov 1993
First Twenty20: N/A

Tests played: 9
India: Won 3, lost 1, drawn 5
Highest team total: 630-6 dec (NZ v Ind 2003)
Lowest team total: 83 (Ind v NZ 1999)
Highest individual total: 179 G Gambhir (for Ind v Eng 2008)
Highest partnership: 314 (G Gambhir & R Dravid, 2nd wicket for Ind v Eng 2008)
Best bowling: 6-27 D Nash (for NZ v Ind 2003)

ODIs played: 16
India: Won 5, lost 4 (neutral games 7)
Highest team total: 339-4 (SL v Pak 1997)
Lowest team total: 89 (Pak v SA 2006)
Highest individual total: 117 NJ Astle (for NZ v Pak 1997) & Younis Khan (for Pak v Ind 2007)
Highest partnership: 173 (SR Tendulkar & G Gambhir, 2nd wicket for Ind v Pak 2007)
Best bowling: 5-27 M Ntini (for SA v Pak 2006)

MUMBAI (BOMBAY)

Above: *Mumbai is surrounded by water. The city was originally seven islands that were joined together through land reclamation projects.*

Capital of cool

Lying on the west coast of India, Mumbai (Bombay) is India's capital of cool, with good food and nightlife, a large middle-class, Bollywood and a vibrant commercial centre. Getting around is not easy, with congestion (and pollution) slowing down your movement, but as you sit in your taxi wondering if you'll ever move forward again the energy of everyone else as they go about their life, whether in an air-conditioned office suite or selling food under a plastic canopy on the street, will keep your heart beating. It's that type of city.

The energy and congestion is not surprising – Mumbai is one of the biggest urban areas in the world with around 14 million people bursting from its city seams.

Mumbai is a centre for television, publishing and, of course, the famed Bollywood film industry, the Hindi-language industry that is one of the largest producers of films in the world. The movie industry has a rich heritage in the city dating back to 1913 when the first silent movie was produced here. Today the all-singing, all-dancing, all-romancing genre of film produces dozes of films in the city every year.

Nightlife in Mumbai is among the best in the country and you'll find no shortage of places to keep you entertained. Many good bars and restaurants can be found in the city's top hotels, while the Bandra is a popular district for food, drink and dance.

Wankhede Stadium is located towards the southern tip of the city, not much more than a big six from the Arabian Sea.

3 THINGS YOU MUST DO...

1 PARTY

Mumbai certainly knows how to party. Join it. Try Vie Lounge (102 Juhu Tara Rd, tel: +91 22 2660 3003) for music, food, cocktails and cool people. When: daily 07.00–01.30. To get there: on the west coast near Juhu Beach.

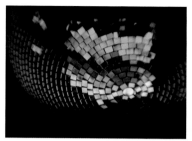

2 GATEWAY TO INDIA

Built for the visit of King George VI and Queen Mary in 1911, this 26-metre-high (85 feet) archway has provided a welcome to India for anyone arriving by ship. To get there: to the south by BEST Bhavan bus depot.

3 BOLLYWOOD

Where better to watch the genre of film known as Bollywood than in the huge Imax Theatre (Bhakti Marg, Ankit Wadala Link Rd, tel: +91 22 2403 6606). When: films shown from 10.00–23.00 approx. To get there: nearest train station is Wadala.

Above: Let the music play.

WEATHER	LOW (°C)	HIGH (°C)	RAIN (MM)	SUNSET
January	19	28	3	18.13
February	19	28	2	18.32
March	23	30	4	18.43
April	24	32	0	18.52
May	27	33	22	19.02
June	26	32	498	19.12
July	25	30	622	19.20
August	25	29	342	19.15
September	24	28	278	18.54
October	24	32	71	18.25
November	22	32	18	18.04
December	21	31	1	18.01

WANKHEDE STADIUM

Kings of swing

The Wankhede Stadium is found 3 km (2 miles) from the centre of Mumbai and a short work from Colaba, an area popular with visiting cricket supporters. It became the third ground in the city to host Test cricket after the Bombay Gymkhana and the Brabourne Stadium in 1975 when the West Indies captain Clive Lloyd marked the occasion by hitting 242.

The stadium was established because of a dispute between the Cricket Club of India and Mumbai Cricket Association. An argument over ticket allocations for the Test between England and India in 1973 led SK Wankhede, a politician and Secretary of MCA, to authorise the building of a new arena in the south of the city. It is now the premier venue in Mumbai, and the centre of Indian cricket administration, with the BCCI moving their offices into the ground in 2006.

England's Ian Botham took a liking to the ground in the 1980 Jubilee Test, scoring a century and taking 13 wickets to guide his team to a ten-wicket win and in 1985 Ravi Shastri hit six sixes in an over off Baroda's Tilak Raj whilst playing for Bombay in a Ranji Trophy match.

Situated near the sea, the ground has proved a happy hunting ground for swing bowlers such as Botham, especially early in the day and in the second innings of day-night matches. The main gates to the Wankhede ground are named after former cricketers – Polly Umrigar and Vinoo Mankad – and the stands are tributes to other cricketing luminaries.

Having already been improved ahead of the 1996 World Cup, when it hosted group matches, the ground was further renovated in preparation for the 2011 World Cup final and was out of action from July 2008. Apart from cricket the ground has also hosted concerts, including one by Shakira in 2007.

Below: Wankhede Stadium, scene of Ravi Shastri's six sixes in one over in 1985.

MATTER OF FACT
Ground: Wankhede Stadium
Capacity: 45,000
Located: Mumbai, India
Address: D Road, Churchgate, Mumbai, 400020
Telephone: +91 22 2279 5500
E-mail: mcacrik@vsnl.com
To get there: Churchgate Station (train)
Stands: Vijay Merchant, Sachin Tendulkar, Sunil Gavaskar

GARWARE PAVILION END

TATA END

First Test: India v West Indies 23-29 Jan 1975
First ODI: India v Sri Lanka 17 Jan 1987
First Twenty20: N/A

Tests played: 21
India: Won 9, lost 6, drawn 6
Highest team total: 604-6 dec (WI v Ind 1975)
Lowest team total: 93 (Aus v Ind 2004)
Highest individual total: 242 CH Lloyd (for WI v Ind 1975)
Highest partnership: 298 (DB Vengsarkar & RJ Shastri, 6th wicket for Ind v Aus 1986)
Best bowling: 7-48 IT Botham (for Eng v Ind 1980) & Harbhajan Singh (for Ind v WI 2002)

ODIs played: 15
India: Won 8, lost 5 (neutral games 2)
Highest team total: 299-4 (Ind v SL 1987)
Lowest team total: 115 (Ban v Ind 1998)
Highest individual total: 151 not out ST Jayasuriya (for SL v Ind 1997)
Highest partnership: 138 (ST Jayasuriya & MS Atapattu, 2nd wicket for SL v Ind 1997)
Best bowling: 6-27 M Kartik (for Ind v Aus 2007)

Above: Devotion to the game of cricket in India.

CRICKET NET
Mumbai's Sachin Tendulkar is the highest earning cricketer in the world. With his sponsorships and business interests, including local restaurants, his income per annum is estimated as £10million. In 2002 *Wisden* rated him the second best batsman ever, behind Don Bradman.

NEW ZEALAND

THE

3

MINUTE
GUIDE

Capital: *Wellington.* **Language:** *English.* **Beers:** *Tui, Speight's.* **Food:** *Lamb, Hokey pokey ice cream, ANZAC biscuits.* **National Anthem:** *God Defend New Zealand.* **Population:** *4.3 million.* **Time zone:** *GMT +12.* **Emergency number:** *111.* **Did you know?** *Bong. New Zealand is the first major country to celebrate New Year every year. Bong.* **Cricket body:** *Level 6, 164 Hereford Street, Christchurch, New Zealand. Tel: +64 3 366 2964. E-mail: info@nzcricket.org.nz. Web: www.blackcaps.co.nz.*

Below: Great skiing can be found at Coronet Peak to the north of Queenstown.

The rise of the Black Caps

Although New Zealand did not play their first Test match until 1930 cricket was mentioned by the naturalist Charles Darwin in his diary in 1835 after he saw a game being played by children in the Bay of Islands.

Despite having a population of just over 4 million, and cricket playing second fiddle to rugby union in the affections of the public, the national side have consistently punched above their weight since winning their first match, against the West Indies, in 1956.

One of the major factors in their improvement in the in the 1970s and 1980s was the emergence of a clutch of talented players spearheaded by the world-class talents of fast bowler Richard Hadlee and batsman Martin Crowe. Hadlee was, for a time, the leading wicket taker in Test history with 431 victims, whilst Crowe scored 5,444 runs in just 77 Tests. At Brisbane in 1985, Crowe scored 188 in New Zealand's only innings and Hadlee took a total of 15 wickets to give New Zealand their first away win against Australia. Men such as Geoff Howarth, John Wright, Jeremy Coney, Jeff Crowe and John Bracewell added to the quality.

Crowe was also an innovative captain, opening the bowling with a spinner, Dipak Patel, as New Zealand got to the semi-finals of the 1992 World Cup, one of five occasions they have made the last four without qualifying for the final. In recent years Stephen Fleming, the best captain New Zealand, or the Black Caps as they are also known, has had, led his side to 28 wins in 80 Tests before retiring in 2008.

Above: *Humboldt Mountains on the South Island of New Zealand.*

TEST RECORD

Versus	First Test	Matches	Won	Lost	Drawn
Australia	Mar 1946	48	7	24	17
Bangladesh	Dec 2001	8	7	0	1
England	Jan 1930	94	8	45	41
India	Nov 1955	47	9	15	23
Pakistan	Oct 1955	48	7	22	19
South Africa	Feb 1932	35	4	20	44
Sri Lanka	Mar 1983	111	32	23	65
West Indies	Feb 1952	37	9	10	18
Zimbabwe	Nov 1992	28	12	2	14

Most runs: SP Fleming (1994-2008) 7,172 runs, 111 Tests, average 40.07
Most wickets: RJ Hadlee (1973-1990) 431 wickets, 86 Tests, average 22.30
Most catches: AC Parore (1990-2002) 197 catches, 78 Tests

WORLD CUP RECORD

Year	Venue	Finished
1975	England	Semi-final
1979	England	Semi-final
1983	England	Pool
1987	India and Pakistan	Pool
1992	Australia and N Zealand	Semi-final
1996	Ind, Pak and S Lanka	Quarter-final
1999	England	Semi-final
2003	South Africa	5th
2007	West Indies	Semi-final

Most ODI runs: SP Fleming (1994-2007) 8,037 runs, 29 matches, average 32.41
Most ODI wickets: DL Vettori (1997-) 256 wickets, 247 matches, average 31.72
Most ODI catches: BB McCullum (2002-) 178 catches, 162 matches

WELLINGTON

Above: A Wellington parade.

The windy city

F amous for its weather (not good; it's known as the Windy Wellington), the capital of New Zealand is located at the bottom of the North Island, looking out across the Cook Strait towards the South Island. It is from here that Interislander ferries run south to Picton.

The small city centre area supports a population of about 400,000 and is home to many of the nation's important buildings – political and legal landmarks such as Parliament House and the Beehive (the executive wing), Government House, the official home of the Governor-General, and the Supreme Court of New Zealand,

The city supports a busy arts and cultural scene with the Museum of New Zealand Te Papa Tongarewa, Museum of Wellington City & Sea, the National Library of New Zealand, as well as being home to the Royal New Zealand Ballet and the New Zealand Symphony Orchestra. The film industry is an important one for the city and its profile has risen in recent

years thanks to the work of producer and director Peter Jackson, a local man who operates from the eastern suburb of Miramar. Jackson is well known for his work on the Lord of the Rings trilogy, the 2005 version of King Kong and sci-fi movie District 9.

Wellington has lively nightlife, with most revellers heading to the central Courtenay Place, especially on the weekends, which has no shortage of bars, live music venues and clubs. Cuba Street and Cuba Mall is another popular area among the city partygoers. There are also some great bars to be found on the Wellington Waterfront. But Wellington really comes into its own with its range of restaurants, with Malaysian, Japanese and Indian cuisine particularly popular. Check out Oriental Bay, Cuba Street and the Newtown suburb and enjoy.

Basin Reserve is 2 km (1 mile) to the south of the city centre.

3 THINGS YOU MUST DO...

1 CUBA STREET

Cafes, bars and restaurants line this popular street along with its bohemian shops and it attracts Wellington's hip crowd. Try the superbly kitsch Mighty Mighty (Level 1, 104 Cuba St, tel: +64 4 385 2890). When: Wed–Sat 16.00–late. To get there: centrally located.

2 CABLE CAR

A gentle 600-metre ride with great views. The Cable Car (tel: +64 4 472 2199) runs from Lambton Quay. When: cars run every 10 mins, Mon–Fri 07.00–22.00, Sat 08.30–22.00, Sun and holidays 09.00–22.00. Price: $5 return adults, $2 child 5–15. To get there: most buses pass through Lambton Quay.

3 MUSEUM OF NEW ZEALAND TE PAPA TONGAREWA

The national museum (55 Cable St, tel: +64 4 381 7000) for everything you ever wanted to know about New Zealand. When: daily 10.00–18.00 (21.00 Thur). Price: free, but some special exhibitions have charges. To get there: a short walk from the centre or bus 24 to Te Papa Museum.

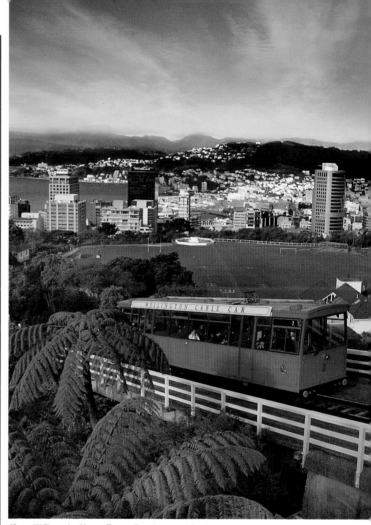

Above: Wellington's cable car offers excellent views across the city.

WEATHER	LOW (°C)	HIGH (°C)	RAIN (MM)	SUNSET
January	14	21	80	20.57
February	14	21	81	20.42
March	12	19	85	20.07
April	11	18	97	19.13
May	9	13	119	17.29
June	7	13	117	17.00
July	6	12	139	17.02
August	6	12	122	17.28
September	9	14	97	17.56
October	9	15	102	19.27
November	10	17	87	20.01
December	12	19	89	20.37

BASIN RESERVE

'Rising' from an earthquake

Standing in the shadows of Mount Victoria and Mount Cook, Wellington's Basin Reserve is the most picturesque ground in New Zealand and the only sporting arena in the country to be on the National Heritage List.

The Basin Reserve is an accident of nature. In 1855 the Wairapa earthquake flattened enough land to build a cricket ground and 13 years later the first match was played between the Wellington Volunteers and HMS Falcon.

It hosted its first Test match in 1930 against Alfred Gilligan's touring England side when Stewie Dempster and Jack Mills opened up with a stand of 276 for the hosts, both scoring centuries. In 1991 Martin Crowe and Andrew Jones were among the runs scoring 299 and 186 respectively for New Zealand against Sri Lanka, sharing a then-world record stand of 467 for the third wicket. Sir Richard Hadlee, New Zealand's greatest bowler, took his 300th Test wicket on the ground when he dismissed the Australian captain Allan Border in 1986, one of 53 wickets he took at the Basin Reserve.

The RA Vance Stand was opened in 1980, and the Museum Stand, to the west of the ground, houses the New Zealand Cricket Museum, which also boasts a reference library which is open daily during the summer.

Apart from the stands there is a grassy embankment from which to watch the cricket on the east of the ground, however it is exposed to the sun and the heat can take its toll over a full day's play.

The ground, which is 2 km (1.25 miles) to the south of Wellington's Central Business District, is surrounded by several places of historical interest including the Wellington National War Memorial Carillon, which is over 50 metres high and holds 74 bells, the Mount Cook Barracks and the Dominion Museum.

Below: Basin Reserve.

MATTER OF FACT

Ground: Allied Nationwide Finance Basin Reserve
Capacity: 11,600
Located: Wellington, New Zealand
Address: Rugby Street, Mount Cook 6021, Wellington
Telephone: +64 4 471 3171
E-mail: Contact form through
www.cricketwellington.co.nz
To get there: Basin Reserve Adelaide Road (bus)
Stands: RA Vance, Museum

VANCE STAND END

SCOREBOARD END

First Test: New Zealand v England 24-27 January 1930
First ODI: New Zealand v England 9 March 1975
First Twenty20: N/A

Tests played: 49
New Zealand: Won 14, lost 16, drawn 19
Highest team total: 671-4 (NZ v SL 1991)
Lowest team total: 42 (NZ v Aus 1946)
Highest individual total: 299 MD Crowe (for NZ v SL 1991)
Highest partnership: 276 (CS Dempster & JE Mills, 1st wicket for NZ v Eng 1930)
Best bowling: 7-23 RJ Hadlee (for NZ v Ind 1976)

ODIs played: 26
New Zealand: Won 9, lost 11, no result 3, (neutral games 3)
Highest team total: 297-6 (Aus v NZ 1998)
Lowest team total: 74 (NZ v Aus 1982)
Highest individual total: 126 not out Shoaib Mohammad (for Pak v NZ 1989)
Highest partnership: 152 (GM Turner & BA Edgar, 1st wicket for NZ v Eng 1983 and Shoaib Mohammad & Ramiz Raja, 3rd wicket for Pak v NZ 1989)
Best bowling: 5-17 TM Alderman (for Aus v NZ 1982)

Above: *All-rounder Tim Southee made his debut for New Zealand against England as a raw 19 year old.*

CRICKET NET

The William Wakefield Memorial, a domed temple inside the Basin Reserve, celebrates the achievements of Colonel William Wakefield, considered the first leader of the Wellington settlement, who died in 1848. It fell into disrepair but was restored by Wellington City Council and replaced back in the stadium in 2006.

AUCKLAND

Above: *Swim with a view at the Hilton Hotel in Auckland.*

City of sails

Auckland is commonly known as the 'city of sails' and it is sometimes said that there are more boats per head of population then anywhere else in the world (it beats the more sheep than people joke, at least). A quick visit to the Westhaven Marina, the largest in the city, and you'll see the sailing passion of the city at first hand. To emphasise this sailing backdrop, Auckland was the centre of the international yachting world when it hosted the prestigious America's Cup regatta in 2000 and again in 2003.

Auckland is a very multi-cultural city and is, in fact, the largest Polynesian city in the world, as well as being home to many with an Asian background, a group whose numbers have grown rapidly in recent years.

The hills in and around Auckland are mostly extinct volcanoes, including Mount Eden, which itself looks over Eden Park. The cricket stadium is 4 km (2.5 miles) southwest of the city centre.

The relatively low-level nightlife scene is spread around the city but the Viaduct Harbour, close to the water, is a great place to hang out with its many bars, restaurants and cafes. This is one of the liveliest parts of Auckland. The Sky City complex, off Federal Street, also boasts a numbers of bars and lively restaurants.

The city is situated to the north of the North Island and is the dominant city area in the country with over 1.3 million in the greater urban area.

3 THINGS YOU MUST DO...

1 SKY TOWER

You can enjoy 360-degree views from the tower (Cnr Victoria and Federal Sts, tel: +64 9 363 6000). When: Sun–Thurs 08.30–22.00, Fri–Sat 08.30-23.30. Price: for observation, sky deck and café, $28 adult, $18 concessions, $11 child 5–14. To get there: 10-min walk from train and bus stations.

2 HARBOUR FERRY TO DEVONPORT

Take a 15-min harbour cruise over to historical Devonport, a small village full of restaurants, cafes, galleries, boutiques and some pretty beaches. When: departures every 15 mins from 06.15–23.00 (Mon–Thur), every 30 mins from 06.15–01.00 (Fri–Sat), 07.15–10.00 (Sun). Price: $10 adult.

3 KELLY TARLTON'S ANTARCTIC ENCOUNTER AND UNDERWATER WORLD

Antarctica exhibition (23 Tamaki Dr, tel: +64 9 531 5065) with penguins, piranhas, sharks. When: daily 09.30–17.30. Price: $31.50 adult, $15.80 child 4–14. To get there: free shuttle bus from opposite the ferry terminal (172 Quay St).

Above: Auckland city.

WEATHER	LOW (°C)	HIGH (°C)	RAIN (MM)	SUNSET
January	16	23	79	20.44
February	15	23	94	20.33
March	15	22	81	20.01
April	13	18	97	19.18
May	11	17	131	17.36
June	9	13	137	17.13
July	8	13	145	17.14
August	9	14	122	17.35
September	9	16	102	18.00
October	12	17	101	19.23
November	12	20	89	19.54
December	14	21	79	20.26

EDEN PARK

The Kiwi home of rugby and cricket

Eden Park, close to the centre of Auckland, has hosted Test cricket since 1930, Test rugby union since 1921 and is the biggest sporting arena in New Zealand. It was the venue for the first Rugby World Cup final in 1987, which was won by New Zealand, hosted the 1988 Rugby League World Cup final and is the home of the Blues Super 14 rugby union franchise.

In 1981, the rugby union Test between the All Blacks and South Africa at the ground was disrupted by anti-apartheid protesters dropping flour bombs on the pitch from a light aircraft.

It was also the stage for one of the darkest days in New Zealand cricket history when the national team were bowled out for just 26 by England in 1955. Bob Appleyard took 4-7 and Brian Statham 3-9 to help the tourists to a win by an innings and 20 runs. New Zealand fared slightly better the next year when they recorded their first ever win in Tests by beating the West Indies by 190 runs. Pakistan defeated New Zealand on the ground in the semi-finals of the 1992 World Cup which they eventually went on to win.

Other notable feats include Walter Hammond's 336 not out for England in 1933 and Daniel Vettori's match figures of 12-149 against Australia in 2000, albeit it in a losing cause.

The terraces at one end of the ground is the liveliest place to watch the cricket whilst the massive ASB Bank Stand, which was opened in 1999, dominates the skyline

The South Stand underwent an extensive renovation in preparation for the 2011 Rugby World Cup but the ground nearly lost out when it was proposed to build a new stadium on the Auckland waterfront. But the New Zealand government eventually threw its weight behind rebuilding Eden Park.

Below: Eden Park.

MATTER OF FACT

Ground: Eden Park
Capacity: 42,000 (60,000 by 2011)
Located: Kingsland, Auckland, New Zealand
Address: Reimers Avenue, Kingsland, Auckland, 1024
Telephone: +64 9 815 5551
E-mail: mdixon@edenpark.co.nz
To get there: Kingsland Station (train), shuttle bus on major match days
Stands: ASB Bank, Terraces, West, North East

BROADCASTING END

TERRACING END

First Test: New Zealand v England 14-17 February 1930
First ODI: New Zealand v India 22 February 1976
First Twenty20: New Zealand v Australia 17 February 2005

Tests played: 47
New Zealand: Won 9, lost 15, drawn 23
Highest team total: 621-5 dec (SA v NZ 1999)
Lowest team total: 26 (NZ v Eng 1955)
Highest individual total: 336 not out WR Hammond (for Eng v NZ 1933)
Highest partnership: 266 (MH Denness & KWR Fletcher, 4th wicket for Eng v NZ 1975)
Best bowling: 8-76 EAS Prasanna (for Ind v NZ 1976)

ODIs played: 59
New Zealand: Won 28, lost 29, tied 1, no result 1
Highest team total: 340-5 (NZ v Aus 2007)
Lowest team total: 73 (NZ v SL 2007)
Highest individual total: 140 GM Turner (for NZ v SL 1983)
Highest partnership: 160 (GP Howarth & MD Crowe, 3rd wicket for NZ v Eng 1984)
Best bowling: 6-30 Waqar Younis (for Pak v NZ 1994)

Above: Got your kit? Left-handed opening batsman Craig Cumming prepares for a training session.

CRICKET NET

Martin Crowe, a product of Auckland Grammar School, is regarded as New Zealand's finest ever batsmen. He made 17 hundreds in 77 Tests, was a revolutionary captain and invented Cricket Max, a precursor to Twenty20 cricket because it takes a short time to play. His brother Jeff also played for New Zealand.

CHRISTCHURCH

Above: *Oxford Terrace in Christchurch.*

Southern charm

The main city on New Zealand's South Island, Christchurch lies on the east coast by the Pacific Ocean. To the north is the Waimakariri River and to the south east the volcanic slopes of Port Hills, a popular recreation area and great place for views across the city.

Sitting at the heart of the city in Cathedral Square is the 19th century ChristChurch Cathedral. A few streets to the west are the city's Art Gallery and Arts Centre, the Canterbury Museum and the Botanic Gardens. For culture of a different sort the 24/7 Christchurch Casino is also nearby, as is the main shopping street, the pedestrianized Cashel Street, and the popular Regent Street, with its small shops and brightly coloured facades.

The main area for nightlife in Christchurch is by the river along the Oxford Terrace. The quaint tram, which originally started running in 1905 (although it had to be resurrected in 1995), runs a small city loop and is a popular way to get around the central sights.

Christchurch is generally a gentle, sedate place, known as the Garden City, and is the launch pad for visitors looking to explore the rugged South Island. It is also known as the gateway to the Antarctic, with explorers Ernest Shackleton and Robert Scott both having set off from the port for expeditions into the iceland to the south.

The Lancaster Park is centrally located a short distance southeast of Cathedral Square.

3 THINGS YOU MUST DO...

1 ADDINGTON RACEWAY
Get hooked on the strange but addictive sport of Trotting Racing at the raceway (75 Jack Hinton Dr, tel: +64 3 338 9094). When: usually Fri at 17.30 but some Thurs. Price: free except big race days. To get there: nearest train station is Addington or short taxi ride from the centre.

2 CHRISTCHURCH CASINO
Win your fortune. Or lose your shirt. This is your author reminding you to bet responsibly boys and girls (34 Victoria St, tel: +64 3 365 9999). Open: 24/7. Price: free entry. To get there: centrally located.

3 CHRISTCHURCH GONDOLA
Take the 500 metre ride up in the gondola for views across the Pacific Ocean, the city and towards the snowy Southern Alps (10 Bridle Path Rd, Heathcote Valley, tel: +64 3 384 0700). When: daily 10.00–21.00. Price: $24 adult, $10 child 5–15. To get there: buses 28, 35 run from outside the City Exchange.

Above: The area around Christchurch is perfect for adventure sports.

WEATHER	LOW (°C)	HIGH (°C)	RAIN (MM)	SUNSET
January	12	22	56	21.05
February	12	21	45	20.47
March	10	19	48	20.09
April	8	17	48	19.11
May	4	12	66	17.27
June	3	11	70	16.52
July	2	10	66	16.57
August	2	12	48	17.25
September	5	14	44	17.55
October	7	17	44	19.28
November	8	19	48	20.03
December	12	21	56	20.41

LANCASTER PARK

More than just cricket

Better known to cricket and rugby fans as Lancaster Park, the ground has more recently been titled Jade Stadium and, since 2001, AMI Stadium after a sponsorship deal with an insurance company. Home to the Canterbury cricket and rugby teams, and found a short walk from the centre of Christchurch, it has also staged Davis Cup tennis, swimming and athletics and, rather differently, was turned into a potato patch during the Second World War.

Built in 1880, and situated in the suburb of Phillipstown, the ground staged its first Test in 1930, and has hosted some remarkable cricket ever since. In 2002 England's Graham Thorpe hit, the-then third fastest double century in Tests, making 200 after 231 balls, although his effort was trumped by New Zealand's Nathan Astle later in the match. Astle's clean-hitting brought him 222 runs off 168 balls but England went on to win the Test by 98 runs. The tourists complained about having to field under floodlights, with a red ball, but the ICC dismissed their claims.

Richard Hadlee, a Christchurch boy, was not worried about bowling at his local ground taking 76 wickets in Tests at an average of just 21.5 and played a pivotal role in one of New Zealand cricket's greatest moments. In March 1987 he took nine wickets in the game, against a West Indies line up including Viv Richards and Gordon Greenidge, to help New Zealand to a five-wicket win. There is a bronze bust of Hadlee outside Christchurch Arts Centre.

For the spectator the AMI Stadium is a perfect place to watch cricket as fans are close to the action unlike some of the concrete bowls found elsewhere in the world. In 2010 redevelopment started at the ground to increase its capacity to over 40,000 ahead of staging matches in the 2011 Rugby World Cup and the 2015 Cricket World Cup.

Below: Chris Cairns reached 200 wickets and 3,000 Test runs in his 58th Test match. Only Ian Botham got to the milestone quicker.

MATTER OF FACT

Ground: AMI Stadium
Capacity: 36,500
Located: Phillipstown, Christchurch
Address: Stevens Street, Phillipstown, Christchurch, 8011
Telephone: +64 3 379 1765 (freecall 0800 4 AMI STADIUM from New Zealand)
E-mail: info@vbase.co.nz
To get there: number 3 (bus)
Stands: PKMC, Hadlee, Smiths City, Tui, Deans

HADLEE STAND END

PORT HILLS END

First Test: New Zealand v England January 10-13 1930
First ODI: New Zealand v Pakistan 11 February 1973
First Twenty20: New Zealand v England 7 February 2008

Tests played: 40
New Zealand: Won 8, lost 16, drawn 16
Highest team total: 580-9 dec (Eng v NZ 1992)
Lowest team total: 65 (NZ v Eng 1971)
Highest individual total: 258 SM Nurse (for WI v NZ 1969)
Highest partnership: 315 (HH Gibbs & JH Kallis, 2nd wicket for SA v NZ 1999)
Best bowling: 7-47 PCR Tufnell (for Eng v NZ 1992)

ODIs played: 46
New Zealand: Won 25, lost 19, (neutral 2)
Highest team total: 392-4 (Ind v NZ 2009)
Lowest team total: 94 (NZ v Aus 1990)
Highest individual total: 163 not out SR Tendulkar (for Ind v NZ 2009)
Highest partnership: 192 (CG Greenidge & DL Haynes, 1st wicket for WI v NZ 1987)
Best bowling: 5-13 SP O'Donnell (for Aus v NZ 1990)

Above: *Not to be confused with Coldplay's singer, Christchurch's Chris Martin holds the record for pairs (six).*

CRICKET NET
Jesse Ryder, the New Zealand batsman, hit the headlines when he punched a window at the Stock Exchange Bar in Cashel Street, Christchurch, in 2008, severing tendons and putting himself out of action. The landlords have replaced the glass, in an outside toilet, with an etching saying 'Jesse's Window'.

DUNEDIN

Students and sport

This is the city of 'S' – students and sport. Both dominate this small southeast coast city of less than 250,000 people (as well as the cold winters). The well-regarded University of Otago provides more than a tenth of those and its students have built a reputation for heavy partying. You'll find no shortage of students (except in the summer) or partying wherever you look, especially around the central Octagon and the streets off it, especially the main George Street.

But sports fans will know Dunedin as the beating heart of New Zealand rugby because Carisbrook, the city's legendary sporting arena (to be replaced by Forsyth Barr, a new covered stadium) was known as the House of Pain, a well-deserved tag as many visiting teams who have taken on the All Blacks here have attested. The city is also home to the Highlanders who represent Otago and Southland in the Super 14 rugby competition.

University Ground is 2.5 km (1.5 miles) northeast of the central Octagon.

Above and below: The rugged South Island.

WEATHER	LOW (°C)	HIGH (°C)	RAIN (MM)	SUNSET
January	10	18	86	21.11
February	10	19	75	20.51
March	9	17	76	20.13
April	7	15	70	19.08
May	5	12	81	17.21
June	3	9	81	16.47
July	3	10	79	16.50
August	3	11	78	17.21
September	5	13	69	17.52
October	7	15	78	19.31
November	7	17	81	20.08
December	9	18	89	20.48

3 THINGS YOU MUST DO...

1 BALDWIN STREET

This is the steepest street in the world according to the Guinness Book of Records with a slope of 1 to 2:9. Run up it, cycle up it or walk up it for great views. To get there: 4 km (2.5 miles) to the north of the city off the North Road.

2 BREWERY TOUR

Speight's is the beer brewed in Dunedin. Take a 90-minute tour, with tasting (200 Rattray St, tel: + 64 3 4777 697). When: Mon–Thur 10.00, 12.00, 14.00, 18.00, 19.00, Fri–Sun 10.00, 12.00, 14.00, 16.00, 18.00. Price: $20 adult, $8 child 5-18. To get there: a five-minute walk from the Octagon.

3 WILDLIFE

Otago is home to a diversity of wildlife including the Royal Albatross, fur seal, sea lion and Yellow-Eyed penguin. Tour companies offer a chance to get up close. Try Back to Nature Tours (tel: + 64 3 479 2009) who offer a six-hour Discover the Peninsula Tour. Price: $89 adult, $45 child under 14.

UNIVERSITY OVAL

New boy on the block

A round 100 years ago, Logan Park, the site of the University Oval in Dunedin was under water and the area was known as Pelichet Bay. Land reclamation started in 1913, continuing after World War One. The first first-class game was not played on the site until 2004, and it staged its first Test match when Bangladesh were beaten in 2008, on a pitch made from Kananui clay, brought in from an area around 80 km (50 miles) north of Dunedin.

Home to the Otago Cricket Association and a training base for the Highlanders rugby team, the University Oval is New Zealand's seventh Test venue, replacing Carisbrook as Dunedin's leading cricket venue after a NZ$6million refurbishment. The new rugby stadium, Forsyth Barr, will be located nearby.

The venue attracted criticism ahead of its first Test when a state match between Otago and Auckland lasted less than two days, leading to New Zealand authorities sending their leading pitch assessor to Dunedin.

Its second Test, when New Zealand hosted the West Indies, highlighted an inadequate drainage system when the match was ruined by rain but its third Test, when Pakistan visited, went ahead without hitches and New Zealand won by 32 runs. The short boundaries have also attracted comment from New Zealand captain Daniel Vettori, the smallest boundary is just 52 metres (170 feet) from the middle of the square, but plans were put in place in 2009 to expand the playing area so the ground could attract more major Test matches.

A tree-lined arena, University Oval has flat grassy banks for spectators to picnic on.

Below: University Oval.

MATTER OF FACT
Ground: University Oval
Capacity: 6,000
Located: Logan Park, Dunedin
Address: Logan Park Drive, Dunedin, Otago,
Telephone: +64 3 477 9056
E-mail: Contact form through www.otagocricket.co.nz
To get there: a 15-min walk from the centre

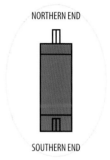

NORTHERN END

SOUTHERN END

First Test: New Zealand v Bangladesh 4-6 January 2008
First ODI: N/A
First Twenty20: N/A

Tests played: 3
New Zealand: Won 2, lost 0, drawn 1
Highest team total: 429 (NZ v Pak 2009)
Lowest team total: 137 (Ban v NZ 2008)
Highest individual total: 129 Umar Akmal (for Pak v NZ 2009)
Highest partnership: 176 (Umar Akmal & Kamran Akmal, 6th wicket for Pak v NZ 2009)
Best bowling: 6-56 DL Vettori (for NZ v Pak 2009)

ODIs played: N/A

HAMILTON

Coffee time

Although built on a site of former Moari villages, Hamilton, some 135 km (80 miles) south of Auckland, is a relatively new city having achieved its status only in 1945. Today the urban area is home to around 200,000 people.

Built along both sides of the Waikato River, Hamilton has been nurturing its reputation for a coffee culture, and in the area along, and off, Hood Street and Victoria Street in particular you will find any number of places for your espresso, machiato or cappuchino fix, as well as a number of bars and restaurants should coffee not be your thing. A large student population, thanks to the University of Waikato, which is situated on the east side of the river, ensures things can get pretty lively. Close by is Hamilton Lake, and although the city is an inland one, it has a strong culture of sailing.

Seddon Park is centrally located, a short walk from the Waikato River.

Above: The Hamilton Gardens. *Below:* The annual Balloons Over Waikato Festival.

WEATHER	LOW (°C)	HIGH (°C)	RAIN (MM)	SUNSET
January	16	23	72	20.44
February	15	23	90	20.33
March	15	22	79	20.01
April	14	18	92	19.18
May	11	18	125	17.36
June	10	14	130	17.13
July	9	14	142	17.14
August	9	14	112	17.35
September	9	16	98	18.00
October	12	18	98	19.23
November	12	20	83	19.54
December	14	21	75	20.26

3 THINGS YOU MUST DO...

1 WATERWORLD

Get wet, have fun, with pools, slides, plus spa, sauna and steam rooms (Garnett Ave, tel: +63 7 958 5860. When: Mon−Fri 06.00−21.00, Sat 07.00−21.00. Sun and holidays 09.00−21.00. Price: $5 adult, $2.50 child 2−15. To get there: bus Te Rapa 18.

2 RIFF RAFF

Richard O'Brien, creator of the Rocky Horry Show, used to live in Hamilton and this statue (Victoria St) stands as celebration to the show. To get there: centrally located.

3 BALLOON

Enjoy some peace and quiet and beautiful scenery with a four-hour balloon trip (Kiwi Balloon Company, 29a Corrin St, tel: +63 7 843 8538). When: daily, weather permitting. Price: $290 each person.

SEDDON PARK

Hamilton's village green

Seddon Park is an idyllic place to watch cricket as it is surrounded by contoured grassy banks for fans to stretch out on and is famous for its 'country' atmosphere. Home to the Northern Districts Cricket Association, and its flagship team, the State Northern Knights, the ground, named after the former New Zealand Prime Minister Richard Seddon, has been known as Trustbank Park, Westpac Trust Park and Westpac Park before reverting back to its original name in 2006.

Found a ten-minute walk from the south of Hamilton, Seddon Park staged its first Test match in 1991 when New Zealand drew with Sri Lanka and it has a reputation as a good batting wicket – India's Rahul Dravid made two centuries here against New Zealand in 1999. In 2008 Seddon Park held its first Twenty20 international with the people of Hamilton turning out in their droves and hundreds locked out before the game against the West Indies.

In 2005 a major upgrade of the stadium started with a new outfield, wicket and practice facilities added. A temporary television box caused a stir in 2008 when Sir Ian Botham refused to commentate, on a one-day international, from what was a Portakabin mounted on 30 metres (100 feet) of scaffolding. The media facilities have since been upgraded.

The stadium has also hosted rugby union with Waikato and the Chiefs playing at the ground in 2001 before moving to the newly-built Waikato Stadium. Hockey, rugby league and rock concerts are other events that have been staged here.

Below: Seddon Park.

MATTER OF FACT
Ground: Seddon Park
Capacity: 11,500
Located: Hamilton Central, Hamilton, New Zealand
Address: 50 Seddon Road, Hamilton
Telephone: +64 7 958 5800
E-mail: info@seddonpark.com, alayne@ndca.co.nz sheldon@ndca.co.nz
To get there: centrally located
Stands: Embankment, City Embankment

MEMBERS' END

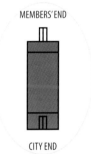

CITY END

First Test: New Zealand v Sri Lanka 22-26 February 1991
First ODI: New Zealand v India 15 February 1981
First Twenty20: New Zealand v West Indies 28 December 2008

Tests played: 15
New Zealand: Won 6, lost 3, drawn 6
Highest team total: 563 (NZ v Pak 2003)
Lowest team total: 93 (NZ v Pak 1993)
Highest individual total: 192 SP Fleming (for NZ v Pak 2003)
Highest partnership: 276 (AFG Griffith & SL Campbell, 1st wicket for WI v NZ 1999)
Best bowling: 7-27 CL Cairns (for NZ v WI 1999)

ODIs played: 15
New Zealand: Won 10, lost 2, (neutral 3)
Highest team total: 350-9 (NZ v Aus 2007)
Lowest team total: 122 (Ind v NZ 2003)
Highest individual total: 181 not out ML Hayden (for Aus v NZ 2007)
Highest partnership: 201 (G Gambhir & V Sehwag, 1st wicket for Ind v NZ 2009)
Best bowling: 4-21 AR Adams (for NZ v Ind 2003)

NAPIER

Above: Napier is famous for its Art Deco style of architecture.

A spell of love

The small city of Napier (city population of less than 60,000) lies on the east coast of the North Island in Hawke's Bay. The port town is an important centre for wool, fruit production and wine, and is famed for its Art Deco style architecture.

Along Marine Parade is Napier's main tourist attraction – a 1.5-metre bronze of Pania of the Reef. The much-photographed figure is to Napier what the Mannekin Pis is to Brussels and the Little Mermaid is to Copenhagen. According to Maori mythology, Pania was a beautiful ocean maiden who spent her days in the sea but at night rested by a stream in the place on which Napier now sits. Karitoki, the son of a Maori chief, used to drink at the stream and after Pania cast a spell they fell in love and were married. They lived together happily but Pania used to return to the sea each day. After a while Karitoki wanted to stop her leaving him and after consulting a village elder he learnt that if she ate cooked food she would not be allowed to return to the sea. He tried to feed her as she slept but

an owl screamed a loud warning to her in time. She fled and returned to her ocean people and although Karitoki swam to search for her, Pania was never seen again. Until the statue was erected in 1954 that is.

But the city of Napier is best known for its Art Deco architecture, attracting tourists and photographers from around the world, especially in February when there is an Art Deco event to celebrate the style of this small city. Few cities have had a chance to build (or rebuild) themselves in the way Napier did with one dominant style; for this city the opportunity arose out of tragedy. In 1931 an earthquake hit, killing many people and destroying the city's buildings. Rebuilding began, and with Art Deco the popular style of the time, it dominated the new look of the city, and to this day gives Napier its attractive style.

3 THINGS YOU MUST DO...

1 PANIA OF THE REEF
You've heard the tale of the beautiful Napier maiden, now go get your photo of her. To get there: the statue is on Marine Parade.

2 NATIONAL AQUARIUM OF NEW ZEALAND
You'll see fish, turtles, stingrays and more at the aquarium (Marine Parade, tel: +64 6 834 1404). And you can swim with the sharks. When: daily 09.00–17.00. Shark swimming at 09.00, 11.00. 15.00. Price: $16.20 adult, $8.30 child under 15. Shark swimming $50. To get there: centrally located.

3 WINE TOUR
Hawke's Bay, Marlborough and Wairarapa are all popular wine producing areas. Go taste. Try a day tour with Flat Earth (tel: +64 4 977 5805). When: 09.30–17.00. Price: $325 each includes transport, tasting, lunch and guide.

Above: The Gilray Fountain, found along Marine Parade, is better known as the Spirit of Napier.

WEATHER	LOW (°C)	HIGH (°C)	RAIN (MM)	SUNSET
January	14	24	70	20.50
February	14	23	86	20.38
March	13	21	74	20.03
April	10	19	76	19.15
May	8	17	89	17.33
June	4	14	86	17.07
July	5	14	112	17.08
August	5	14	84	17.32
September	6	17	59	18.02
October	8	18	56	19.25
November	11	21	64	19.57
December	13	23	58	20.31

MCLEAN PARK

To the east

McLean Park, situated close to the international date line and the world's most easterly Test venue, is the home of the Central Districts Cricket Association and the Hawke's Bay rugby team. A picturesque ground, the stadium has the Pacific Ocean and Marine Parade as a backdrop and hosted its first Test match in 1979 when Pakistan were the visitors.

In 1905, Sir Douglas McLean, the owner of the Maraekakaho sheep station and stock farm in Hawke's Bay, got together a syndicate to raise funds for a sports ground. He gave 10 acres of land, in memory of his father, which was named the 'Sir Donald McLean Park' in 1911. Now just known as McLean Park the ground is a ten-minute walk from the centre of Napier and is a regular host of Test and one-day cricket.

In March 2009 the pitch had to be changed ahead of New Zealand's Test match against India because of a fungal growth. Fears that it would not last the course were eased when Jesse Ryder hit 201 as New Zealand amassed 619-9 dec and India made 305 and 476-4 to force a draw. The draw was a familiar scenario for cricket-watchers in Napier with the first eight Tests played at the ground yielding six stalemates and not one win for the hosts. In 2008 England's Ryan Sidebottom took 7-47 to bowl his side to victory and in 1995 Sri Lanka won by 241 runs.

Helped by a grant of NZ$2.9 million from the New Zealand government the ground underwent extensive redevelopment ahead of being used as a venue for the 2011 Rugby World Cup. Floodlights were added and a new Graeme Lowe Stand, housing media and corporate facilities, replaced the old wooden McKenzie Stand, and opened in 2009 when Hawke's Bay played Auckland in the Air New Zealand Cup rugby tournament. The renovations took the seating capacity of the ground up to 21,000 and gave the stadium a horseshoe configuration of stands.

Below: Searching for the next New Zealand cricketing hero.

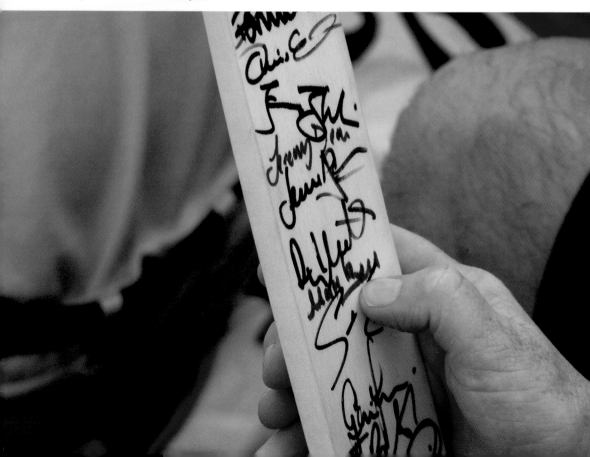

MATTER OF FACT

Ground: McLean Park
Capacity: 21,000
Located: Napier, New Zealand
Address: Latham Street, Napier, New Zealand
Telephone: +64 6835 7617
E-mail: admin@cdcricket.co.nz
To get there: Napier Station (train)
Stands: Graham Lowe, Harris, Centennial

CENTENNIAL END

EMBANKMENT END

First Test: New Zealand v Pakistan 16-21 February 1979
First ODI: New Zealand v Sri Lanka 19 March 1983
First Twenty20: N/A

Tests played: 9
New Zealand: Won 0, lost 2, drawn 7
Highest team total: 619-9 dec (NZ v Ind 2009)
Lowest team total: 109 (NZ v SL 1995)
Highest individual total: 201 JD Ryder (for NZ v Ind 2009)
Highest partnership: 271 (LR Taylor & JD Ryder, 4th wicket for NZ v Ind 2009)
Best bowling: 7-47 RJ Sidebottom (for Eng v NZ 2008)

ODIs played: 31
New Zealand: Won 18, lost 10, tied 2, no result 1
Highest team total: 347-5 (Aus v NZ 2005)
Lowest team total: 126 (Pak v NZ 2004)
Highest individual total: 141 not out RT Ponting (for Aus v NZ 2005)
Highest partnership: 201 (WU Tharanga & ST Jayasuriya, 1st wicket for SL v NZ 2006)
Best bowling: 5-30 M Muralitharan (for SL v NZ 2001)

Above: Daniel Vettori, New Zealand's gritty all-rounder.

CRICKET NET

The McLean Park Memorial Gates were opened on 13 December 1934 as a memorial to all the Hawke's Bay athletes killed in the Great War of 1914-1918. Designed by JA Louis Hay the inscription contains the words 'Their last great game of all'.

PAKISTAN

Capital: *Islamabad.* **Languages:** *Urdu, English, Punjabi.* **Drinks:** *Tea, sugar cane juice.* **Food:** *Korma, chicken tikka.* **National Anthem:** *Qaumi Tarana.* **Population:** *168 million.* **Time zone:** *GMT +5.* **Emergency numbers:** *15/1122.* **Did you know?** *Pakistan's K2, the world's second tallest mountain, is 8,611 metres high. That's 237 metres lower than Everest.* **Cricket body:** *Gaddafi Stadium, Ferozpur Road, Lahore, 54600, Pakistan. Tel: +92 42 571 7231/2/3/4. E-mail: mail@pcb.com.pk. Web: www.pcb.com.pk.*

Below: Pakistani fans certainly know how to celebrate a win.

A constant rise and fall

Awful one day, world beaters the next – the one thing you can say about Pakistani cricket is that it is never dull. Winners of the World Cup in 1992 and the World Twenty20 in 2009 the side has traditionally been capable of spectacular collapses as well as brilliance – but controversy is never far from the surface. In 2006 they were embroiled in the ball-tampering row in the Oval Test match against England and in 1987 Mike Gatting had his infamous, finger-wagging row with umpire Shakoor Rana at Faisalabad.

You can't deny the country's passion for cricket – which sometimes gets out of hand. Effigies of former captain Wasim Akram were burned after a World Cup loss in 1999 and more recently a government minister accused the team of throwing a match in the 2009 Champions' Trophy.

Pakistan played their first Test match in 1952 in Delhi against India and their first overseas tour was to England two years later. Since then they have given the world game some of the most exciting cricketers ever seen, most notably Imran Khan – now involved in politics – who captained them to the 1992 World Cup, Waqar Younis, who formed a deadly partnership with Akram, the leg-spinner Abdul Qadir and the big-hitting Shahid Afridi who was the star turn in their World Twenty20 triumph.

International cricket was put on hold in Pakistan after gunmen attacked the Sri Lankan team on their way to the Gaddafi Stadium in Lahore, for a Test match, in March 2009 and the side had to start playing matches on neutral venues.

Above: Shalimar Gardens were built under the reign of Mughal Emperor Shah Jahan, who also built the Taj Mahal in Agra.

TEST RECORD

Versus	First Test	Matches	Won	Lost	Drawn
Australia	Oct 1956	55	11	27	17
Bangladesh	Aug 2001	6	6	0	0
England	Jun 1954	67	12	19	36
India	Oct 1952	59	12	9	38
New Zealand	Oct 1955	45	21	6	18
South Africa	Jan 1955	16	3	8	5
Sri Lanka	Mar 1982	37	15	9	13
West Indies	Jan 1958	44	15	14	15
Zimbabwe	Dec 1993	14	8	2	4

Most runs: Javed Miandad (1976-1993) 8,832 runs, 124 Tests, average 52.57
Most wickets: Wasim Akram (1985-2002) 414 wickets, 104 Tests, average 23.62
Most catches: Wasim Bari (1967-1984) 201 catches, 81 Tests

WORLD CUP RECORD

Year	Venue	Finished
1975	England	Pool
1979	England	Semi-final
1983	England	Semi-final
1987	India and Pakistan	Semi-final
1992	Australia and N Zealand	Winners
1996	Ind, Pak and S Lanka	Quarter-final
1999	England	Runners-up
2003	South Africa	Pool
2007	West Indies	Pool

Most ODI runs: Inzamam-ul-Haq (1991-2007) 11,739 runs, 378 matches, average 39.53
Most ODI wickets: Wasim Akram (1984-2003) 502 wickets, 356 matches, average 23.53
Most ODI catches: Moin Khan (1990-2004) 214 catches, 219 matches

KARACHI

A city to sea

Pakistan's largest city is home to just under 12 million people and, being located on the Arabian Sea, the water naturally plays an important part in the city's business and cultural life. Being the largest port, Karachi is an important hub for the dhows that trade around the Indian Ocean; while the city's many beaches act as a magnet for locals and visitors alike. Clifton Beach is easy to reach and always popular, the nearby Bagh-e-Ibn-e-Qasim is where you will find the water jet fountain, the world's largest fountain, while French Beach to the southwest is reputed to be the cleanest and best of all the beaches. There are a number of islands off the coast of the city, including Churna Island, well-known for its marine life, to the west, while Bundle Island and Manora Island are both close to Clifton Beach.

The National Cricket Stadium is 16 km (10 miles) north of Clifton Beach.

*Above: Painted faces support Pakistan. **Below:** Clifton Beach.*

WEATHER	LOW (°C)	HIGH (°C)	RAIN (MM)	SUNSET
January	13	25	13	17.54
February	14	26	10	18.18
March	19	30	8	18.34
April	23	32	3	18.49
May	26	34	3	20.02
June	28	34	18	20.17
July	28	33	79	20.26
August	26	32	45	20.17
September	24	31	13	19.52
October	21	31	0	19.19
November	18	30	5	17.53
December	14	27	5	17.42

3 THINGS YOU MUST DO...

1 CLIFTON BEACH

Do your Lawrence of Arabia thing without leaving the city. The popular Clifton Beach (Beach Avenue) is where you can test your ability to sit on a camel without falling off. Haggle, haggle and haggle over the distance of your ride and its cost. To get there: book a radio cab (111 222 178).

2 PAKISTANI FOOD

Some of the tastiest food in the world can be found in Pakistan. For great barbecued lamb, chicken, kebabs and more head to BBQ Tonight (Com. 5/1, Boating Basin, tel: +92 21 583 2841). When: daily midday–midnight. To get there: near the Boat Basin. Book a radio cab (111 222 178).

3 MURREE'S WHISKY

Muree's (National Park Road, PO Box No 13, Rawalpindi, tel: +92 51 5567 0417) is only allowed to sell to non-Muslims and due to law is not allowed to export their whisky, so if you find it in one of the few bars that sell alcohol this is going to be your only chance to taste it.

NATIONAL STADIUM

The Pakistani fortress

The Pakistan cricket team were unbeaten at the National Stadium in Karachi for 34 Tests from 1955 to 2000 when Nasser Hussain's England touring side won a memorable match in light so gloomy the batsmen and fielders could hardly see the ball. The ground is the second biggest in Pakistan after Lahore's Gaddafi Stadium.

Inside, the ground enclosures are named after some of the stars of Pakistani cricket such as Javed Miandad, Zaheer Abbas, Wasim Bari and Intikhab Alam – who took a wicket on the ground with his first ball in Test cricket in 1959. Most of the locals head for the huge Mohammad Brothers enclosure at the north side of the ground and eat the local Pakistani food provided by the sellers who wander around the stadium.

The first one-day international at the ground, in 1980, went to the last ball – with Gordon Greenidge hitting Imran Khan for four to win the match for the West Indies. It also staged a quarter-final in the 1996 World Cup when Brian Lara scored 111 as the West Indies knocked out South Africa.

In February 2009 Younis Khan became the third Pakistani player to make a triple hundred in Test matches when he scored 313 against Sri Lanka. In the same game the visiting batsman Mahela Jayawardene and Thilan Samaraweera made 240 and 231 respectively, putting on 437 for the fourth wicket, on a pitch that was widely criticized for being too flat.

Below: *Umar Gul was the leading wicket taker in both the 2007 and 2009 World Twenty20 tournaments.*

MATTER OF FACT

Ground: National Stadium
Capacity: 34,228
Located: Karachi, Pakistan
Address: Stadium Road, Gulshan-e-Iqbal, Karachi
Telephone: +92 21 3482 1219 or +92 21 3496 3990
E-mail: arshadkhan@yahoo.com
To get there: 16-F, 50-C, 7 (bus)
Stands: Javed Miandad, Intikhab Alam, Wasim Bari, Zaheer Abbas, Fazal Mahmood, Mohammad Brothers, Majid Khan, Asif Iqbal

PAVILION END

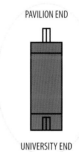

UNIVERSITY END

First Test: Pakistan v India 26 Feb-1 Mar 1955
First ODI: Pakistan v West Indies 21 Nov 1980
First Twenty20: Pakistan v Bangladesh 20 Apr 2008

Tests played: 41
Pakistan: Won 21, lost 2, drawn 18
Highest team total: 765-6 dec (Pak v SL 2009)
Lowest team total: 80 Aus v Pak 1956
Highest individual total: 313 Younis Khan (for Pak v SL 2009)
Highest partnership: 437 (M Jayawardene & T Samaraweera, 4th wicket for SL v Pak, 2009)
Best bowling: 8-60 Imran Khan (for Pak v India 1982)

ODIs played: 46
Pakistan: Won 20, lost 17, no result 2, (7 neutral games)
Highest team total: 374-4 (Ind v HK 2008)
Lowest team total: 115 (Ban v Pak 2008)
Highest individual total: 181 IVA Richards (for WI v SL 1987)
Highest partnership: 201 (ST Jayasuriya & KC Sangakkara, 1st wicket for SL v Ban 2008)
Best bowling: 6-13 BAW Mendis (for SL v Ind 2008)

LAHORE

City of culture

The ancient city of Lahore, situated in the northeast of the country near the Indian border, is rich with cultural and architectural history.

On the edge of the main part of the city, near the Ravi River, is the Minar-e-Pakistan, a minaret that is an important symbol to the creation of Pakistan. Built at the place where the Muslim League passed the Lahore Resolution in 1940, demanding a homeland for the Muslims in India, this 60-metre-high (197 feet) concrete structure is found in the Iqbal Park.

Nearby is the imposing Badshahi Mosque and the Lahore Fort. The Mosque, built during the reign of the sixth Mughal Emperor Aurangzeb Alamgir, was completed in 1673 and is one of the largest on the subcontinent. The fort, on the edge of the Walled City, dates back to the 16th century. The Gaddafi Stadium is situated to the south of these monuments.

For modern culture the Gulberg Main Boulevard has the top shopping centres, while the Anakarli Bazaar offers something more traditional. Lahore is a centre for hand-made carpets so prepare yourself for some magic offers.

Above: *Lahore Fort.* **Below:** *A daily flag-lowering ceremony.*

WEATHER	LOW (°C)	HIGH (°C)	RAIN (MM)	SUNSET
January	5	19	22	17.10
February	8	22	28	17.37
March	13	28	40	18.00
April	19	35	20	18.22
May	23	40	22	19.42
June	27	40	35	20.02
July	27	35	205	20.12
August	26	35	165	19.59
September	24	34	61	19.27
October	17	33	12	18.48
November	10	27	1	17.14
December	5	21	2	16.59

3 THINGS YOU MUST DO...

1 COCO'S CAFE

This iconic cafe (2168-9/A Roshnai Gate, Fort Road, tel: +92 42 766 2228) offers delicious food and great views from the rooftop across to the Badshahi Mosque and the Lahore Fort. Formerly a brothel, it is situated in the red-light district (Heera Mandi). To get there: book a radio cab (111 222 178).

2 FOOD STREETS

The people of Lahore love food, and you will love their food – seekh kebab, biryani and samoosas and more. Certain streets close down to traffic at nights so even if you don't fancy the food, just take a stroll and soak up the atmosphere. Try the food streets of Gawalmandi or restaurants of MM Alam Road.

3 LAHORE RACE CLUB

The city's horse racing club (Khayaban-e-Amin Road) was established in 1924, although there was racing in the city before that. It was one of only two racetracks in the country (the other was Karachi) when Pakistan was formed in 1947.

GADDAFI STADIUM

Nation's cricket HQ

Formerly known as the Lahore Stadium, the ground was renamed after the Libyan leader Colonel Gaddafi in 1974 after he gave a speech at the Organization of the Islamic Conference supporting Pakistan's right to have nuclear weapons. Designed by the architect Nayyar Ali Dada, and opened in 1959, the stadium was completely renovated for the 1996 World Cup when it hosted the final in which Sri Lanka beat Australia. Thirteen years later the Sri Lankans took away more tragic memories when the bus taking them to the ground for a Test match was attacked by gunmen, killing seven policemen and the driver, as well as injuring several players.

The first ground in Pakistan to have floodlights, the Gaddafi Stadium houses shops and offices in the lower portion of its stands and is situated in Gulberg, a residential and commercial area to the south of Lahore. The Pakistan Cricket Board also has its headquarters here.

Once in the ground spectators can buy food and water at the fence around the ground and visitors to Test matches can often choose where they want to sit because the ground is rarely full for five-day games.

Australia were the first tourists to play a Test match at the ground, in 1959, when they ran out winners by seven wickets, but Pakistan fans had more to cheer about in 2002 when Inzamam-ul-Haq hit 329 against New Zealand. England were the victims when Abdul Qadir, the leg-spinner, took 13 wickets in the match, including 9-56 in the first innings to bowl Pakistan to victory in the first Test of the controversial 1987 series.

Below: Pakistani fans.

MATTER OF FACT
Ground: Gaddafi Stadium
Capacity: 62,645
Located: Lahore, Pakistan
Address: Gaddafi Road, Gulberg, Lahore 54600
Telephone: +92 42 3571 7231/2/3/4
E-mail: tickets@pcboard.com.pk (Pakistan Cricket Board)
To get there: Buses 5, 5A
Stands: Fazal Mahmood, Kadar Nazar, Wasim Akram, Mohammad Hussein, Kham Mohammad, Saeed Anwar, Imran Khan, Hanif Mohammad, Intiaz Ahmed, Waqar Younis

PAVILION END

COLLEGE END

First Test: Pakistan v Australia 21-26 Nov 1959
First ODI: Pakistan v England 13 Jan 1978
First Twenty20: N/A

Tests played: 40
Pakistan: Won 12, lost 6, drawn 22
Highest team total: 699-5 (Pak v Ind 1989)
Lowest team total: 73 (NZ v Pak 2002)
Highest individual total: 329 Inzamam-ul-Haq (for Pak v NZ 2002)
Highest partnership: 410 (V Sehwag & R Dravid for 1st wicket Ind v Pak 2006)
Best bowling: 9-56 Abdul Qadir (for Pak v Eng 1987)

ODIs played: 58
Pakistan: Won 29, lost 18, tied 1 (neutral games 10)
Highest team total: 357-9 (SL v Ban 2008)
Lowest team total: 75 (Pak v SL 2009)
Highest individual total: 139 Ijaz Ahmed (for Pak v Ind 1997)
Highest partnership: 213 (ST Jayasuriya & PA de Silva for third wicket SL v Pak 1997)
Best bowling: 6-49 L Klusener (for SA v SL 1997)

FAISALABAD

The Union Jack designed city

Faisalabad is approximately 130 km (81 miles) from Lahore in the northeast of Pakistan, and is the third largest city in the country. The city was bizarrely built around a Union Jack design (check out an aerial photo!) that was proposed by a young British officer in 1880. Eat your heart out town planners. The ornate Faisalabad Clock Tower, built during the British Raj, sits at the centre of the city and eight roads (as per the lines in the Union flag) stretch out from here in interesting symmetry. Ghenta Ghar, as the clock tower is known, is also the major market, as well as being the oldest part of the city. As per the design of the Union flag there are eight bazaars, one in each section.

Faisalabad is an important industrial city in the region, especially for cotton and silk textiles, but the region is also important for agriculture, being a major producer of sugarcane, maize, wheat, barley and rice, among other crops.

The Iqbal Stadium is centrally located to the north.

Above: A camel eats from a hand decorated with henna. Below: Clay lamps at a street shrine.

WEATHER	LOW (°C)	HIGH (°C)	RAIN (MM)	SUNSET
January	5	19	22	17.10
February	8	22	28	17.37
March	12	27	40	18.00
April	18	35	20	18.22
May	23	39	22	19.42
June	27	41	35	20.02
July	27	37	205	20.12
August	27	36	165	19.59
September	24	36	61	19.27
October	17	34	12	18.48
November	10	28	1	17.14
December	6	21	2	16.59

3 THINGS YOU MUST DO...

1 TANDOORI CHICKEN

This succulent and popular marinated (in yoghurt and masala spices) chicken dish is a Punjabi speciality. Tuck in . . .

2 GHENTA GHAR

Smack in the centre of one of the most uniform pieces of urban planning you will ever find. Bazaars to satisfy the most ardent of shoppers and hagglers.

3 LASSI

This thick and refreshing yogurt drink is a Punjabi speciality. Made with ice, you can choose from either a spicy lassi or a sweet lassi, which has sugar added. You'll find the drink all over the city for about Rs20–25.

IQBAL STADIUM

Poet's corner

The Iqbal Stadium in Faisalabad, named after Allama Muhammad Iqbal, an Urdu poet, in 1977, staged its first Test match in 1978 but it was nine years later that it hit the headlines during England's tour of 1987. In one of the most controversial episodes in Test history the England captain, Mike Gatting, and the Pakistani umpire Shakoor Rana had an on-field argument that nearly led to the cancellation of the Test match and cost a day's play. Rana had refused to allow play to carry on until he had received an apology from Gatting. The England skipper's short letter of apology was finally accepted by Rana and the game continued although the time lost from the row and rain meant England could not press home their advantage and it finished in a draw. England did not tour Pakistan for another 13 years after the incident.

Less controversially Zimbabwe recorded their first series win when the third Test against Pakistan, in 1998, was completely wiped out by fog – only the ninth Test history to be abandoned without a single ball being bowled. The ground also saw the great West Indies of Viv Richards and Gordon Greenidge bowled out for 53, in 1986, with Abdul Qadir taking 6-16.

Found in the northern province of Punjab, around 2 km (1 mile) from the city centre, this is an impressive modern stadium with stands named after world-renowned Pakistani cricketers although local heroes such as Ijaz Ahmed and Taslim Arif also have areas named in their honour.

Below: Shahid Afridi, Pakistan's most exciting all-rounder since Imran Khan, is mobbed by his team yet again.

MATTER OF FACT
Ground: Iqbal Stadium
Capacity: 25,000
Located: Faisalabad, Punjab, Pakistan
Address: Stadium Road, Faisalabad
Telephone: +92 41 920 0558
E-mail: navednazir@yahoo.com
To get there: 2 km (1 mile) rickshaw ride from centre
Stands: Imran Khan, Hanif Mohammad, Wasim Akram, Zaheer Abbas, AH Karder, Ijaz Ahmed, Taslim Arif, Javed Miandad

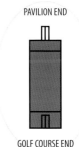

PAVILION END

GOLF COURSE END

First Test: Pakistan v India 16-21 October 1978
First ODI: Pakistan v New Zealand 23 November 1984
First Twenty20: N/A

Tests played: 24
Pakistan: Won 6, lost 5, drawn 13
Highest team total: 674-6 (Ind v Pak 1984)
Lowest team total: 53 (WI v Pak 1986)
Highest individual total: 253 ST Jayasuriya (for SL v Pak 2004)
Highest partnership: 397 (Qasim Omar & Javed Miandad 3rd wicket for Pak v SL 1983)
Best bowling: 7-52 C Pringle (for NZ v Pak 1990)

ODIs played: 16
Pakistan: Won 9, lost 3 (4 neutral)
Highest team total: 314-7 (NZ v Pak 2003)
Lowest team total: 151 (WI v Pak 2006)
Highest individual total: 108 Mohammad Yousuf (Pak v Zim 2008)
Highest partnership: 147 (Ijaz Ahmed & Basit Ali 5th wicket for Pak v SA 1994)
Best bowling: 4-57 Mudassar Nazar (Pak v NZ 1984)

SOUTH AFRICA

| THE
3
MINUTE
GUIDE | | **Capitals:** *Cape Town (Legislative), Pretoria (Administrative), Bloemfontein (Judicial).*
Languages: *11 official languages: Afrikaans, English, Ndebele, Northern Sotho, Sothi, Swazi, Tswana, Tsonga, Venda, Xhosa, Zulu.* **Beers:** *Castle, Carling Black Label, Bosun's Bitter.*
Food: *Braais (barbecues), boerewors (sausage), pap and vleis (porridge and meat).*
National Anthem: *Nkosi Sikilel' iAfrica (God Bless Africa).* **Population:** *49 million.*
Time zone: *GMT +2.* **Emergency numbers:** *1011 (police and fire), 10177 (medical).*
Did you know? *The largest diamond in the world was found near Pretoria in 1905. It was 3,106 carat.* **Cricket body:** *The Wanderers Club, 21 North Street, Illovo, Johannesburg 2196, South Africa. Tel: +27 11 880 2810. E-mail: csa@cricket.co.za. Web: www.cricket.co.za.* |

Below: Visit South Africa, see the cricket, then see a lion.

Back with a bang

South African cricket was scarred by its exclusion from the international game between 1970 and 1991 because of its government's apartheid policy. Their suspension denied the public the chance to see stars such as Graeme Pollock, Mike Proctor and Barry Richards and led to players like Robin Smith, Tony Greig and Allan Lamb playing for England and Kepler Wessels for Australia.

Since readmission they've established themselves as a leading side in the world although they have gained a reputation as chokers especially in big one-day games having played, and lost, three World Cup semi-finals.

Alan Donald, Shaun Pollock and Jacques Kallis have been the stars of the post-apartheid era with Kallis topping 10,000 runs and 200 wickets in Tests and one-day internationals. Hansie Cronje, captain in 53 Tests up until 2000 was another central figure in their re-emergence although he admitted taking a bribe in 2000, was banned from the game for life and died in a plane crash, aged 32, in June 2002. Some parties still claim he was murdered by a cricket betting syndicate.

South Africa played their first Test in 1889 and their absence from the game has sharpened the enthusiasm of the fans, although rebel sides did tour the country during their exile. Most grounds in South Africa are filled with the aroma of barbecues as fans cook the local sausages, boerewors, and huge steaks on braais around the pitch, whilst sinking the local lager.

Above: *Farmers in the Helderberg area, north of Cape Town, enjoy a casual match.*

TEST RECORD

Versus	First Test	Matches	Won	Lost	Drawn
Australia	Oct 1902	83	18	47	18
Bangladesh	Oct 2002	8	8	0	0
England	Mar 1889	138	29	56	53
India	Nov 1992	22	10	5	7
New Zealand	Feb 1932	35	20	4	11
Pakistan	Jan 1995	16	8	3	5
Sri Lanka	Aug 1993	17	8	4	5
West Indies	Apr 1992	22	14	3	5
Zimbabwe	Oct 1995	7	6	0	1

Most runs: JH Kallis (1995-) 10,640 runs, 135 Tests, average 54.56
Most wickets: SM Pollock (1995-2008) 421 wickets, 108 Tests, average 23.12
Most catches: MV Boucher (1997-) 469 catches, 130 Tests

WORLD CUP RECORD

Year	Venue	Finished
1975	England	Did not play
1979	England	Did not play
1983	England	Did not play
1987	India and Pakistan	Did not play
1992	Australia and N Zealand	Semi-final
1996	Ind, Pak and S Lanka	Quarter-final
1999	England	Semi-final
2003	South Africa	Pool
2007	West Indies	Semi-final

Most ODI runs: JH Kallis (1996-) 10,409 runs, 295 matches, average 45.26
Most ODI wickets: SM Pollock (1996-2008) 393 wickets, 303 matches, average 24.51
Most ODI catches: MV Boucher (1998-) 393 catches, 288 matches

CAPE TOWN

Above: Cape Town central and the harbour area against the backdrop of Table Mountain.

A beautiful life

Life's pretty good for Capetonians. Nestled against the imposing Table Mountain and flanked by the Atlantic Ocean and Indian Ocean, visitors very quickly declare that this is a city that has it all. Warm summers, plentiful rains, an abundance of wine farms nearby, good restaurants, a vibrant nightlife, sandy beaches and beautiful scenery, international sporting events, excellent shopping, affordable prices, and it has to be said, very beautiful people. The locals even put a positive spin on the wind that can whistle down the streets with ferocity sometimes, dubbing it the Cape Doctor because it blows away all the germs and keeps the city healthy. It's no wonder that so many visitors end up staying or buying holiday homes in the city.

The V&A Waterfront, an ever-growing complex of shops, offices, restaurants and bars, is a magnet for tourists who enjoy the waterside location, the working harbour and the relaxed, cosmopolitan atmosphere. This is said to be the busiest tourist attraction in the country and it's easy to see why. It is from here that you can get ferries to Robben Island, where Nelson Mandela and other leaders of today's South Africa were imprisoned as they fought to free the country from apartheid.

Heading away from the city, you will find wine farms till your vino heart's content in the Stellenbosch, Constantia, Paarl, Robertson and Worcester areas. Popular city beaches are Camp's Bay and Clifton, while Bloubergstrand, Noordhoek and Boulder's Beach (where you can sometimes swim with penguins) are found out of town.

Newlands is about 10 km (6 miles) south of the city centre.

3 THINGS YOU MUST DO...

1 CABLE CAR
Take the revolving car to the top of Table Mountain for great walks and views (Tafelberg Rd, tel: +27 21 424 2121). When: varies depending on light but approx 08.30–18.00 (winter) and 08.00–21.30 (summer). Price R160 return adult, R80 child 4-17. To get there: try Rikki Taxis (tel: +27 21 418 6713).

2 LA MED
Simply the best place to drink cocktails while looking at beautiful views and beautiful people (off Victoria Rd, tel: +27 21 438 5600). When: Mon–Fri noon–late, Sat–Sun 09.00–late. To get there: Camps Bay buses stop nearby or try Rikki Taxis (tel: +27 21 418 6713).

3 WINE FARM
If you like wine you'll love the Stellenbosch wine route. Try Morgenhof Estate (Klapmuts Rd, R44, tel +27 21 889 5510) for a tasting and lunch. When: daily for tastings. Lunch, Jun–Sept, Tues–Sun 12.00–14.30, Oct–May, daily 12.00–15.00. To get there: 55 km (34 miles) east of Cape Town.

Above: Beach huts on Muizenberg Beach. Which is your favourite colour?

WEATHER	LOW (°C)	HIGH (°C)	RAIN (MM)	SUNSET
January	16	26	15	20.01
February	16	26	8	19.53
March	14	24	23	19.23
April	12	22	48	18.41
May	10	19	79	18.06
June	8	18	78	17.45
July	7	17	89	17.48
August	8	18	66	18.06
September	10	19	41	18.29
October	11	22	31	18.49
November	13	23	19	19.14
December	14	24	10	19.43

NEWLANDS

Picture perfect

One of the most picturesque grounds in the world, Newlands, overlooked by Table Mountain and Devil's Peak, is home of Western Province Cricket Club and was the venue for South Africa's second ever Test match, against England, in 1889. Originally a swampy patch of farmland given to the Vicomtesse de Montmort as a wedding present, it staged its first game on 2 January 1888 with a match between teams called Mother Country and Colonial Born.

Close to the Newlands Stadium, used for rugby union and football, the cricket ground is easily reached by train from the centre of Cape Town.

Renovations have seen some of the grassy embankments that used to be so popular with spectators replaced by stands which have increased the seating capacity to 25,000 but Newlands is still ranked alongside the Adelaide Oval by many as one of the most beautiful stadiums in the world to watch cricket.

The first Test match in 1889 saw a remarkable bowling performance by England's Johnny Briggs, who took 8-11 in the second innings, to add to seven first innings wickets, as the tourists triumphed by an innings and 202 runs. Briggs, a left-arm spinner, was the first in a line of many slow bowlers to have enjoyed bowling on the Newlands wicket. In 1957 Australia's Lindsay Kline became the 12th bowler to take a hat-trick in Test cricket as Ian Craig's tourists won by an innings.

The ground staged five games in the 2003 Cricket World Cup and the opening ceremony, and eight games in the 2007 World Twenty20, including the semi-final between New Zealand and Pakistan.

Capetonians are enthusiastic about their cricket and the climate in the area makes watching the sport in December or January, in the African sunshine, one of the highlights of the year.

The ground is next door to the Castle Brewery, the long-term sponsors of the game in South Africa, which ensures spectators will never run out of refreshment.

Below: Newlands, one of the most picturesque cricket grounds in the world. South Africa have only lost three times in 21 matches at Newlands since Test readmission. All to Australia.

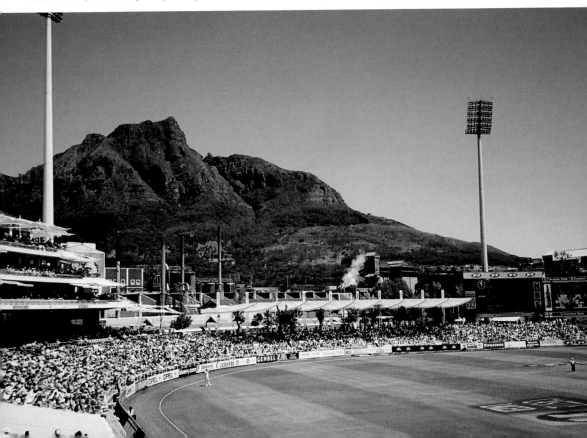

MATTER OF FACT

Ground: Sahara Park Newlands
Capacity: 25,000
Located: Cape Town, South Africa
Address: 146 Campground Road, Newlands, Cape Town, South Africa, 7700
Telephone: + 27 21 657 3300
E-mail: members@wpcc.co.za
To get there: Newlands Station (train)
Stands: Railway, President's Stand, Oaks, The Planes, North, Members'

WYNDBERG END

KELVIN GROVE END

First Test: South Africa v England 25-26 March 1889
First ODI: South Africa v India 7 December 1992
First Twenty20: Australia v Zimbabwe 12 September 2007

Tests played: 45
South Africa: Won 17, lost 19, drawn 9
Highest team total: 651 (SA v Aus 2009)
Lowest team total: 35 (SA v Eng 1899)
Highest individual total: 262 SP Fleming (for NZ v SA 2006)
Highest partnership: 368 (GC Smith & HH Gibbs, 1st wicket for SA v Pak 2003)
Best bowling: 8-11 J Briggs (for Eng v SA 1889)

ODIs played: 34
South Africa: Won 25, lost 3, (neutral 6)
Highest team total: 354-3 (SA v Ken 2001) & 354-6 (SA v Eng 2009)
Lowest team total: 43 (Pak v WI 1993)
Highest individual total: 131 not out ND McKenzie (for SA v Ken 2001)
Highest partnership: 209 (G Kirsten & ND McKenzie, 2nd wicket for SA v Ken 2001)
Best bowling: 6-19 HK Olonga (for Zim v Eng 2000)

Above: *Graeme Smith established the ground's highest partnership of 368 with Herschelle Gibbs in 2003.*

CRICKET NET

The scoreboard at Newlands is a memorial to all South African cricketers killed in the Second World War. Opened in 1948 by Governor-General, Gideon Brand van Zyl it was funded by donations including one from the Bantu Cricket Union.

BLOEMFONTEIN

The land of cheetahs

The heart of Afrikanerdom, Bloemfontein is one of the three capitals of the country (this is the judicial capital) and is seat of the Supreme Court of Appeal, the highest court in the country. Located in the centre of the country it is 400 km (250 miles) south of Johannesburg, 160 km (100 miles) east of mining town Kimberley, and 140 km (88 miles) west of Maseru, the capital of Lesotho. You may also hear the city called Manguang, which is the Sesotho name, meaning place of the cheetahs.

Cheetahs is the name of the Super 14 rugby side based here. The city also supports the Eagles cricket team and Bloemfontein Celtic, who play in football's Premier League. All the teams play in the centrally located Free State sports complex. Near here is the popular Waterfront shopping centre, called Loch Logan, with its many retail outlets and restaurants. Also near here is Second Street where you will find plenty of bars and eating places.

Above: City Hall. **Below:** *The city centre.*

WEATHER	LOW (°C)	HIGH (°C)	RAIN (MM)	SUNSET
January	16	26	15	19.18
February	16	26	7	19.12
March	13	25	18	18.48
April	12	22	51	18.12
May	9	18	79	17.42
June	8	18	84	17.26
July	7	17	89	17.28
August	8	18	64	17.45
September	10	19	43	18.01
October	11	21	31	18.17
November	13	23	16	18.36
December	14	24	10	19.00

3 THINGS YOU MUST DO...

1 SKYDIVING

You've always fancied jumping out of a plane and hanging by a thread, haven't you? Now's your chance thanks to Bloemfontein Skydiving Centre (Tempe Airfield, tel: +27 51 451 1143 or +27 76 394 6059). When: Sat and holidays but other days can be booked.

2 ANGLO BOER WAR MUSEUM

The museum (Monument Road, tel: +27 51 447 0079) gives an insight into the war of 1899-1902 including the concentration camps. When: Mon–Fri 08.30–16.30, Sat 10.00–17.00, Sun 11.00–17.00, holidays 09.00–17.00. To get there: south of the centre, nearest train station is Showground.

3 GAME

Beef or chicken sir? Fed up with the usual? Then taste game: springbok, ostrich, gemsbok and more. Try the Famous Butcher's Grill (Holiday Inn Garden Court, cnr Nelson Mandela and Melrose Drive, tel: +27 51 444 4980). When: 12.00–23.00 (12.00–01.00 bar). To get there: west of the centre.

SPRINGBOK PARK

MATTER OF FACT
Ground: OUTsurance Oval
Capacity: 20,000
Located: Bloemfontein, South Africa
Address: OUTsurance Oval, Att Horak Avenue, Bloemfontein, Free State, South Africa
Telephone: +27 51 447 5715
E-mail: petriw@cricket.co.za
To get there: Bloemfontein Station (coach)
Stands: Centenary, Northern Pavilion

Where cricket parties

The OUTsurance Oval, better known as Springbok Park, and previously called Goodyear Park, is a 20,000-seater stadium that also has popular grassy banks where fans cook up the traditional braai, or barbecue, whilst play progresses. A 10-minute walk from the centre of Bloemfontein, the ground is the home of the Free State Cricket Union and the Diamond Eagles, a team formed by the amalgamation of Free State Cricket and Griqualaland-West Cricket that plays in the Standard Bank Pro20 Series and the SuperSport Series.

It staged its first international cricket, a one-dayer, when South Africa beat India in 1992 and in 1999 it hosted its first Test match when Zimbabwe were the visitors.

The city was a fitting venue for Allan Donald, the great fast bowler from Free State, to take his 300th Test wicket, becoming the first South African to reach the milestone, against New Zealand in 2000. It was also the scene of a tied one-day international between South Africa and England in 2005 when Geraint Jones stumped Andrew Hall off the last ball. The ground was used as a venue for the 2009 Indian Premier League when it was moved at short notice to South Africa.

Aside from international cricket it was also the venue of an epic innings by Hansie Cronje of 251, for Orange Free State against the touring Australians in 1994. Set 457 to win, the locals finished just 60 short against a bowling attack including Shane Warne and Merv Hughes.

Spectator-friendly, the stadium is part of a complex that includes facilities for athletics, hockey, rugby, tennis and swimming and has excellent floodlights making it a particularly good venue for day-night games when a party atmosphere fills the ground.

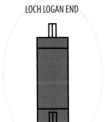

LOCH LOGAN END

WILLOWS END

First Test: South Africa v Zimbabwe 29 October 1999
First ODI: South Africa v India 15 December 1992
First Twenty20: N/A

Tests played: 4
South Africa: Won 4, lost 0, drawn 0
Highest team total: 563 (SA v Ind 2001)
Lowest team total: 153 (Ban v SA 2008)
Highest individual total: 160 JH Kallis (for SA v NZ 2000)
Highest partnership: 225 (GC Smith & HM Amla, 2nd wicket for SA v Ban 2008)
Best bowling: 6-56 SM Pollock (for SA v Ind 2001)

ODIs played: 24
South Africa: Won 11, lost 6, tied 1, (neutral games 6)
Highest team total: 336-7 (SA v Ken 2008)
Lowest team total: 90 (Ken v Ind 2001)
Highest individual total: 141 SB Styris (for NZ v SL 2003)
Highest partnership: 228 (JF Kloppenburg & KJ van Noortwijk, 2nd wicket for Ned v Nam 2003)
Best bowling: 5-42 L Klusener (for SA v Ind 1997)

Below: Herschelle Gibbs, South Africa's controversial opening batsman, signs autographs.

PRETORIA

Jacaranda City

Lying some 70 km (44 miles) to the north of Johannesburg, the city of Pretoria is South Africa's administrative capital (there are three capitals, Cape Town and Bloemfontein being the other two). Known as the Jacaranda City for the explosion of pink when the thousands of jacaranda trees lining the streets bloom in the springtime, Pretoria is a more relaxed place than its large neighbour to the south.

The Union Buildings, is the seat of the South African government and famously is the place where Nelson Mandela was inaugurated as the country's first democratically elected president. The large, semi-circular shaped buildings, and indeed the city itself (sometimes referred to as Tshwane, although this is the metropolitan area) are increasing becoming a symbol of democracy in the country. However, Pretoria has fierce Afrikaner roots. It was founded by Marthinus Pretorius, one of the leaders of the Voortrekkers who sought out a homeland, and it was named after his father Andries, who led his people to victory over the Zulus in the Battle of Blood River. The city is home to the monolithic Voortrekker Monument, which pays honour to the pioneers.

Centurion lies 15 km (9 miles) to the south of Pretoria.

Above: Pretoria's jacaranda trees in bloom. ***Below:*** The Voortrekker Monument.

WEATHER	LOW (°C)	HIGH (°C)	RAIN (MM)	SUNSET
January	19	28	130	19.02
February	18	27	101	18.49
March	18	26	80	18.37
April	14	24	45	18.07
May	10	22	21	17.38
June	8	18	6	17.25
July	7	19	7	17.28
August	9	21	7	17.42
September	14	24	20	17.56
October	15	25	71	18.07
November	17	26	110	18.23
December	18	27	111	18.45

3 THINGS YOU MUST DO...

1 ELEPHANT SANCTUARY
Get up close with African elephants (Hartbeespoort Dam, tel: +27 12 258 0423). When: educational programmes at 08.00, 10.00, 14.00 (and 12.00 from June–Oct). Price: R325–525 adults, R165–R215 child 3–14. Rides: R350 adult, R250 child (must be 8). To get there: 32 km (20 miles) west of Pretoria.

2 THE ANN VAN DYK CHEETAH CENTRE
See cheetah, wild dog, hyena, vultures and more (De Wildt, tel: +27 12 504 9906). When: cheetahs run Tues, Thur, Sat, Sun 08.00, three-hour tours Tues, Wed, Thur, Sat, Sun, 13.30 (plus 08.30 Wed). Price: R220. To get there: De Wildt is 37 km (23 miles) northwest of Pretoria on the R566.

3 HATFIELD
Boosted by the large student population (the university is nearby) Hatfield is the area to head to for bars, restaurants and clubs. Try the Drop Zone (Hatfield Sq, tel: +27 12 362 6528). To get there: Hatfield is to the east of the city centre.

CENTURION PARK

Where Cronje fell

Centurion Park, officially known as SuperSport Park after its sponsors, is a ten-minute walk from the centre of Centurion, a city that is reachable by bus from Johannesburg and Pretoria. Home of the Northerns Cricket Union, it made its debut as a provincial cricket venue in 1986 and is one of the few privately-owned grounds in South Africa after it was bought back from Centurion City Council.

It staged its first Test in 1995 when Mike Atherton's England were the visitors, the match ending in a draw after rain restricted the teams to 130 overs. Shaun Pollock, the South African fast bowler, made his Test debut in the match.

But Centurion is better known in cricket history as the ground that destroyed the reputation of former South African captain Hansie Cronje after it was revealed he had taken a bribe to throw the final Test match against England in 2000. After four days of rain, both teams forfeited an innings with England winning by two wickets. Only later did the truth come out.

SuperSport Park hosted the Champions Trophy final in 2009 when Shane Watson's century helped Australia beat New Zealand and five games during the 2003 Cricket World Cup, including two Super Six games. In 2008 it also staged an AFL match between Carlton and Freemantle.

The ground is spectator friendly with grassy banks, braai areas where fans can cook their own food, beer kiosks dotted around the stadium and a beer garden just behind the main scoreboard. Although spectators can take food into the ground they cannot take in any drinks, alcoholic or otherwise.

Below: The hard-hitting Pretoria-born AB de Villiers never knowingly hangs around when he comes out to bat.

MATTER OF FACT
Ground: SuperSport Park
Capacity: 22,000
Located: Centurion, South Africa
Address: Supersport Park, Cnr South and West Ave, Centurion, South Africa
Telephone: +27 12 663 1005
E-mail: titans@cricket.co.za
How to get there: 15 km (9 miles) south from Pretoria along the Ben Schoeman Highway
Stands: Grandstand, Eastern Embankment, Western Embankment

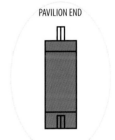

PAVILION END

HENNOPS RIVER END

First Test: South Africa v England 16-20 November 1995
First ODI: South Africa v India 11 December 1992
First Twenty20: South Africa v Australia 29 March 2009

Tests played: 15
South Africa: Won 11, lost 1, drawn 3
Highest team total: 604-6 dec (SA v WI 2004)
Lowest team total: 119 (SL v SA 2001)
Highest individual total: 192 HH Gibbs (for SA v WI 2004)
Highest partnership: 301 (GC Smith & HH Gibbs, 1st wicket for SA v WI 2004)
Best bowling: 6-39 M Zondeki (for SA v Zim 2005)

ODIs played: 40
South Africa: Won 17, lost 9 (neutral 13, no result 1)
Highest team total: 392-6 (SA v Pak 2007)
Lowest team total: 119 (Zim v SA 2009)
Highest individual total: 169 not out DJ Callaghan (for SA v NZ 1994)
Highest partnership: 252 (SR Watson & RT Ponting, 2nd wicket for Aus v Eng 2009)
Best bowling: 5-14 DT Johnston (for Ire v Can 2009)

DURBAN

Above: Durban beachfront. It's long and it's sandy.

Where East meets West

Durban is a vibrant city, in the province of KwaZulu-Natal, and is often referred to as a place where East meets West. There are prominent Zulu and Asian populations which makes for an interesting mix of cultures. The city has one of the busiest ports in Africa and is a magnet for tourists, although like the rest of the South Africa the division between poverty and wealth is huge with many Zulus living in shanty towns out of the city.

Durban has sunshine for approximately 320 days a year and 100 km (62 miles) of coastline with superb beaches, some of which are protected by shark nets. Away from the sun and sea visitors flock to the Durban North Japanese Gardens, Mitchell Park Zoo, Umgeni River Bird Park and the Durban Botanic Gardens. uShaka Marine Park on Bell Street is the largest attraction of its type in Africa and many tour operators offer helicopter trips over the stunning Drakensberg Mountains, with a glass of champagne when you land on top of the range to top it off.

Like all South Africans, Durban people love their sport. The ABSA Stadium is home to the Natal Sharks rugby team, and the impressive Moses Mabhiba Stadium was built to host games in the 2010 soccer World Cup. Golf is also popular with Durban Country Club, Zimbali and Selbourne being among the leading courses in the area.

By night the city is full of busy bars, restaurants and clubs with one of the most popular being Joe Kools on North Beach which is open from the morning until late.

Like any part of South Africa travellers have to exercise common sense about which areas in Durban they go to and are warned not to venture onto the beaches in the dark.

3 THINGS YOU MUST DO...

1 ZULU BATTLEFIELDS

Visit Fugitive's Drift (tel: +27 34 642 1843 or +27 34 271 8051) and take in the battlefields of Rorke's Drift, where 11 Victoria Crosses were won in 1879, and take a tour of Isandlwana where the British were routed a day earlier. To get there: 3.5 hour drive from Durban (N3 and R33).

2 THE GOLDEN MILE

The most popular tourist spot in Durban (tel: Tourism KwaZulu-Natal, +27 86 010 1099) running from South Beach to the Suncoast Casino and Entertainment World. Features the Blue Lagoon, Mini Town (a replica of Durban) and many vendors selling Zulu art, plus bars and restaurants.

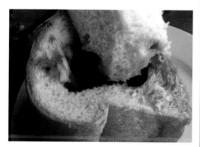

3 BUNNY CHOW

Durban speciality made of curried meat or vegetable cased in a hollowed out loaf of bread. Served with carrot, onion and chilli salad, they come in quarter, half and full loaves. Use your fingers and enjoy the mess. Stalls and Bunny Chow shops are all over Durban.

Above: Rickshaw drivers can be found touting for business along the beachfront.

WEATHER	LOW (°C)	HIGH (°C)	RAIN (MM)	SUNSET
January	21	27	109	19.00
February	22	27	121	18.54
March	20	27	124	18.30
April	18	26	76	17.53
May	14	24	51	17.22
June	13	24	32	17.04
July	11	22	28	17.08
August	13	23	38	17.24
September	15	23	69	17.42
October	17	24	109	17.57
November	18	25	122	18.18
December	19	26	119	18.43

KINGSMEAD

The venue of the last timeless Test

Kingsmead, officially known as Sahara Stadium, became Durban's Test venue in 1923 when England were the visitors. Previously Tests in the city had been played at the Lord's ground which was demolished in 1922.

Home to the KwaZulu-Natal Cricket Union, and the Nashua Dolphins, the ground was scene of the famous timeless Test between England and South Africa in 1939 that was abandoned as a draw, after nine days play, because the England team had to catch their boat home. The South African Ken Viljoen remarked that it was the only time he had had two haircuts in a game and nearly 5,500 deliveries were bowled in what was to be the last timeless Test in history.

Other highlights include South Africa's innings and 129-run demolition of Australia in 1970 when Graeme Pollock and Barry Richards hit 274 and 140 respectively and India being bowled out for 66 in 1996 when Allan Donald took 4-14.

In 2007 India's Yuvraj Singh became the first batsman to hit six sixes in an over in a Twenty20 international, with England's Stuart Broad the luckless bowler as Singh reached his 50 off 12 balls.

For spectators the open East Stand has a grass bank, favoured by England fans, and 'Castle Corner' is a bar at the South West End that England's Barmy Army once drank dry by tea on the first day of a Test match. There are plenty of refreshment stalls, some selling the famous Kingsmead Curry that soaks up the lager.

Kingsmead's location, on the east coast of Africa, means it is vulnerable to bad light and thunderstorms and its closeness to the sea helps swing bowlers. According to the locals the best conditions for the seamers are when the tide comes in during the late afternoon. The ground hosts the Boxing Day Test match and is the finishing point, every other year, for the Comrades Marathon, run over 89 km (56 miles) from Pietermaritzburg.

Below: Mark Boucher, South African wicket-keeper.

MATTER OF FACT

Ground: Sahara Stadium Kingsmead
Capacity: 25,000
Located: Greyville, Durban, South Africa
Address: 2 Kingsmead Close, Durban 4062 South Africa
Telephone: +27 31 335 4200
E-mail: dolphins@cricket.co.za
To get there: Durban Station (train)
Stands: North, East, South, West

UMGENI END

OLD FORT END

First Test: South Africa v England 18-22 January 1923
First ODI: South Africa v India 17 December 1992
First Twenty20: Kenya v New Zealand 12 September 2007

Tests played: 37
South Africa: Won 13, lost 11, drawn 13
Highest team total: 658-9 dec (SA v WI 2003)
Lowest team total: 66 (Ind v SA 1996)
Highest individual total: 275 G Kirsten (for SA v Eng 1999)
Highest partnership: 280 (WJ Edrich & PA Gibb, 2nd wicket for Eng v SA 1939)
Best bowling: 8-69 HJ Tayfield (for SA v Eng 1957)

ODIs played: 35
South Africa: Won 14, lost 8, tied 1, no result 4 (neutral games 7, no result 1)
Highest team total: 351-4 (Pak v SA 2007)
Lowest team total: 91 (Ind v SA 2006)
Highest individual total: 128 BC Lara (for WI v Pak 1993)
Highest partnership: 197 (BC Lara & PV Simmons, 2nd wicket for WI v Pak 1993)
Best bowling: 6-23 A Nehra (for Ind v Eng 2003)

Above: Morné Morkel's pace and bounce bagged him 19 wickets in the 2009/10 Test series against England.

CRICKET NET

Graeme Pollock, a son of Durban, was one of South Africa's finest batsmen, but his career was curtailed by apartheid and he played only 23 Tests (he averaged over 60). His brother Peter also played Test cricket for South Africa, and was later a selector, and his nephew Shaun played 108 Tests and 303 ODIs.

EAST LONDON

Buffalo City

East London, or Buffalo City, as has been rebranded, is 1,000 km (620 miles) from Cape Town on South Africa's southeast coast. Squeezed between the Buffalo River and Nahoon River and situated on the Indian Ocean, it is a popular destination for international and South African tourists alike.

The long beaches are some of the finest in South Africa with Nahoon Reef being a top surfing venue. Bonza Bay sand dunes are also a popular attraction, as are the Queen's Park Zoo, the East London Aquarium and East London City Hall, that was built in 1897 to celebrate the Diamond Jubilee of Queen Victoria. There are several good golf courses in the area including the Gary Player-designed Fish River Sun, which is an hour's drive from East London and which hosted the inaugural African Open in 2008 and East London Golf Club which has been a regular venue for the South African Open.

East London (and surrounds) is the scene of the great anti-apartheid film, *Cry Freedom*, about a friendship between black activist Steve Biko and Donald Woods, editor of the city's newspaper the *Daily Dispatch*.

Above: A fun fair in the city. *Below:* East London harbour.

WEATHER	LOW (°C)	HIGH (°C)	RAIN (MM)	SUNSET
January	14	31	68	19.21
February	15	33	94	19.12
March	13	32	104	18.44
April	11	32	83	18.04
May	8	32	53	17.31
June	7	29	45	17.10
July	5	31	48	17.13
August	6	32	78	17.32
September	8	32	87	17.52
October	9	30	10	18.11
November	11	29	10	18.35
December	13	31	63	19.02

3 THINGS YOU MUST DO...

1 EAST LONDON MUSEUM

Home to the world's only surviving dodo egg, the museum (Oxford Street, tel: +27 43 743 0686) also features the original coelacanth, a prehistoric fish thought to be extinct until discovered in East London Harbour in 1938. When: Mon–Fri 09.30–17.00, Sat 14.00–17.00, Sun/holidays 11.00–16.00.

2 SHIPWRECK DIVING

The Indian Ocean that laps the beaches of East London hides shipwrecks that provide fascinating dives for those who are competent (tel: the Border Undersea Club, +27 43 748 2958).

3 WILD COAST

East London is the gateway to the Wild Coast (tel: Wild Coast Tourism Office, +27 47 531 5290) an area of spectacular scenery with hiking and riding amongst the most popular activities. Wild is the correct description for the rugged land that houses spectacular beaches and coves.

BUFFALO PARK

One-dayers at the Buffs

Buffalo Park, a 10-minute walk from the centre of East London, has the Indian Ocean as its backdrop, is a picturesque arena and became the tenth Test ground in South Africa when Bangladesh were beaten by an innings and 107 runs in 2002. Graeme Smith top-scored in that match with a double hundred.

Mainly used for one-day games, Buffalo Park staged its first international in 1992 and hosted matches during the 2003 World Cup, the 2009 Indian Premier League, when it was the venue for three games, and England used the ground to play two warm-up games ahead of the Test series against South Africa the same year. In 1996 Mike Atherton's England tourists were bowled out for 115, having been set just 130 to win a one-day international against South Africa with the spinner Paul Adams taking three wickets to set up the victory.

In 2005 England's Kevin Pietersen nearly pulled off a record-breaking win for England in a match of 615 runs that did not finish until 11pm. Pietersen's 100 not out was not quite enough for the tourists to overhaul South Africa's 311-7 as they finished seven runs short.

Home to the Border Bears, the Warriors in the SuperSport Series, and the South African wicketkeeper Mark Boucher, the stadium has grassy embankments for fans to stretch out on and plenty of fast food outlets and bars around the ground. The ground is known to locals as 'The Buffs' or 'The Carpark' after a sponsorship deal with Mercedes-Benz, who also promote cricket development in the area.

Below: Hashim Amla's dogged style and long beard has made him an iconic figure in the South African team.

MATTER OF FACT
Ground: Buffalo Park
Capacity: 28,000
Located: East London, South Africa
Address: Buffalo Park Drive, Arcadia, East London 5200
Telephone: +27 43 743 7757
E-mail: bevw@bordercricket.co.za
To get there: the city train station and bus station are both a few minutes away
Stands: Main and Supporters' Club, Buffalo City Pavilion, Mercedes-Benz Pavilion.

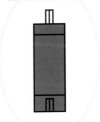

BUFFALO PARK DRIVE END

BUNKERS HILL END

First Test: South Africa v Bangladesh 18-21 October 2002
First ODI: South Africa v India 19 December 1992
First Twenty20: N/A

Tests played: 1
South Africa: Won 1, lost 0, drawn 0
Highest team total: 529-4 dec (SA v Ban 2002)
Lowest team total: 170 (Ban v SA 2002)
Highest individual total: 200 GC Smith (for SA v Ban 2002)
Highest partnership: 272 (GC Smith & G Kirsten, 2nd wicket for SA v Ban 2002)
Best bowling: 5-19 M Ntini (for SA v Ban 2002)

ODIs played: 19
South Africa: Won 11, lost 4, (neutral 4)
Highest team total: 311-7 (SA v Eng 2005)
Lowest team total: 115 (Eng v SA 1996)
Highest individual total: 150 S Chanderpaul (for WI v SA 1999)
Highest partnership: 226 (S Chanderpaul & CL Hooper, 4th wicket for WI v SA 1999)
Best bowling: 6-35 SM Pollock (for SA v WI 1999)

JOHANNESBURG

Above: *Johannesburg attracts people from across Africa and the rest of the world looking for their share of the golden life.*

The city of gold and hopes

Welcome to the city of gold. *Egoli*, meaning the place of gold, is a popular name for Johannesburg (as is Jo'burg and Jozi) and it lives up to its name having built a reputation as the place to do serious business.

The city also attracts migrants from across Africa and the rest of the world attracted by the hope and opportunities offered by South Africa's biggest city. The hills around Jo'burg are rich with gold and diamonds, driving the wealth and allure of the city. It's hard not to get caught up in the energy of the place.

With the urban decline of the city centre (with its skyline dominated by the high-rise Carlton Tower, Hillbrow Tower and Ponte City) in the late 1980s and early 1990s, the de facto centre shifted north to Sandton where you will find gleaming office blocks, huge shopping centres, hotels, and many restaurants and bars. This is also the home to the Johannesburg Stock Exchange, Africa's largest exchange, which moved here in 2000 from the city centre.

To the east are the areas of Benoni, Brakpan and Boksburg in an area known collectively as the East Rand, and dominated by the giant slag heaps of earth that have been emptied from the ground in search of riches. To the southwest is Soweto, the famous township that is home to well over a million people. Another well-known but smaller township area, Alexandra, is to the northeast.

The Wanderers is north of the city centre towards Sandton.

3 THINGS YOU MUST DO...

1 BALLOON SAFARI

Watch game while drifting along in a balloon. Book at Mabula Lodge in the Northern Province with Bill Harrop's Balloon Safaris (tel: +27 11 705 3201). Includes accommodation, meals, game drives and balloon safari. Price: R5,040–R6,520 each. To get there: a 2.5-hour drive from Jo'burg.

2 THE CRADLE OF HUMANKIND

Visit the birthplace of mankind and discover the history of humanity at Maropeng (Sterkfontein, tel: +27 14 577 9000). When: daily 09.00–17.00. Price: R105 adults, R60 child 4–14. To get there: 40 km (25 miles) northwest of Jo'burg.

3 STEAK

Jo'burg has some great restaurants and steak is juicy, tender and affordable. Try Turn 'n Tender (Cnr 3rd and 7th Ave, tel: +27 11 788 7933) which has been cooking steaks since 1977. When: daily from 11.30. Price: a 300g is R98. To get there: in Parktown North, between the city centre and Sandton.

Above: Painted wooden statues can be found on sale at most street and covered markets.

WEATHER	LOW (°C)	HIGH (°C)	RAIN (MM)	SUNSET
January	14	26	114	19.04
February	14	25	116	19.00
March	13	24	87	18.38
April	10	22	38	18.07
May	7	19	28	17.38
June	5	17	7	17.24
July	4	17	8	17.28
August	6	21	8	17.43
September	9	23	23	17.57
October	12	25	62	18.06
November	14	25	107	18.24
December	14	26	125	18.46

THE WANDERERS

The Bullring

Known as the Bullring because of its intimidating atmosphere, Wanderers Stadium, about 7 km (4 miles) to the north of Johannesburg, is the most high-profile cricket ground in South Africa and hosted the World Cup final in 2003, the final of the 2007 World Twenty20 and the final of the Indian Premier League in 2009.

It was also the scene of one of the most extraordinary games of one-day cricket in history, in 2006, when South Africa, thanks to 175 by Herschelle Gibbs, chased down Australia's world record total of 434 to make 438-9, with one ball to spare.

In Test cricket, it was the scene of Mike Atherton's epic 185 not out, as he batted for more than 10 hours in 1995 to salvage a draw for England against the might of Allan Donald and Shaun Pollock in 1995 and in 2002, Australia's Adam Gilchrist hit 204 not out, from 213 balls as the tourists crushed South Africa by an innings and 360 runs.

Home of the Highveld Lions, and the base of Cricket South Africa, the ground had its first taste of international cricket in 1956 when it became the third ground in Johannesburg to be used for Tests, after the old Wanderers and Ellis Park, and Peter May's England beat the South Africans.

More than R60 million has been lavished on the stadium since South Africa were re-admitted to international cricket in 1991, with the Centenary Pavilion, the Unity Pavilion and Memorial Pavilion Stand all being built and the Western Pavilion being refurbished. Five 65-metre tall floodlight towers have also been installed making it an ideal venue for night cricket.

Fans are well catered for at the ground. There are braai (barbecue) areas near the Western Pavilion to cook meat, which can be brought into the ground or purchased at the Cadac Butchery.

Below: The Wanderers cricket ground. Visiting teams should prepare to be intimidated by the fiercely patriotic crowd.

MATTER OF FACT

Ground: Bidvest Wanderers Stadium
Capacity: 34,000
Located: Illovo, Johannesburg, South Africa
Address: Corlett Drive, Illovo, Johannesburg 2196, South Africa
Telephone: +27 11 340 1500
E-mail: general@cricketgauteng.co.za
To get there: Rosebank Station (train)
Stands: Centenary Pavilion, Unity Pavilion, Memorial Pavilion, Grass Embankment, Taverners Pavilion, Open East

GOLF COURSE END

CORLETT DRIVE END

First Test: South Africa v England 24-29 Dec 1956
First ODI: South Africa v India 13 December 1992
First Twenty20: South Africa v New Zealand 21 October 2005

Tests played: 32
South Africa: Won 13, lost 9, drawn 10
Highest team total: 652-7 (Aus v SA 2002)
Lowest team total: 72 (SA v Eng 1956)
Highest individual total: 214 GS Blewett (for Aus v SA 1997)
Highest partnership: 385 (SR Waugh & GS Blewett, 5th wicket for Aus v SA 1997)
Best bowling: 9-113 HJ Tayfield (for SA v Eng 1957)

ODIs played: 37
South Africa: Won 18, lost 6 (neutral 13)
Highest team total: 438-9 (SA v Aus 2006)
Lowest team total: 109 (Pak v SA 1995 & SL v Ind 2003)
Highest individual total: 175 HH Gibbs (for SA v Aus 2006)
Highest partnership: 234 (RT Ponting & DR Martyn, 3rd wicket for Aus v Ind 2003)
Best bowling: 5-20 SM Pollock (for SA v Eng 2000)

Above: Herschelle Gibbs smashed 175 runs as South Africa scored 438-9 in an ODI v Australia in 2006.

CRICKET NET
In October 2004 a fire swept through the Wanderers' clubhouse destroying much memorabilia relating to the history of SA cricket including the bat Graeme Pollock used to score 274 against Australia in 1970. The fire brigade checked the scene, gave the OK and were leaving when the clock tower on the pavilion collapsed.

PORT ELIZABETH

Friendly and windy

If you like the wind and friendly people you'll like PE, as most people call Port Elizabeth, a seaport in the Eastern Cape Province with a population of over 700,000. The city is known both as the Friendly City, thanks to the generous nature of the locals, and the Windy City, thanks to gusts that whip around the urban area.

The city is also well known for its excellent sandy beaches and the warm Indian Ocean temperatures. Popular city beaches are Summerstrand and Hobie Beach, while Jeffrey's Bay, some 80 km (50 miles) away attracts surfers from around the world. But the long stretch of Algoa Bay, on which PE sits, has no shortage of decent beaches.

The Eastern Cape is home to the Xhosa people and significantly was the birthplace of Nelson Mandela (a village called Mvezo), and black activist Steve Biko (King William's Town) who was questioned in PE before the journey to Pretoria and his ultimate death. Both men have left an indelible mark on the region and the country.

St George's Park is centrally located near the Port Elizabeth Harbour.

Above: The beachfront at dusk. Below: Traditional dancers are always a popular attraction for tourists.

WEATHER	LOW (°C)	HIGH (°C)	RAIN (MM)	SUNSET
January	16	26	31	19.33
February	17	26	33	19.23
March	16	24	48	18.54
April	14	23	46	18.13
May	10	22	66	17.36
June	8	21	46	17.17
July	7	19	52	17.20
August	8	20	51	17.39
September	10	20	56	18.01
October	12	22	57	18.20
November	14	22	56	18.46
December	15	24	43	19.14

3 THINGS YOU MUST DO...

1 BARNEYS TAVERN

Meet the famous friendly people of PE and enjoy a beer. You'll do a lot worse than the beachfront venue of Barneys (Shop 6, The Boardwalk, Marine Drive, tel: +27 41 583 4500). When: daily 08.30–late.

2 ADDO ELEPHANT NATIONAL PARK

The elephants will get you there but you'll see warthog, eland, buffalo and kudu at Addo (tel: +27 42 233 8600). When: daily 07.00–19.00 but varies depending on season. Price: R130 adult (non-African passports) per day, R65 child (non-African passports). To get there: about 70 km (44 miles) north of PE.

3 BAYWORLD

A museum, oceanarium and snake park all rolled into one (Beach Rd, tel: +27 41 584 0650). When: daily 09.00–16.30. Price: R40 adult, R25 child. To get there: south of the city in Humewood, the nearest train station is Humewood Road.

ST GEORGE'S PARK

South Africa's first Test venue

St George's Park, or Axxess DSL St George's as it is officially known, in Port Elizabeth, was the venue of the first Test match staged outside England or Australia, when England beat South Africa by eight wickets in 1888.

One of the most historic grounds in South Africa, it staged the Springboks first rugby union international, with England also the opponents in 1891 and was the scene of a remarkable feat of bowling by England's George Lohmann, who took 15-45 in the 1896 Test match with the hosts bowled out for 30 in their second innings. It was also the ground where South Africa played its last Test match, in 1970, before they were banned from international cricket.

Found close to the city centre St George's was vastly improved for the 2003 Cricket World Cup, when it hosted a semi-final amongst five games, and boasts grassy embankments for fans, as well as more conventional stands. Like many other grounds in South Africa, however patrons are not allowed to take alcoholic drinks into the stadium and any cutlery must be plastic.

For spectators, there are ample refreshment stalls and bars and the St George's Park band have been entertaining the crowd at matches since 1994, although they were barred from the 2003 World Cup because of security concerns. The Centenary Pavilion contains a display of cricketing memorabilia that is worth a visit during a break in play.

The ground is surrounded by 73 hectares of gardens that feature the 1882 Edwardian Pearson Conservatory, a national monument, and hosts a craft fair every second Sunday of the month.

Below: *The South African cricket team of 1888 that played in the first Test hosted at Port Elizabeth.*

MATTER OF FACT
Ground: Axxess DSL St Georges
Capacity: 19,000
Located: Port Elizabeth, South Africa
Address: Park Drive, St George's Park, Central, Port Elizabeth, South Africa
Telephone: +27 41 585 1646
E-mail: leighd@cricket.co.za
To get there: Centrally located near Port Elizabeth Harbour. A short walk from Port Elizabeth Station (train)
Names of Stands: Duckpond Pavilion; Centenary Pavilion; Frielinghaus

DUCKPOND END

PARK DRIVE END

First Test: South Africa v England 12-13 March 1889
First ODI: South Africa v India 9 December 1992
First Twenty20: South Africa v West Indies 16 December 2007

Tests played: 24
South Africa: Won 8, lost 11, drawn 5
Highest team total: 549-7 dec (Aus v SA 1950)
Lowest team total: 30 (SA v Eng 1896)
Highest individual total: 196 HH Gibbs (for SA v Ind 2001)
Highest partnership: 187 (AR Morris & RN Harvey, 3rd wicket for Aus v SA 1950)
Best bowling: 8-7 GA Lohmann (for Eng v SA 1896)

ODIs played: 32
South Africa: Won 16, lost 8, no result 1, (neutral games 7)
Highest team total: 335-6 (Pak v SA 2002)
Lowest team total: 112 (NZ v Aus 2003)
Highest individual total: 135 Saleem Elahi (for Pak v SA 2002)
Highest partnership: 257 (Saleem Elahi & Abdul Razzaq, 2nd wicket for Pak v SA 2002)
Best bowling: 7-20 AJ Bichel (for Aus v Eng 2003)

POTCHEFSTROOM

The Boer's first capital

This small city of just over 120,000 people is situated only 120 km (75 miles) southwest of Johannesburg and locals frequently shorten its name simply to 'Potch'. It was the first capital (briefly) of the South African Republic, the independent state ruled by the Boers in the late 1800s. It was, of course, these people who fought against the British in the two Anglo-Boer Wars in an attempt to retain their independence, and the city was the site of a British concentration camp, so the city naturally has fierce Afrikaner roots.

Visitors who have been to the larger cities in South Africa may enjoy the gentler pace of the Potchefstroom, which today has strong academic links (thanks in particular to the North West University) and acts as a centre for the agricultural surrounding areas.

The North West Stadium is to the north of the city.

Above: Wire and bead street art. Below: The area is an excellent base for game viewing excursions.

WEATHER	LOW (°C)	HIGH (°C)	RAIN (MM)	SUNSET
January	16	29	99	19.04
February	15	28	102	19.00
March	15	26	73	18.38
April	9	24	31	18.07
May	4	21	19	17.38
June	1	18	3	17.24
July	0	19	3	17.28
August	3	22	5	17.43
September	8	25	18	17.57
October	11	27	55	18.06
November	13	28	98	18.24
December	15	29	121	18.46

3 THINGS YOU MUST DO...

1 POTCHEFSTROOM COUNTRY CLUB
If you've got time for golf on a course that has held the South African Open, then head to the country club (Mooi River Ave, tel: +27 18 297 7875). Price: from R100. To get there: the country club is centrally located.

2 PILANSBERG NATIONAL PARK
South Africa's fourth largest park (tel: +27 14 555 1600) has a good population of the Big Five. Gate open: 06.00–18.00/19.00. Price: R45 adult, R20 child, R20 vehicle. To get there: 220 km (137 miles) to the north.

3 MAFIKENG
Site of the 217-day siege by Boer soldiers on the British who were led by Robert Baden-Powell, the man who later created Boy Scout movement, is now popular on the battlefield tour of South Africa (tel: tourism office, +27 18 381 3155). To get there: 200 km (125 miles) to the northwest.

NORTH WEST STADIUM

Here be Dragons

Found about a 15-minute walk from the centre of Potchefstroom and around 120 km (75 miles) from Johannesburg, Senwes Park is home of the North West Cricket Association, which was founded in 1922. It became South Africa's 11th Test venue when hosting Bangladesh in October 2002. The South African batsmen took an immediate liking to the pitch with Jacques Kallis, Herschelle Gibbs and Gary Kirsten all scoring hundreds to take their team to victory by an innings and 160 runs.

Historically known as North West Cricket Stadium, it was first used for international cricket in October 2000 when the one-dayer between South Africa and New Zealand was rained off despite the hosts' Nicky Boje hitting an unbeaten 105 off 93 deliveries.

In the 2003 World Cup the ground hosted three games, most significant of which was the contest between South Africa and Kenya during which Jonty Rhodes broke his hand and had to retire from the international game.

The ground has plenty of grassy mounds for spectators to stretch out on and has been used as a training camp by the South African national team as well as many touring sides. The ground also has a museum containing much cricket memorabilia. Senwes Park is the second home to the Highveld Lions and the main ground for the North-West Dragons side.

Potchefstroom is known as the 'Home of Sport' and the city houses the provincial headquarters for 17 of the most prominent sports in the region and Senwes Park is also the home of the South African national Australian Rules team.

Below: Wayne Parnell is aiming to join Shaun Pollock and Allan Donald as one of South Africa's bowling greats.

MATTER OF FACT
Ground: Senwes Park
Capacity: 10,000
Located: Pochefstroom, SA
Address: Senwes Park, Loopstreet, Potchefstroom
Telephone: +27 18 294 6666
E-mail: christelleg@cricket.co.za
To get there: M12 from Johannesburg
Stands: Grandstand, President's Suite (contains Bacher Room)

CARGO MOTORS END

UNIVERSITY END

First Test: South Africa v Bangladesh 25-27 October 2002
First ODI: South Africa v New Zealand 20 October 2000
First Twenty20: N/A

Tests played: 1
South Africa: Won 1, lost 0, drawn 0
Highest team total: 482-5 dec (SA v Ban 2002)
Lowest team total: 107 (Ban v SA 2002)
Highest individual total: 160 G Kirsten (for SA v Ban 2002)
Highest partnership: 234 (G Kirsten & JH Kallis, 3rd wicket for SA v Ban 2002)
Best bowling: 5-21 JH Kallis (for SA v Ban 2002)

ODIs played: 15
South Africa: Won 4, tied 1, no result 1, (neutral games 9)
Highest team total: 418-5 (SA v Zim 2006)
Lowest team total: 45 (Nam v Aus 2003)
Highest individual total: 153 H Gibbs (for SA v Ban 2002)
Highest partnership: 186 (RN ten Doeschate & B Zuiderent, 4th wicket for Ned v Ken 2009)
Best bowling: 7-15 GC McGrath (for Aus v Nam 2003)

SRI LANKA

THE

3

MINUTE
GUIDE

Capitals: *Sri Jayawardenepura Kotte.* **Languages:** *Sinhalese, Tamil.* **Beers:** *Lion lager, Lion stout.* **Food:** *Curry, Kiribath (rice with coconut milk), dhal (lentils).* **National Anthem:** *Sri Lanka Matha (Mother Sri Lanka).* **Population:** *20 million.* **Time zone:** *GMT +5.30.*
Emergency numbers: *119/118 (police), 110 (medical), 111 (fire).* **Did you know?** *Although the country gained Independence in 1947 the Colonial name of Ceylon was not changed until 1972.* **Cricket body:** *35 Maitland Place, Colombo 7, Sri Lanka. Tel: +94 112 681 601/2/3/4. E-mail: info@srilankacricket.lk. Web: www.srilankacricket.lk.*

Below: Fishermen on stilts in Galle.

Cricket's revolutionaries

Touring sides from England and Australia have been stopping in Sri Lanka, or Ceylon as it was known before 1972, since 1882 but the island's team was not granted Test status until a century later. Since then the national team has become formidable and has given the world the likes of the freakish spinner Muttiah Muralitharan, who would become the leading wicket-taker in Test cricket, the explosive batting of Sanath Jayasuriya and the elegance of Kumar Sangakkara and Mahela Jayawardene.

Sri Lanka's first Test match was against England, in 1982, at the P Saravanamuttu Stadium in Colombo which the tourists won by seven wickets. Three years later they beat India at the same ground to record their first Test win, by 149 runs, and Sri Lankan cricket was up and running.

The emergence of a crop of world-class players in the early 1990s saw Sri Lanka become a more difficult side to beat but they really came of age by winning the World Cup in 1996, beating Australia in the final in Lahore. Sri Lanka were supposedly co-hosts of that tournament, with India and Pakistan, but the Australian and West Indian teams refused to travel to the island because of the threat of the Tamil terrorists who had just bombed the Central Bank in Colombo. When they did get onto the pitch the Sri Lankans changed the face of one-day cricket by employing Jayasuriya and Romesh Kaluwitharana as 'pinch hitters' at the top of the order to take advantage of the fielding restrictions. Now 'pinch-hitting' is used by every one-day side in the world.

Above: *A Kandyan dancer. The dance form originated in Kandy but has spread and become popular throughout Sri Lanka.*

TEST RECORD

Versus	First Test	Matches	Won	Lost	Drawn
Australia	Apr 1983	20	1	13	6
Bangladesh	Sep 2001	12	12	0	0
England	Feb 1982	21	6	8	7
India	Sep 1982	32	5	13	14
New Zealand	Mar 1983	26	7	9	10
Pakistan	Mar 1982	37	9	15	13
South Africa	Aug 1993	17	4	8	5
West Indies	Dec 1993	12	6	3	3
Zimbabwe	Oct 1994	15	10	0	5

Most runs: Mahela Jayawardene (1997-) 9,120 runs, 110 Tests, average 53.96
Most wickets: Muttiah Muralitharan (1992-) 792 wickets, 132 Tests, average 22.71
Most catches: Mahela Jayawardene (1997-) 152 catches, 110 Tests

WORLD CUP RECORD

Year	Venue	Finished
1975	England	Pool
1979	England	Pool
1983	England	Pool
1987	India and Pakistan	Pool
1992	Australia and N Zealand	Pool
1996	Ind, Pak and S Lanka	Winners
1999	England	Pool
2003	South Africa	Semi-final
2007	West Indies	Runners-up

Most ODI runs: Sanath Jayasuriya (1989-) 13,428 runs, 443 matches, average 32.43
Most ODI wickets: Muttiah Muralitharan (1993-) 512 wickets, 333 matches, average 22.93
Most ODI catches: KC Sangakkara (2000-) 254 catches, 266 matches

COLOMBO

Above: *The train from Colombo to Kandy.*

Three's company

Uniquely of any cricketing city, Colombo is home to three recently active Test grounds – P Saravanamuttu Stadium, the Sinhalese Sports Club Ground and R Premadasa Stadium. Another venue, the Colombo Cricket Club Ground, also held a Test as recently as 1987. It is an indication of the dominance of the city when it comes to the country's beloved sport of cricket, and indeed in all spheres of life on this island in the sub-continent. It's the dominant city of the country (the small, neighbouring Sri Jayawardenepura Kotte is the administrative capital) with its greater urban area being home to around a quarter of the entire population of Sri Lanka.

Water plays a central role in the make-up of the city and its daily life, with the harbour attracting traders to this area for hundreds years. The Kelani River runs through the city to the north, while downtown there are a series of canals and waterways and, importantly for recreation, the Beira Lake.

The skyline is dominated by the World Trade Center, two 40-storey towers which can be found near the Indian Ocean in the Galle Face area. Nearby to these is the smaller but still impressive Bank of Ceylon tower. Stretching away from here to the south is one of the city's famous open spaces, the Galle Face Green, a large strip of grassland and promenade that is wedged between the ocean and the Galle Road. The area is popular among locals who want to walk by the sea, or simply relax with friends and family.

Further south still is the city's main recreation area, the Viharamahadevi Park, a large-scale park that is flanked by the Town Hall and the Colombo National Museum.

The Sinhalese Sports Club Ground is nearby to the park. The R Premadasa Stadium is 4 km (2.5 miles) northeast of here and the P Saravanamuttu Stadium is 3 km (2 miles) to the east.

3 THINGS YOU MUST DO...

1 ZANZIBA CLUB
For a cool, laid-back night of drinking and chilling to music head to Zanziba (1st & 2nd Floor, Huejay Court 32B, 1/1 Sir Mohamed Macan Markar Rd. When: Wed–Sat. To get there: next to the Holiday Inn in the Galle Face area.

2 ODEL
For all your Sri Lankan goodies in one department store (No 5, Alexandra Place +94 11 2682 712/3. When: daily 10.00–20.00. To get there: near the World Trade Center.

3 MOUNT LAVINA HOTEL
Enjoy casual seafood dining on the beach but with the backdrop of Mount Lavania Hotel's (100 Hotel Rd, tel: +94 11 2711 711) colonial splendour. When: Seafood Cove Sun–Thur 19.00–22.30, Fri–Sat 19.00–23.00. To get there: 12 km (7.5 miles) south of Colombo.

Above: An ornate temple in Colombo.

WEATHER	LOW (°C)	HIGH (°C)	RAIN (MM)	SUNSET
January	22	30	89	18.36
February	22	31	69	18.49
March	23	31	147	18.53
April	24	31	231	18.50
May	26	31	371	18.50
June	24	30	224	18.53
July	24	30	135	19.00
August	25	29	109	19.00
September	25	29	160	18.48
October	24	29	348	18.32
November	23	29	315	18.20
December	22	29	147	18.22

R PREMADASA

The bowlers' graveyard

Built in 1986 and renamed after the former Sri Lankan President, Ranasinghe Premadasa, in 1994, the one-time Khetterama Cricket Stadium became the island's fifth Test cricket ground in 1992 when the match against the touring Australians ended in stalemate.

The fourth Test played at the ground, between Sri Lanka and India in 1997 captured the attention of the cricketing world with a host of records being broken. Sri Lanka made a world-record innings total of 952-6 with Sanath Jayasuriya making 340, Roshan Mahanama 225 and Aravinda de Silva 126. The Indians, who made 537-8 themselves, were in the field for three days as the Sri Lankans piled on the runs and Jayasuriya and Mahanama's partnership of 576 for the second wicket was at the time the highest for any stand in the history of Test cricket.

Five years earlier in 1992 the Sri Lankans had given a Test debut to a young spinner on the ground in the game against Australia. The novice took 3-141 in the match and the world of cricket did not take too much notice. They know all about him now, his name was Muttiah Muralitharan.

Most bowlers would be reluctant to play at the ground, given the events of 1997, but New Zealander Paul Wiseman took 5-82 to hand Sri Lanka their first defeat at the stadium in 1998. There was no more Test cricket at the ground for seven years but plenty of one-day cricket and the stadium was due to host a semi-final in the 2011 World Cup.

Found in the suburb of Maligawatta, to the northeast of the Fort area, the ground is a far cry from some of the modern concrete bowls found in world cricket with the three-tier grandstand catching the eye as it is decked out with flowers and plants. The stadium was constructed on swampland that was once used by monks as they ferried across to the Khettarama temple that is next to the ground.

Below: The guard of honour is given to Sri Lankan legend Muttiah Muralitharan (in Zimbabwe).

MATTER OF FACT

Ground: R Premadasa Stadium
Capacity: 35,000
Located: Maligawatta, Colombo, Sri Lanka
Address: Khettarama Road, Maligawatta, Colombo
Telephone: +94 112 681 601/2/3/4 (SLCB)
To get there: Dematagoda Station (train)
Stands: A, B, C, D

SCOREBOARD END

First Test: Sri Lanka v Australia 28 August-
2 September 1992
First ODI: Sri Lanka v Pakistan 9 March 1986
First Twenty20: Sri Lanka v India 10 February 2009

Tests played: 6
Sri Lanka: Won 2, lost 1, drawn 3
Highest team total: 952-6 (SL v Ind 1997)
Lowest team total: 86 (Ban v SL 2005)
Highest individual total: 340 ST Jayasuriya (for SL v Ind 1997)
Highest partnership: 576 (ST Jayasuriya & RS Mahanama, 2nd wicket for SL v Ind 1997)
Best bowling: 6-18 M Muralitharan (for SL v Ban 2005)

ODIs played: 96
Sri Lanka: Won 50, lost 25, no result 6
(neutral games 15)
Highest team total: 363-5 (Ind v SL 2009)
Lowest team total: 86 (Neth v SL 2002)
Highest individual total: 150 G Ghambir (for Ind v SL 2009)
Highest partnership: 252 (SC Ganguly & SR Tendulkar, 1st wicket for Ind v SL 1998)
Best bowling: 6-20 AD Mathews (for SL v Ind 2009)

Above: India's Sourav Ganguly made his first ODI hundred at the R Premadasa Stadium in 1997.

CRICKET NET

President Ranasinghe Premadasa, who commissioned the building of the ground, was in power from 1988 to 1993 during some of the most turbulent times in Sri Lanka's history. The ground was renamed after Premadasa was assassinated by a suicide bomber, in Colombo in May 1993.

SINHALESE SPORTS CLUB

Sri Lankan HQ

The Sinhalese Sports Club, formerly known as Maitland Place, staged its first Test match in 1984, with New Zealand and Sri Lanka playing out a draw and was the country's third Test venue. It is the home of the Sri Lankan Cricket Board and for many years it was Sri Lanka's premium stadium. Recently, however, it has been overtaken by the R Premadasa Stadium as Colombo's main cricket venue. Used as an airfield by the Allies in the Second World War the ground is found in Cinnamon Gardens, a 15-minute drive south of the central Fort area of the city, and surrounded by shops and cafes.

It was the scene of the highest partnership in Test and first class cricket when Kumar Sangakkara and Mahela Jayawardene put on 624 for the third wicket against South Africa in 2006 with Jayawardene coming within 26 runs of equalling Brian Lara's record for an individual Test score.

In 2001 England edged home in a tense finish. After being set just 74 to win the match and the series, Graham Thorpe scored 32 not out, to add to his first-innings century, as they scraped home by four wickets.

In one-day cricket Chaminda Vaas, the Sri Lankan left-arm pace bowler, took 8-19 against Zimbabwe in 2001 as the tourists were bowled out for just 38.

The Sinhalese Sports Club has its own long room and is known as the Lord's of Colombo – it is a far cry from some of the modern concrete bowls and combines Sri Lankan characteristics with top-class facilities.

Below: The Sinhalese Sports Club.

MATTER OF FACT
Ground: Sinhalese Sports Club
Capacity: 10,000
Located: Cinnamon Gardens, Colombo
Address: 35 Maitland Place, Colombo 07
Telephone: +94 112 681 601/2/3/4 (SLCB)
To get there: 15-min drive south of central Fort
Stands: Lanka Bell Stand, Seylan Bank Pavilion

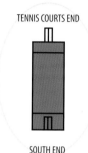

TENNIS COURTS END

SOUTH END

First Test: Sri Lanka v New Zealand 16-21 March 1984
First ODI: Sri Lanka v England 13 February 1982
First Twenty20: N/A

Tests played: 33
Sri Lanka: Won 17, lost 6, drawn 10
Highest team total: 756-5 dec (SL v SA 2006)
Lowest team total: 81 (SL v Eng 2001)
Highest individual total: 374 DPM Jayawardene (for SL v SA 2006)
Highest partnership: 624 (KC Sangakkara & DPM Jayawardene, 3rd wicket for SL v SA 2006)
Best bowling: 8-87 M Muralitharan (for SL v Ind 2001)

ODIs played: 56
Sri Lanka: Won 20, lost 11, no result 6
(neutral games 19)
Highest team total: 343-5 (Pak v HK 2004)
Lowest team total: 38 (Zim v SL 2001)
Highest individual total: 144 Younis Khan (for Pak v HK 2004)
Highest partnership: 223 (Shoaib Malik & Younis Khan, 3rd wicket for Pak v HK 2004)
Best bowling: 8-19 WPU Vaas (for SL v Zim 2001)

P SARAVANAMUTTU STADIUM

Where it all started

The P Saravanamuttu Stadium, formerly known as the Colombo Oval, is named after the first President of the Board of Control for Cricket in Sri Lanka who masterminded the construction of the ground during the Second World War. Situated about a ten-minute drive from the Fort area, it is built on marshland and was ready to host cricket in 1943. It staged Sri Lanka's, first Test in 1982 when England were the visitors. Home of the Tamil Union, the ground was also the venue for Sri Lanka's first Test win, against India in 1985 and in 2002 the ground staged a Test between Australia and Pakistan when their series was shifted from Pakistan because of security fears. The other Test in the series was played in Sharjah.

A small ground, the P Sara Oval is host to the Tamil Union Cricket and Athletic Club, inaugurated in 1899 and is the home club ground of world record-breaking spinner Muttiah Muralitharan who, although born in Kandy, played for the Tamil side in the Premier Trophy. The ground's other most famous player is Mahadevan Sathasivam, who has a stand named after him and who Gary Sobers termed 'the greatest batsman ever on earth'.

Don Bradman took his 'Invincibles' side of 1948 to play a game on their way to England – he previously played for the Australians on the ground in 1930 against the All Ceylon team.

The ground has undergone renovations in recent years following criticism of its upkeep, but has retained the feeling of being more of a club ground than a Test venue.

Below: The original pinch-hitter, Sanath Jayasuriya was still playing one dayers for Sri Lanka aged 40.

MATTER OF FACT
Ground: P Saravanamuttu Stadium
Capacity: 15,000
Located: Borella, Colombo
Address: 301 Lesley Ranagala Mawatha, Colombo 8, Sri Lanka
Telephone: +94 112 693 006
E-mail: ceo@tamilunioncricket.com
To get there: Cotta Road Station (train)
Stands: Dr Ranjan Chanmugam, M Sathasivam, T Murugesar, Tryphone Mirando, Sathi Coomarswamy

AIR FORCE FLATS END

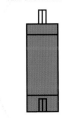

PRESS BLOCK END

First Test: Sri Lanka v England 17-21 February 1982
First ODI: Sri Lanka v Australia 13 April 1983
First Twenty20: N/A

Tests played: 14
Sri Lanka: Won 7, lost 2, drawn 4 (neutral games 1)
Highest team total: 541-9 (SL v Ban 2002)
Lowest team total: 62 (Ban v SL 2007)
Highest individual total: 274 not out SP Fleming (for NZ v SL 2003)
Highest partnership: 280 (TT Samaraweera & TM Dilshan, 5th wicket for SL v Ban 2005)
Best bowling: 7-94 SK Warne (for Aus v Pak 2002)

ODIs played: 12
Sri Lanka: Won 8, lost 2, no result 2
Highest team total: 251-6 (SL v Aus 1992)
Lowest team total: 115 (SL v NZ 1984)
Highest individual total: 105 PA De Silva (SL v Aus 1992)
Highest partnership: 147 (AP Gurusinha & PA de Silva, 3rd wicket for SL v Aus 1992)
Best bowling: 4-24 CRD Fernando (SL v Ban 2007)

GALLE

Above: King coconuts hang off a bike. They taste like regular coconuts, but the outside is yellow rather than green. Now you know.

A city rebuilds

One date will be indelibly marked on the history of Galle forever. The date 24 December 2004 is when the city was devastated by the massive and destructive tsunami that swept through the region. Caused by an earthquake thousands of kilometres away, the disaster left thousands dead in the city; in total more than 200,000 people were killed in the region.

Built on the southern shores of Sri Lanka, Galle is 120 km (75 miles) from Colombo and has a population of around 100,000. It's a city whose character has been forged by outside influences. In recent history it was the Portuguese (who arrived in 16th century) then the Dutch (who took over in 1640) who left the city's best known landmark, the Dutch Fort, which stands proudly by the Indian Ocean guarding the entrance to Galle. British rule began in 1796 and continued until the island's Independence in 1948.

But modern European influence is not the only to have touched this city. Galle's location means it has been an important port for hundreds of years and traders did business with the Greeks, Romans, Arabs, Chinese and of course the Indians.

Today visitors come for the city's relaxed charm, its ancient monuments and the beautiful beaches. Soft sand, sheltered bays, warm Indian Ocean fringed by lush vegetation and palm trees, anyone? Thought so. The nearby Unawatuna Beach to the south and Hikkaduwa Beach to the north are both popular and within easy striking distance from the city. As well as the obvious attractions for those who prefer to laze, the beaches around Galle are also favourites for snorkeling, surfing and deep-sea fishing.

3 THINGS YOU MUST DO...

1 DUTCH FORT
Simply stroll around the fort and rediscover the Dutch colonial era of the city. The fort was built in 1663 and survived the force of the 2004 tsunami.

2 BEACH
You can't come to Galle and not go to a beach. Try Unawatuna Beach. To get there: 5 km (3 miles) to the south along the A2.

3 STILT FISHERMAN
The amazing stilt fishermen can be found out on their stilts early each morning along the southern coast of Sri Lanka around Galle. You'll find them at Ahangama. To get there: 23 km (14 miles) to the south along the A2.

Above: An elephant is moved between towns.

WEATHER	LOW (°C)	HIGH (°C)	RAIN (MM)	SUNSET
January	23	29	102	18.36
February	23	29	81	18.49
March	23	29	117	18.53
April	25	31	242	18.50
May	26	31	296	18.50
June	25	30	206	18.53
July	25	28	164	19.00
August	25	28	157	19.00
September	25	28	213	18.48
October	23	28	343	18.32
November	23	29	302	18.20
December	23	29	177	18.22

GALLE INTERNATIONAL

Rising from the tsunami

Formerly known as the Esplanade and originally built in 1876 as a racecourse, Galle International was one of the most beautiful grounds in the world until it was destroyed by the tsunami of 2004 which is estimated to have claimed the lives of more than 35,000 Sri Lankans and wrecked the homes of millions more.

The stadium was unrecognizable as cars and general debris floated around and it seemed that cricket would never be played there again. Political rows delayed the start of the rebuilding process and it was suggested that the ground should be constructed on another site. But work started in May 2006 and the cricket world threw its weight behind the reconstruction project.

The likes of Shane Warne and Ian Botham helped with fund-raising and the stadium was quickly restored with England playing the first match at the refurbished arena in December 2007. Spinners have fond memories of the ground; Warne took his 500th Test wicket here in 2004 and Muttiah Muralitharan snared his 400th Test victim at Galle in 2002.

The post-tsunami reconstruction included the building of the Mahinda Rajapakse Pavilion, named after the Sri Lankan President who gave permission for the re-construction of the ground. It can house 500 VIPs in air-conditioned comfort as well as 150 members of the media and both teams. The ground is still overlooked by Galle Fort which was built by the Dutch in the 17th century to protect against invading Tamils. It kept the invaders at bay and hundreds of years later repelled the force of the tsunami.

The ground staged its first Test match in 1998 when New Zealand were beaten by an innings and is a particular favourite of Mahela Jayawardene, the Sri Lankan batsman who hit double centuries against South Africa, in the last Test there before the tsunami, and England in the first Test back after the disaster.

Below: Mahela Jayawardene hold the record for the highest individual score at the Galle Ground, hitting 237 against South Africa in 2004.

MATTER OF FACT

Ground: Galle International Stadium
Capacity: 35,000
Located: Galle, Sri Lanka
Address: Wakwalla Road, Galle, 80000
Telephone: +94 112 681 601/2/3/4 (SLCB)
To get there: Galle Station (train) and Galle Central (bus)
Stands: Grandstand, The Hill

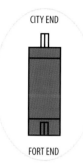

CITY END

FORT END

First Test: Sri Lanka v New Zealand 3-7 June 1998
First ODI: Sri Lanka v India 25 Jun 1998
First Twenty20: N/A

Tests played: 15
Sri Lanka: Won 8, lost 3, drawn 4
Highest team total: 600-8 dec (Pak v SL 2000)
Lowest team total: 79 (Zim v SL 2002)
Highest individual total: 237 DPM Jayawardene (for SL v SA 2004)
Highest partnership: 230 (MS Atapattu & PA de Silva, 3rd wicket for SL v Eng 2001)
Best bowling: 7-46 M Muralitharan (for SL v Eng 2003)

ODIs played: 4
Sri Lanka: Won 2, lost 1 (neutral games 1)
Highest team total: 249-7 (SL v SA 2000)
Lowest team total: 160 (SL v Aus 1999)
Highest individual total: 85 KC Sangakkara (for SL v SA 2000)
Highest partnership: 150 (G Kirsten & AJ Hall, 1st wicket for SA v SL 2000)
Best bowling: 5-28 ST Jayasuriya (for SL v Aus 1999)

Above: *Preparing for a big match.*

CRICKET NET
Jayanda Warnaweera played ten Test matches for Sri Lanka and, as curator at Galle, was at the heart of its rebuilding following the tsunami. His devotion to the project is summed up when he says: "This is my first home. I'm here at 6am and go home at midnight. I only go home to sleep."

KANDY

In the land of tea

The picturesque hill city of Kandy, built around the Kandy Lake, is the second largest in Sri Lanka with a population of over 110,000. The city, which is surrounded by large tea plantations, was capital of an independent kingdom when the Portuguese and Dutch were occupying the coastal areas from the 16th-18th century. It was the base for a series of attacks on the foreign forces, the jungle area providing ideal cover for the local people to withdraw to when needed. The British eventually took control of Kandy in 1815.

The city's major landmarks, the Temple of the Tooth Relic, the Royal Palace, which today houses the National Museum of Kandy, and various Buddhist temples, are found on the north shore of the lake. Close by is the Udawattakele National Forest Reserve, an important sanctuary for flora and fauna. The Royal Botanic Gardens are about 6 km (4 miles) southwest of the city in Peradeniya.

The Asgiriya Stadium is situated to the north of the lake.

Above: A giant Buddhist looks out on the city. Below: Queen's Hotel seen across Kandy Lake.

WEATHER	LOW (°C)	HIGH (°C)	RAIN (MM)	SUNSET
January	18	28	121	18.36
February	18	30	66	18.49
March	20	31	101	18.53
April	21	31	179	18.50
May	22	30	154	18.50
June	21	28	204	18.53
July	21	28	175	19.00
August	21	28	140	19.00
September	20	28	145	18.48
October	20	28	286	18.32
November	20	28	273	18.20
December	19	28	217	18.22

3 THINGS YOU MUST DO...

1 VICTORIA GOLF AND COUNTRY RESORT
Horse riding, massages, dining, nature trails, tennis and, of course, golf (tel: +94 812 376 376). Price: Rs4,500 for 18 holes weekdays, Rs6,000 weekends and holidays. To get there: 22 km (14 miles) east of Kandy along the A26.

2 TEMPLE OF THE TOOTH RELIC
Called Sri Dalada Maligawa, this is an important holy Buddhist site as it is said to house a tooth of Buddha (Palace Sq, tel: +94 812 234 226). There is also a museum. When: dawn–dusk. To get there: centrally located.

3 CEYLON TEA MUSEUM
Everything you ever wanted to know about your favourite drink from an area which certainly knows how to grow it (Hantana Rd, tel: Sri Lanka Tea Board, + 94 11 258 7814). When: Tues–Sat 08.15–16.45, Sun 08.15–12.15. Price: Rs250. To get there: 4 km (2.5 miles) south of the city.

ASGIRIYA STADIUM

Back to school for cricketers

The Asgiriya Stadium, in the hill lands of Sri Lanka, about a ten-minute walk from the centre of Kandy, became the only Test venue in the world to be owned by a school (Trinity College) when a match was played here in 1983. The College has supplied several international cricketers for Sri Lanka, notably Kumar Sangakkara, Ravi Ratnayeke and Ranjan Madugalle, who became a leading Test match referee after retiring. The ground is stunning; it is carved into the hillside and overlooked by the hills of Kandy and a giant Buddha and houses the Old Trinity Clubhouse. It's a good spot to watch the cricket and enjoy a drink.

The Asgiriya Stadium became Sri Lanka's second Test ground when it hosted Greg Chappell's Australians in a one-off game and its first one-day international followed three years later when Pakistan were the visitors.

The ground was opened in 1915 by Sir Robert Chalmers and the MCC, captained by Colin Cowdrey, played a tour match there in 1969, beating Central Province by 61 runs.

But the local hero in Kandy is Muttiah Muralitharan, who was born in the nearby village of Nattarampotha and went on to become the world's leading wicket-taker in Test cricket. He was not a pupil at Trinity (he went to St Anthony's College in Kandy where he was taught by Benedictine monks). He took his 709th Test wicket – England's Paul Collingwood – on the ground in 2007 to pass Shane Warne's tally of victims. He was also the first player to pass 100 wickets at three different grounds – the Asgiriya Stadium, Galle International Stadium and the Sinhalese Sports Ground.

Below: Kumar Sangakkara, Sri Lanka's wicket-keeper batsman.

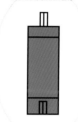

HUNNASGIRIYA END

HANTHANA END

MATTER OF FACT
Ground: Asgiriya Stadium
Capacity: 10,300
Located: Kandy, Sri Lanka
Address: Gamini Dissanayake Mawatha, Kandy
Telephone: +94 112 681 601/2/3/4 (SLCB)
To get there: Asgiriya Station (train)

First Test: Sri Lanka v Australia 22-26 April 1983
First ODI: Sri Lanka v Pakistan 2 March 1986
First Twenty20: N/A

Tests played: 21
Sri Lanka: Won 7, lost 9, drawn 5
Highest team total: 514-4 dec (Aus v SL 1983)
Lowest team total: 71 (SL v Pak 1994)
Highest individual total: 223 MS Atapattu (for SL v Zim 1998)
Highest partnership: 335 (MS Atapattu & ST Jayasuriya, 1st wicket for SL v Pak 2000)
Best bowling: 9-51 M Muralitharan (for SL v Zim 2002)

ODIs played: 6
Sri Lanka: Won 3, lost 1, no result 1 (neutral games 1)
Highest team total: 398-5 (SL v Ken 1996)
Lowest team total: 154 (Zim v WI 2001)
Highest individual total: 145 PA de Silva (for SL v Ken 1996)
Highest partnership: 187 (MS Atapattu & DPM Jayawardene, 3rd wicket for SL v WI 2001)
Best bowling: 3-21 D Brown (for WI v Zim 2001)

WEST INDIES

<table>
<tr>
<td>
THE

3

MINUTE
GUIDE
</td>
<td>

</td>
<td>
Capitals: *St John's (Antigua and Barbuda), Bridgetown (Barbados), St George's (Grenada), Georgetown (Guyana), Kingston (Jamaica), Castries (St Lucia), Basseterre (Saint Kitts & Nevis), Kingstown (Saint Vincent & The Grenadines), Port of Spain (Trinidad & Tobago).* **Languages:** *English, Creole.* **Beers:** *Carib lager, Red Stripe.* **Food:** *Goat curry.* **Time zones:** *GMT -4 and GMT -5 (Jamaica).* **Did you know?** *West Indian umpire Steve Bucknor officiated in 128 Test matches and 181 one-day internationals between 1989 and 2009.* **Cricket body:** *Factory Road, St John's, Antigua. Tel: +1 268 481 2450. E-mail: wicb@windiescricket.com. Web: www.windiescricket.com.*
</td>
</tr>
</table>

Below: Home for tea?

Kings of calypso cricket

Think of cricket in the Caribbean and you think of fans leaping about, fearsome fast bowlers and batsman swatting the ball to all parts of the ground. It all adds up to 'Calypso Cricket'.

That was the case for a couple of decades from the mid-1970s to the mid-1990s when teams captained by Clive Lloyd and Viv Richards dominated world cricket. With bowlers such as Michael Holding, Andy Roberts, Malcolm Marshall, Courtney Walsh and Curtly Ambrose and batsmen like Richards, Lloyd, Gordon Greenidge and Desmond Haynes at their disposal it is hardly surprising that a visit to the Caribbean was not treated as a holiday by most international cricketers. Before those stars they had possibly the greatest player of all time in Garry Sobers, who could command a place in any side in history with his batting, bowling and fielding and held the world Test batting record for 36 years after scoring 365 against Pakistan in 1958.

Since the mid-1990s, despite the brilliance of Brian Lara with the bat, who beat Sobers's Test mark twice, West Indies cricket has declined as many youngsters have been lured away from cricket by the millions of dollars on offer in the American sports that dominate the television schedule in the Caribbean.

West Indies played their first Test in 1928 against England, won their first series, also against England in 1935 and took the first two World Cups in 1975 and 1979. They added the ICC Champions Trophy, held in England, in 2004.

Above: *Most places in the West Indies will find you a jetty into paradise.*

TEST RECORD

Versus	First Test	Matches	Won	Lost	Drawn
Australia*	Dec 1930	108	32	52	23
Bangladesh	Dec 2002	6	3	2	1
England	Jun 1928	145	53	43	49
India	Nov 1948	82	30	11	41
New Zealand	Feb 1952	37	10	9	18
Pakistan	Jan 1958	44	14	15	15
South Africa	Apr 1992	22	3	14	5
Sri Lanka	Dec 1993	12	3	6	3
Zimbabwe	Mar 2000	6	4	0	2

* Includes one tied match v Australia (1960)
Most runs: BC Lara (1990-2006) 11,953 runs, 131 Tests, average 52.89
Most wickets: CA Walsh (1984-2001) 519 wickets, 132 Test, average 24.44
Most catches: PJL Dujon (1981-1991) 267 catches, 81 Tests

WORLD CUP RECORD

Year	Venue	Finished
1975	England	Winners
1979	England	Winners
1983	England	Runners-up
1987	India and Pakistan	Pool
1992	Australia and N Zealand	Pool
1996	Ind, Pak and S Lanka	Semi-final
1999	England	Pool
2003	South Africa	Pool
2007	West Indies	6th

Most ODI runs: BC Lara (1990-2007) 10,045 runs, 299 matches, average 40.49
Most ODI wickets: CA Walsh (1985-2000) 227 wickets, 205 matches, average 30.48
Most ODI catches: PJL Dujon (1981-1991), 183 catches, 169 matches

ANTIGUA & BARBUDA

Above: *A view of Antigua Bay.*

Life's 365 beaches

Situated in the middle of the Leeward Islands, 17 degrees north of the Equator, Antigua, encompassing 280 square kilometres (108 square miles), is larger than its neighbour, Barbuda, which is a flat coral island to the north.

The island's economy is heavily reliant on tourism and visitors will find a warm welcome from the locals, and just as warm a welcome from the sea on the island's 365 beaches which help provide the classic picture-postcard Caribbean break.

Life in Antigua is governed by the sea; it has a huge sailing and yachting scene and Antigua Sailing Week is one of the premier regattas on the planet. But there is more to the island than messing around in boats and lazing on the beach. Popular attractions include Fig Tree Drive, which comprises 32 km (20 miles) of winding roads through the fishing villages and hills, the markets at the south end of the capital, St John's and

exploring the caves at Two Foot Bay in Barbuda. Back to the water, Devil's Bridge is a natural arch carved by the sea in limestone ledges to the north-eastern part of Antigua and is a popular spot for a swim with the locals.

The island gained independence in 1981, having been discovered and claimed for Spain by Christopher Columbus in 1493. There followed periods of English, and a brief French, occupation with Horatio Nelson arriving in 1784 to develop the British naval facilities which resulted in the building of Nelson's Dockyard, a popular visiting place for tourists.

Antigua can be an expensive place to eat and drink, although a visit to a local bar to watch the locals playing Wari, an ancient board game, normally involving bets for the next round of drinks, or a trip to take in the slightly more eccentric pastime of crab racing, also put on at local pubs, comes cheap enough.

3 THINGS YOU MUST DO...

1 ANTIGUA RAINFOREST TOUR

Take a break from the beaches by getting airlifted through the Antiguan rainforests on a harness (tel: +1 268 562 6363). Tours last between 35 minutes and 2.5 hours. When: Mon–Sat 09.00 and 11.00 or by arrangement). To get there: Taxi to Fig Tree Drive.

2 NELSON'S DOCKYARD

Nelson was a captain in the Navy in the Leeward Islands from 1784-1787 and this area (tel +1 268 460 1379) is named in his honour. The yard has many points of interest, with a marina, museum and many examples of Georgian architecture. To get there: 15 km (9 miles) from St John's.

3 TAKE A SUBMARINE TRIP

Board the Subcat Antigua (tel: +1 268 562 7333) and view the stunning stingrays and turtles off the coast of Antigua. After the trip customers receive a certificate to prove they have been to the bottom of the Caribbean Sea. Price: US$100 adult. To get there: 30-minute taxi from St John's.

Above: Getting ready for the big match.

WEATHER	LOW (°C)	HIGH (°C)	RAIN (MM)	SUNSET
January	22	28	61	17.45
February	22	29	39	18.03
March	22	29	46	18.15
April	23	30	67	18.21
May	24	31	112	18.27
June	25	31	49	18.39
July	26	31	86	18.45
August	26	31	100	18.40
September	25	30	135	18.22
October	24	30	130	17.56
November	23	30	137	17.36
December	23	29	79	17.32

ANTIGUA REC

Home of Viv, Chickie and Gravy

A graveyard for bowlers, the Antigua Recreation Ground, was the scene of Brian Lara's world record innings of 375, in 1994, and 400 not out, in 2004, both against England. In 1986 local hero Viv Richards flayed the England attack for a century off just 56 deliveries, the fastest hundred in terms of balls faced in Test history, and in 2003 the West Indies made 418-7 to beat Australia, the highest run chase ever in a five-day international.

It looked like Test cricket had been lost to the ground for ever when it was superseded by the Sir Vivian Richards Stadium as Antigua's premier international venue. However, five-day cricket returned to the ground in February 2009 when the newer stadium's outfield was deemed unfit for play and the Test match against England was abandoned after ten balls. The teams switched to the Recreation Ground, with the game starting two days later, when the West Indies, with nine wickets down in the second innings, clung on for a draw.

Over the years, the spectators have almost provided as much entertainment as the cricket at the Recreation Ground. A local eccentric, known as Gravy, full name Labon Kenneth Blackburn Leeweltine Buckonon Benjamin, who officially retired in 2002, used to dance on a platform in front of the double decker stand, often wearing women's clothing. He celebrated his 'retirement' with a lap of honour wearing a wedding dress. DJ Chickie pounded out music and in 1998, with England slipping to defeat, he put on the track *Captain, Your Ship is Sinking!*

The ground is a five-minute walk from the centre of St John's.

Below: Dwayne Bravo, here in one-day mode, made his maiden Test hundred at Antigua Rec in 2005.

MATTER OF FACT
Ground: Antigua Recreation Ground
Capacity: 12,000
Located: St John's, Antigua
Address: Coronation Road, St John's, Antigua
Telephone: +1 268 462 1219
E-mail: dnicholas@windiescricket.com
To get there: West Bus Station (bus)
Stands: Richie Richardson, Andy Roberts, Sir Viv Richards

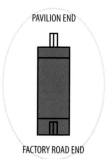

PAVILION END

FACTORY ROAD END

First Test: West Indies v England 27 March-April 1 1981
First ODI: West Indies v Australia 22 February 1978
First Twenty20: N/A

Tests played: 22
West Indies: Won 7, lost 3, drawn 12
Highest team total: 751-5 dec (WI v Eng 2004)
Lowest team total: 127 (Eng v WI 1998)
Highest individual total: 400 not out BC Lara (for WI v Eng 2004)
Highest partnership: 331 (CH Gayle & RR Sarwan, 2nd wicket for WI v SA 2005)
Best bowling: 7-78 JJC Lawson (for WI v Aus 2003)

ODIs played: 11
West Indies: Won 6, lost 1, (neutral games 4)
Highest team total: 313-9 (WI v Aus 1978)
Lowest team total: 144 (Zim v WI 2006)
Highest individual total: 148 DL Haynes (for WI v Aus 1978)
Highest partnership: 179 (HH Gibbs & JH Kallis, 2nd wicket for SA v WI 2001)
Best bowling: 4-24 JE Taylor (for WI v Zim 2006)

SIR VIV RICHARDS STADIUM

Controversial homage to hero

Located halfway between the Antiguan capital, St John's, and VC Bird International Airport, the Sir Vivian Richards Stadium is named after the island's most famous cricketing son and was established in 2006.

The decision to replace the Antigua Recreation Ground as the premier venue on the island was not the most popular one but the needs of the 2007 World Cup, when the ground hosted six matches, demanded it. Unfortunately the ground, whose capacity was increased to 20,000 during the tournament, was never full as the locals refused to travel out of town to watch the cricket.

The state of the outfield caused concerns immediately and it was relaid after the 2008 Test match against Australia. This did not help when England were the visitors a year later and the match was abandoned with only ten balls being bowled and leaving Richards venting his anger at what he saw as an insult to his name. Subsequently the stadium was suspended from hosting international cricket and left having to pass an ICC inspection before further matches were played there again.

Funded largely by a grant from the Chinese government, the ground has two large stands, one, five levels high, to the south and one opposite that houses the media. To the east and west are terraces which have a more Caribbean atmosphere. There is also an artificial beach – named 'Beach 366', (Antigua is famous for having 365 beaches) – and underground passageways for the players to move around the stadium.

Below: Chris Gayle, cricket's coolest man, captained West Indies in the abandoned Test of 2009.

MATTER OF FACT
Ground: Sir Vivian Richards Stadium
Capacity: 10,000 (20,000 for 2007 World Cup)
Located: Antigua
Address: North Sound, St Peter's, Antigua
E-mail: dnicholas@windiescricket.com
To get there: West Bus Station St John's (bus)
Stands: Northern, South

MEDIA CENTRE END

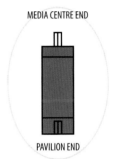

PAVILION END

First Test: West Indies v Australia 30 May-3 Jun 2008
First ODI: West Indies v Australia 27-28 March 2007 (Note: played over two days because of rain)
First Twenty20: N/A

Tests played: 2
West Indies: Won 0, lost 0, drawn 2
Highest team total: 479-7 dec (Aus v WI 2008)
Lowest team total: 352 (WI v Aus 2008)
Highest individual total: 128 RR Sarwan (for WI v Aus 2008)
Highest partnership: 143 (RR Sarwan & S Chanderpaul, 4th wicket for WI v Aus 2008)
Best bowling: 5-59 B Lee (for Aus v WI 2008)

ODIs played: 6
West Indies: Won 0, lost 2, (neutral games 4)
Highest team total: 322-6 (Aus v WI 2007)
Lowest team total: 174 (Ban v NZ 2007)
Highest individual total: 158 ML Hayden (for Aus v WI 2007)
Highest partnership: 140 (IR Bell & KP Pietersen, 3rd wicket for Eng v Aus 2007)
Best bowling: 4-43 SB Styris (for NZ v Ban 2007)

BARBADOS

Above: *Poster perfect Barbados.*

Little England

The island of Barbados is found in the western Atlantic Ocean, east of the Caribbean Sea and was a colony of the United Kingdom for over three centuries before gaining independence in 1966. It is referred to by its neighbours as 'Little England'. A coral island, it boasts 3,000 hours of sunshine annually, warm temperatures all year, and has a population of around 6,000. Fortunately for English, Australian, Indian, Pakistani and South African visitors the locals drive on the left-hand side of the road.

The capital, Bridgetown, is filled with places of historical interest, such as National Heroes Square, where a statue of Lord Nelson stands, and, at the top of Broad Street, the Parliament Buildings.

With tourism a major plank in the local economy, Barbados has a reputation for being expensive but if you are on a budget, you can take one of the free treks, run by the National Trust or visit a Bajan rum shop, where the drink is cheap and the company lively.

Like virtually every other island in the area, Barbados has superb beaches and for golfers is the home of Sandy Lane, which has hosted the World Golf Championship and where the former West Indian cricketer Franklyn Stephenson is a golf professional. On the west coast, in St James, is the highly-regarded Royal Westmoreland.

Bajan food is centred on seafood with flying fish, dorado, red snapper and lobster among the specialties which can be washed down with Mount Gay and Cockspur rums and Banks, a lager made from Austrian and British grains, which is the local brew.

The currency on the island is the Barbados dollar but US dollars are generally accepted.

3 THINGS YOU MUST DO...

1 SUNBURY PLANTATION HOUSE
Tour around Sunbury Plantation House (tel: +1 246 423 6270) built in 1660, destroyed by fire in 1995 and subsequently restored to give a glimpse of life on 18th and 19th century sugar plantations. When: daily 9.00–17,00. To get there: 25-min drive from Bridgetown along Highway 5.

2 MOUNT GAY RUM
Tours and tastings at the distillery (tel: +1 246 425 8757) of the oldest rum in the world which was first produced in 1703. Basic tours last about 45 minutes and include samples but more extensive trips are on offer. When: Mon–Fri 09.30–15.30. To get there: five-min taxi ride from Bridgetown.

3 EMANCIPATION MEMORIAL
Overlooking a cane field where slaves once worked this statue is a figure of Bussa, leader of the 1838 slave uprising that led to the abolition of slavery (tel: tourist information, +1 246 427 2623). To get there: St Barnabus Roundabout, Intersection of ABC Highway and Highway 5.

Above: *Cruise liners are a common sight in Barbados.*

WEATHER	LOW (°C)	HIGH (°C)	RAIN (MM)	SUNSET
January	21	27	72	17.42
February	21	28	31	17.59
March	21	29	33	18.08
April	22	30	38	18.10
May	23	31	59	18.14
June	23	31	112	18.24
July	23	31	149	18.29
August	23	31	147	18.26
September	23	31	169	18.10
October	22	30	178	17.48
November	22	29	211	17.32
December	22	28	97	17.30

KENSINGTON OVAL

Jewel of Barbados

Massively renovated for the 2007 Cricket World Cup, the Kensington Oval, 2 km (1 mile) to the north of Bridgetown staged its first Test match in 1930 when England and West Indies played out a draw, with Clifford Roach scoring the first international century for the hosts.

There have been great Test matches staged at the ground ever since with one of the most remarkable being the 1999 encounter between West Indies and Australia. Then Brian Lara, who described the ground as the 'Mecca of cricket', batting with the tail, made 153 not out to get his team home by one wicket. In 1981 Michael Holding bowled what many have called the greatest over of all time, to England's Geoff Boycott, with the opener being dismissed off the final delivery as the West Indies crowd danced in the stands. Another England opener, Alec Stewart, fared slightly better in 1994, scoring a hundred in both innings as the tourists won by 208 runs.

In the 2007 World Cup the ground staged seven games, including the final, in which Australia beat Sri Lanka, although the occasion was spoiled by rain, and a misinterpretation of the rules by the five match officials that led to their suspension.

The stands are named after heroes of Bajan cricket, with batsmen getting a chilling reminder of the past as they face bowlers from the Joel Garner and Malcolm Marshall ends. The liveliest stand is the Party Stand which contains a swimming pool and beach and for a one-off fee fans can enjoy free drinks and food whilst listening to local DJs. This stand is particularly popular with England's 'Barmy Army' and 'The Fanatics' of Australia as you'd imagine.

Outside the ground spectators can see a statue commemorating the achievements of the island's most famous cricketer, Sir Garfield Sobers, that was moved to the stadium in 2006, having previously stood elsewhere in Wildey.

Below: Kensington Oval was loved by Brian Lara. It was renovated for the 2007 World Cup.

MATTER OF FACT

Ground: Kensington Oval
Capacity: 28,000
Located: Barbados
Address: Fontabell, St Michael, Bridgetown, Barbados
Telephone: +1 246 436 1397
E-mail: theoffice@bca.org.bb
To get there: 2 km (1 mile) to the northwest of Bridgetown
Stands: Worrell, Weekes and Walcott, Hall and Griffith, Hewitt and Inniss, Greenidge and Haynes, Sir Garfield Sobers Pavilion

MALCOLM MARSHALL END

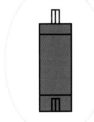

JOEL GARNER END

First Test: West Indies v England 11-16 January 1930
First ODI: West Indies v New Zealand 23 April 1985
First Twenty20: West Indies v Australia 20 June 2008

Tests played: 45
West Indies: Won 21, lost 8, drawn 16
Highest team total: 749-9 dec (WI v Eng 2009)
Lowest team total: 81 (Ind v WI 1997)
Highest individual total: 337 Hanif Mohammad (for Pak v WI 1958)
Highest partnership: 399 (GSA Sobers & FMM Worrell, 4th wicket for WI v Eng 1960)
Best bowling: 8-38 LR Gibbs (for WI v Ind 1962)

ODIs played: 28
West Indies: Won 10, lost 13, (neutral games 5)
Highest team total: 313-6 (SL v WI 2003)
Lowest team total: 91 (Ire v Aus 2007)
Highest individual total: 149 AC Gilchrist (for Aus v SL 2007)
Highest partnership: 200 (SC Williams & S Chanderpaul, 1st wicket for WI v Ind 1997)
Best bowling: 5-18 AJ Hall (for SA v Eng 2007)

Above: Up, up and away.

CRICKET NET

Outstanding batsmen Frank Worrell, Everton Weekes and Clyde Walcott – known as the 'Three Ws' – were born in Barbados within 18 months of each other, between 1924 and 1926. Worrell was the West Indies' first black captain. Walcott became a leading administrator and Weekes served in the Barbados government.

GEORGETOWN

Above: Cruise ships off Georgetown beach.

Where South America comes to the cricket party

Georgetown is the capital city of Guyana, the only English-speaking country in South America, and characterized by its colonial architecture that features 19th-century stilted wooden houses.

After the abolition of slavery in 1834 many Indians moved to Guyana to work as labourers on the plantations and today Indians make up the largest racial group in the country and the country continues to maintain close links to India.

Georgetown is around 1.5 metres below sea level, situated on the mouth of the Demerara River, something that has caused problems with cricket grounds, and the city is protected by a sea wall and canals to prevent flooding. The climate is tropical with two rainy seasons, from May to mid-August and from mid-November to mid-January.

The city is full of historical places of note, including the Parliament Buildings, St George's Cathedral and the 1763 monument, close to the Botanical and Zoological Gardens, a tribute to the African slave, Cuffy, who led the revolt of that year.

At night head to Sheriff Street, said to be a street that never sleeps, where there are plenty of bars and restaurants or by day enjoy some shopping in Regent Street, the main retail area.

Georgetown is a lively city with markets, such as Starbroek sprawling all over the streets and all sorts of traffic fighting for possession of the road. By night, take advice about the best areas to visit as street-crime can be a problem but as with most places in the Caribbean, using common sense will ensure an enjoyable stay. The best way to travel round the city is by using the cheap minibus service.

3 THINGS YOU MUST DO...

1 KAIETEUR FALLS
The Kaieteur Falls, on the Potaro River, drop 226 metres (741 feet) into a deep valley. An hour's flight from Georgetown they are some of the most spectacular falls in the world. Many tour companies (see www.kaieteurpark.gov.gy) offer excursions. To get there: fly from Georgetown.

2 ST GEORGE'S CATHEDRAL
One of the tallest wooden buildings in the world, St George's Cathedral (tel: +1 592 226 5067) is in the centre of Georgetown. The inside of the cathedral is a snapshot of the history of the area. When: 08.30–17.00 except holidays: To get there: Minibus to Carmichael Street.

3 GUYANA NATIONAL MUSEUM
Found on North Road, the museum (tel: +1 592 225 7191) contains a selection of flora and fauna, precious stone and examples of the arts and crafts of the Amerindians. When: 09.00–16.30. Price: free. To get there: minibus to North Road.

Above: T-shirts depicting inspirational figures at the Georgetown market.

WEATHER	LOW (°C)	HIGH (°C)	RAIN (MM)	SUNSET
January	22	29	198	17.49
February	23	29	121	18.01
March	23	29	177	18.05
April	23	29	142	18.02
May	23	29	290	18.00
June	24	29	302	18.05
July	24	30	256	18.13
August	24	32	185	18.12
September	25	32	78	18.00
October	25	32	76	17.44
November	24	31	156	17.34
December	24	30	287	17.34

PROVIDENCE STADIUM

When the world's eyes are on Guyana

Found a ten-minute drive from the centre of Georgetown, on the banks of the Demerara River, the Guyana National Stadium, or Providence Stadium, took over from Bourda as Guyana's premier international venue ahead of the 2007 Cricket World Cup.

Bourda traditionally suffered from flooding but the newer facility is fitted with a state-of-the-art drainage system. Costing around US$25 million the Providence was built with the help of grants and loans from India and hosted Super 8 matches during the 2007 World Cup.

The ground was officially opened by the Indian vice-president Bhairon Singh Shekhawat in 2006. The two countries have long historical links with half the population of Guyana being descendants of immigrants from the sub-continent.

It was during the 2007 World Cup that Sri Lankan fast bowler Lasith Malinga became the first man to take four wickets in four balls in international cricket when he dismissed four South Africans in succession.

His efforts were in vain as the South African team scrambled to a one-wicket win.

Prior to staging its first Test match in 2008, between West Indies and Sri Lanka, the ground also had to host a three-day warm-up game between the tourists and a Guyana President's Select XI which was shifted because Bourda was waterlogged again.

Sri Lanka won that first Test by 121 runs with Mahela Jayawardene setting up the victory with 136 and Chaminda Vaas taking eight wickets in the game.

The ground is made up of three major stands and a grass bank, which is the cheapest place to watch the cricket and can hold around 4,000 fans. The stadium complex also includes a shopping mall and theme park and a hotel, the Princess International, is next to the ground.

Below: Shivnarine Chanderpaul is Guyana's most celebrated cricketer since Clive Lloyd and has scored more than 8,000 Test runs.

MATTER OF FACT

Ground: Guyana National Stadium
Capacity: 15,000
Located: Providence, Guyana
Address: Stadium Road, Georgetown, RI 02906, Guyana
Telephone: +592 265 7083 or +592 265 7084
E-mail: gcb@solutions2000.net
To get there: ten-min drive along East Bank Highway from Georgetown
Stands: Grass Mound, Party

MEDIA CENTRE END

PAVILION END

First Test: West Indies v Sri Lanka 22-26 March 2008
First ODI: South Africa v Sri Lanka 28 March 2007
First Twenty20: N/A

Tests played: 1
West Indies: Won 0, lost 1, drawn 0
Highest team total: 478-6 dec (SL v WI 2008)
Lowest team total: 280 (WI v SL 2008)
Highest individual total: 136 DPM Jayawardene (for SL v WI 2008)
Highest partnership: 134 (DJJ Bravo & RR Sarwan, 2nd wicket for WI v SL 2008)
Best bowling: 5-61 WPU Vaas (for SL v WI 2008)

ODIs played: 8
West Indies: Won 1, lost 2, (neutral games 5)
Highest team total: 303-5 (SL v WI 2007)
Lowest team total: 134 (Ire v NZ 2007)
Highest individual total: 115 ST Jayasuriya (for SL v WI 2007)
Highest partnership: 183 (ST Jayasuriya & DPM Jayawardene, 3rd wicket for SL v WI 2007)
Best bowling: 5-39 CK Langeveldt (for SA v SL 2007)

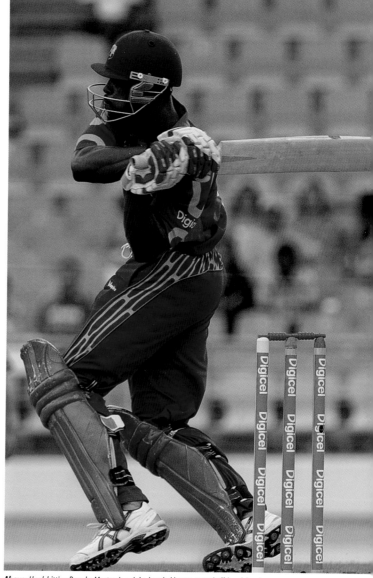

Above: Hard-hitting Runako Morton is a right-handed batsman and off-break bowler.

CRICKET NET

Clive Lloyd, born in Georgetown in 1944, was the captain and driving force behind the dominant West Indies teams in the late 1970s and early 1980s. A brutal left-handed batsman, he favoured using four fast bowlers to batter the opposition and he led the West Indies to World Cup victories in 1975 and 1979.

GRENADA

Spice Island

Just 200 square kilometres (77 square miles) in area, Grenada is the most southerly of the Windward Islands and is known as The Spice Island, with nutmeg being one of its most prominent products. The capital St George's is full of Georgian architecture and is set around a harbour with three forts dominating the skyline.

St George's is a vibrant city with a market at its centre, many religious buildings, the Bay Gardens and a National Museum on Young Street which relives the history of the island.

There are around 45 beaches on the island with the most popular being in the southwest. The coral reefs at some makes them ideal for snorkeling.

Tourism is not rampant, as in Antigua and Barbados, and the pace of life is relaxed and the island is largely unspoiled. The middle of the island is full of valleys and volcanic peaks, creole houses with spice and fruit trees, and Honeymoon Falls is worth a visit if you have got your walking boots.

Grenada is politically attached to two islands to the north, Carriacou and Petit Martinique, which if anything have an even more relaxed lifestyle. The latter has a population of under 1,000 but is said to be one of the wealthiest islands per head in the Caribbean.

Above: The underwater sculpture 'Visissitudes' in Moliniere Bay. **Below:** View of Grenada from a cruise liner.

WEATHER	LOW (°C)	HIGH (°C)	RAIN (MM)	SUNSET
January	20	29	130	17.54
February	20	30	100	18.09
March	20	30	110	18.16
April	21	30	90	18.18
May	22	31	150	18.21
June	21	30	120	18.28
July	21	30	225	18.35
August	21	31	260	18.33
September	22	31	245	18.17
October	21	31	240	17.57
November	21	30	240	17.41
December	20	30	200	17.40

3 THINGS YOU MUST DO...

1 GRAND ETANG FOREST RESERVE

The most popular area for hikers, the Grand Etang Forest Reserve (tel: Grenada Board of Tourism, +1 473 440 2279) is found in the mountains in the middle of Grenada. Flora includes huge mahogany trees and the area is populated by frogs, lizards, armadillos and Mona monkeys.

2 BAY GARDENS

Found in St Paul's the Bay Gardens (tel: +1 473 435 4544) has over 8 hectares (20 acres) of wild flowers and ponds and is a perfect place to relax. When: Mon–Sat 10.00–21.00. To get there: ten-min drive to St Paul's from St George's.

3 CLABONEY VOLCANIC HOT SPRINGS

Relax by taking a dip in the volcanic springs found near Grenville (see www.grenadaexplorer.com). Filled with sulphurous water, the springs is open to everyone. Price: free. To get there: north of St George's.

NATIONAL STADIUM

Reborn after the hurricane

T he National Stadium in Grenada, close to the centre of the capital St George's, was completed in time for Australia's visit to play a one-day international in 1999 and hosted its first Test match in 2002, when New Zealand and West Indies drew and its next one in 2009, when Bangladesh beat the hosts by four wickets.

The visit of Bangladesh was plagued by poor crowds, mainly due to a strike by the West Indian players that forced them to field a weakened side and the attendances were described by the Grenada Cricket Association as a 'disaster'.

In between those two Tests the ground was devastated by Hurricane Ivan in 2004 and had to be completely renovated for the 2007 Cricket World Cup, with the help of a Chinese team of builders and engineers. It was the venue for six Super 8 games in the tournament. During that World Cup South Africa's AB de Villiers hit 146 to help his team to 356 and a crushing win over the West Indians.

In 2009 a West Indies Cricket Heritage centre was opened at the ground which showcases cricket memorabilia from the 1800s onwards. For spectators there are plenty of vendors walking around the ground selling food, beers and the locally made rum as well as numerous stalls around the stadium.

The stadium, also known as Queen's Park, is used to stage football, hosts events during Grenada's carnival, otherwise known as Spicemas, and is the venue for games in the Grenada Cricket Classics tournament, a popular event featuring former international cricketers.

Below: Cricket legend Brian Lara (left) shows USA President Barack Obama how to swing a bat properly.

MATTER OF FACT
Ground: National Cricket Stadium
Capacity: 15,000
Located: Grenada
Address: Queens's Park, St George's, Grenada
Telephone: +1 473 435 2007
E-mail: dnicholas@windiescricket.com
To get there: 15-min drive from Grand Anse

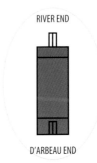

RIVER END

D'ARBEAU END

First Test: West Indies v New Zealand 28 Jun-2 July 2002
First ODI: West Indies v Australia 14 April 1999
First Twenty20: N/A

Tests played: 2
West Indies: Won 0, lost 1, drawn 1
Highest team total: 470 (WI v NZ 2002)
Lowest team total: 209 (WI v Ban 2009)
Highest individual total: 204 CH Gayle (for WI v NZ 2002)
Highest partnership: 143 (CH Gayle & S Chanderpaul, 5th wicket for WI v NZ 2002)
Best bowling: 6-48 KJA Roach (for WI v Ban 2009)

ODIs played: 16
West Indies: Won 4, lost 6, (neutral games 6)
Highest team total: 356-4 (SA v WI 2007)
Lowest team total: 77 (Ire v SL 2007)
Highest individual total: 146 AB de Villiers (for SA v WI 2007)
Highest partnership: 191 (SR Watson & RT Ponting, 2nd wicket for Aus v WI 2008)
Best bowling: 5-46 CH Gayle (for WI v Aus 2003)

JAMAICA

Above: Jamaica includes a tribute museum to Bob Marley where visitors can play out their reggae dreams. Man.

Where reggae rules

Jamaica is the third largest island in the Caribbean with a population of over 2.5 million, mainly consisting of people of African descent. Independent from Britain since 1962, Jamaica has a rich heritage of producing sports figures such as champion sprinter Usain Bolt, cricketer Courtney Walsh and boxer Trevor Berbick. Soccer is also hugely popular with the national team, the Reggae Boyz, gaining a worldwide following when they qualified for the 1998 World Cup.

The island has plenty of relaxing beaches in areas such as Montego Bay, Port Antonio, Negril and Ocho Rios. James Bond Beach to the northeast of Jamaica, is home to the Golden Eye Hotel, where the author Ian Fleming once lived and is where the film Dr No was made.

The capital Kingston also has its share of beautiful beaches, and plenty of accommodation to fit most budgets. Set against the stunning backdrop of Blue Mountain Peak, a piece of land known as the Palisaodes connects the city to the old pirate haunt of Port Royal.

By night the centre of activity is Knutsford Boulevard, or the 'Kingston Strip', which has many bars, hotels, restaurants and clubs, such as Asylum where reggae and hip-hop tunes blast out until the early hours.

Other attractions include the National Gallery of Art, the Craft Market on King Street, the Hope Botanical Gardens and the White Marl Arawak Museum. St Peter's Church, near the Kingston Harbour contains memorabilia from the days when pirates ran riot in the Caribbean and exhibits silver that is believed to have been donated by 17th century Welsh pirate Henry Morgan.

Kingston has a reputation for violent crime, as does Montego Bay, so tourists should not walk around alone after dark. The best advice is to ask your hotel which areas to avoid.

3 THINGS YOU MUST DO...

1 BOB MARLEY MUSEUM

The Bob Marley Museum (tel: +1 876 978 2929) celebrates the life of Jamaica's most famous musician. Tours last about an hour. When: Mon–Sat 09.30–16.00. Price: US$20 adult, US$10 child. To get there: taxi to Hope Road.

2 CAYMANAS PARK

Jamaicans love a bet and Caymanas Park racetrack (St Catherine, tel: +1 876 988 2523) gives them their fix. There are about 900 races run here each year and fans can also bet on simulcast races from other tracks. When: Wed, Sat 12.00–18.00. To get there: taxi to Gregory Park.

3 JAMAICA JERK TRAIL

Jamaica is home of jerk cooking with spicy pork and chicken being a staple on the island. Eat your way round Jamaica at ten specialist jerk restaurants on the newly created Jerk Trail (tel: Jamaican Tourist Board +1 876 929 9200).

Above: Jamaican fast bowler Michael Holding. In 1989 he famously kicked the stumps (in New Zealand).

WEATHER	LOW (°C)	HIGH (°C)	RAIN (MM)	SUNSET
January	19	30	23	17.43
February	20	30	11	18.03
March	20	31	24	18.13
April	21	31	31	18.21
May	22	31	99	18.29
June	22	32	91	18.40
July	23	32	89	18.47
August	23	32	91	18.40
September	23	32	97	18.21
October	23	31	179	17.56
November	22	31	74	17.35
December	21	31	36	17.30

SABINA PARK

Scene of Sobers' record

Sabina Park, home to Kingston Cricket Club since 1880, hosted its first Test match in 1930, when England, helped by Andy Sandham's 325 (Test cricket's first triple century) drew with the West Indies in a timeless match lasting nine days. The tourists eventually had to catch their boat home. Twenty-eight years later Garry Sobers made another treble hundred at the ground, 365 not out against Pakistan, to claim the world record for runs in a Test innings, a mark that lasted for 36 years.

Traditionally a fast, bouncy wicket, the pitch was re-laid after a farcical Test in 1998 when the England innings, and the match, was abandoned with just 10.1 overs bowled after several batsman were hit in the opening session by misbehaving deliveries. England's Alec Stewart described his nine not out as worth a double century! That was not the first time the ground saw controversy. In 1968 fans rioted during England's visit and in 1976 Indian captain Bishen Bedi called off his side's second innings at 97

to spare his tailenders having to face Malcolm Marshall and Wayne Daniel. The surface has been relaid several times but they have not been able to rediscover the old pace and fair bounce that pitches of old possessed and the wicket was blameless when England were shot out for 51 in 2009.

Redeveloped for the 2007 World Cup when a new North Stand was erected, Sabina Park has the Blue Mountains as a backdrop to the north and Kingston Harbour to the south and is found 2 kilometres (1 mile) to the south west of New Kingston. Many fans stay in New Kingston when the Test matches are on and it is advisable to take taxis to the ground.

Once there spectators can party in the Mound Stand, one of the first all-inclusive stands (entry includes food and drink) in world cricket, watch from the elevated North Stand or look at the Blue Mountains from the George Headley Stand.

Below: Jamaica's David Bernard was recalled to the West Indies side against Bangladesh in 2009 when the first-choice players were on strike.

MATTER OF FACT

Ground: Sabina Park
Capacity: 20,000
Located: Jamaica
Address: South Camp Road, Kingston 4, Jamaica, WI
Telephone: +1 876 922 8423 or +1 876 967 0322
E-mail: jamcricket@cwjamaica.com
To get there: 2 km (1 mile) southwest of New Kingston (taxi advised)
Stands: George Headley, Northern, Mound

BLUE MOUNTAINS END

HEADLEY STAND END

First Test: West Indies v England 3-12 April 1930
First ODI: West Indies v Australia 26 April 1984
First Twenty20: N/A

Tests played: 44
West Indies: Won 22, lost 9, drawn 13
Highest team total: 849 (Eng v WI 1930)
Lowest team total: 47 (WI v Eng 2004)
Highest individual total: 365 not out GSA Sobers (for WI v Pak 1958)
Highest partnership: 446 (CC Hunte & GSA Sobers, 2nd wicket for WI v Pak 1958)
Best bowling: 7-12 SJ Harmison (for Eng v WI 2004)

ODIs played: 27
West Indies: Won 15, lost 7, no result 1 (neutral won 3, tied 1)
Highest team total: 349 (Pak v Zim 2007)
Lowest team total: 99 (Zim v Pak 2007)
Highest individual total: 160 Imran Nazir (for Pak v Zim 2007)
Highest partnership: 187 (RB Richardson & AL Logie, 3rd wicket for WI v Pak 1988)
Best bowling: 4-23 MD Marshall (for WI v Eng 1986)

Above: *England needed more than helmets as they were bombarded in the abandoned 1998 Test at Sabina Park.*

CRICKET NET

Kingston-born George Headley, who has a stand named after him at Sabina Park, is one of a handful of players to average over 60 in Test cricket. He finished with 2,190 runs at 60.83 from 22 Tests. His son, Ron, played twice for the West Indies and his grandson, Dean, played 15 Tests for England. He died in 1983 aged 74.

SAINT LUCIA

Beaches, parties and a drive-in volcano

St Lucia is a volcanic island in the southeast Caribbean, part of the Windward Islands and it gained independence from England in 1979.

Apart from tourism, the local economy is based on growing crops such as bananas and copras and some of the estates on the island are open to the public. However, increased worldwide competition has seen some of these plantations struggling to survive.

The island is characterized by superb beaches, rainforests and coral reefs and Sulphur Springs are known as the world's only drive-in volcano.

The capital, Castries, is not large but makes up for lack of size by being a vibrant city with its streets filled with market stalls. There are several points of interest, including the Cathedral of the Immaculate Conception, in Derek Walcott Square, which was named after the 1992 winner of the 1992 Nobel Prize for Literature.

The premier tourist area is Rodney Bay where you can visit one of the ships used in the Hollywood film *Pirates of the Caribbean*. Those in party mood should head to Gros Islet for the Friday Night Street Party, which goes on for most of the night as local DJs entertain locals and tourists all night long.

Above: Jalousie Beach St Lucia. Below: Sailing into Saint Lucia.

WEATHER	LOW (°C)	HIGH (°C)	RAIN (MM)	SUNSET
January	23	29	75	17.47
February	23	29	49	18.04
March	24	29	58	18.12
April	24	30	59	18.15
May	25	30	69	18.20
June	25	31	99	18.30
July	25	32	150	18.36
August	25	32	161	18.31
September	24	32	196	18.15
October	24	31	201	17.54
November	24	30	176	17.37
December	23	29	109	17.34

3 THINGS YOU MUST DO...

1 PIGEON ISLAND
Lying north of Castries is Pigeon Island National Park (tel: St Lucia National Trust, +1 758 452 5005), linked to the mainland by a causeway, which was once a British garrison and in the 1500s was used as a hideout by the French private Jambe de Bois. When: daily. Price: US$5.

2 GROS PITON
Gros Piton, at nearly 800 metres (2,169 feet), is the biggest peak on the island and dominates the west coast (tel: St Lucia National Trust, +1 758 452 5005). The fit can hike up it, a 6.5 km (4 miles) round trip that requires a permit from the St Lucia Forest and Lands Department and a qualified guide.

3 MOUNTAIN BIKING
Mountain bike around the Anse Mamim Plantation, through tropical vegetation and historical sites (tel: +1 758 459 2453). Trails are made for first-timers and experienced bikers. The fittest cyclists will face the challenging Tinker's Trail designed by world champion Tinker Juarez.

BEAUSEJOUR

Picture postcard cricket

The Beausejour Cricket Ground, found to the north of the St Lucian capital of Castries, near to the tourist resort of Rodney Bay staged its first Test in 2003 becoming the eighth Test venue in the West Indies when Sri Lanka drew with the hosts. It was also the scene of the first floodlit one-day international in the Caribbean in 2006 when the hosts thrashed Zimbabwe by ten wickets.

Set in 22 acres at the foot of the Beausejour Hills, the ground, a home venue for the Windward Islands, was constructed in 2001 to replace Mindoo Phillip Park in Castries, which had drainage problems, as the island's premier international venue. It hosted England, Kenya, Canada and New Zealand's group in the 2007 Cricket World Cup, as well as the semi-final between Australia and South Africa which Australia won by seven wickets.

The ground is considered one of the best in the Caribbean to watch cricket with the Piton Party Stand, sponsored by the makers of the local beer, being the liveliest area. The stand lives up to its name, with music pumping out all day from local DJs and St Lucian cricket fans making visitors welcome as the island comes to a standstill when there is a match on. This fanaticism for the game is remarkable as St Lucia traditionally does not supply many players to the West Indies team. The first islander to play Test cricket was Darren Sammy who made his debut on the tour of England in 2007.

Below: All-rounder Dwayne Bravo's best bowling at Beausejour is 3-24 against Zimbabwe in 2006.

MATTER OF FACT
Ground: Beausejour Cricket Ground
Capacity: 15,000
Located: St Lucia
Address: Beausejour, Gros Islet St Lucia
Telephone: +1 758 457 8851
E-mail: sportsstlucia@yahoo.com or jersonronan@yahoo.com
To get there: Bus 1A or shuttle to Beausejour
Stands: Laborie, Choiseul, Soufriere, Canaries, Castries, Gros Islet

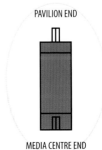

PAVILION END

MEDIA CENTRE END

First Test: West Indies v Sri Lanka 20-24 June 2003
First ODI: West Indies v New Zealand 8 June 2002
First Twenty20: N/A

Tests played: 3
West Indies: Won 0, lost 0, drawn 3
Highest team total: 588-8 dec (Ind v WI 2006)
Lowest team total: 215 (WI v Ind 2006)
Highest individual total: 209 BC Lara (for WI v SL 2003)
Highest partnership: 179 (R Dravid & Mohammad Kaif, 5th wicket for Ind v WI 2006)
Best bowling: 5-66 CD Collymore (for WI v SL 2003)

ODIs played: 19
West Indies: Won 5, lost 5, no result 2, (neutral games 7)
Highest team total: 363-5 (NZ v Can 2007)
Lowest team total: 146 (WI v Eng 2009)
Highest individual total: 130 ME Trescothick (for Eng v WI 2004)
Highest partnership: 156 (CH Gayle & S Chattergoon, 1st wicket for WI v Zim 2006)
Best bowling: 5-19 A Flintoff (for Eng v WI 2009)

SAINT KITTS & NEVIS

The secret Caribbean

Found in the north part of the Leeward Islands and separated by a 3 km (2 miles) channel, St Kitts and Nevis were originally settled in by South American Indians until, after brief squabbles between France and Spain, the British took control in 1623. The islands were granted independence in 1983.

The capital of St Kitts, Basseterre, still has much of the Georgian character from the days of British rule and has historical landmarks such as The Treasury Building and The Circus, modelled on London's Piccadilly, the centrepiece of which is an ornate iron tower with four clock faces.

In Nevis, the largest city, Charlestown, was built so it could be protected by Fort Charles and Fort Black Rocks, and it is the site of the Caribbean's oldest synagogue, a reminder of how many Jews were involved in the sugar industry in the 1700s and boasts a lively Market Place which opens three days a week.

Often known as the 'Secret Caribbean' the islands offer good golf, fishing, boating and snorkeling as well as plantation inns. It almost goes without saying that there are plenty of eye-catching beaches on both islands.

Above: Nisbet Plantation Inn, Nevis. Below: Brimstone Hill Fortress, St Kitts.

WEATHER	LOW (°C)	HIGH (°C)	RAIN (MM)	SUNSET
January	21	27	120	17.48
February	21	28	95	18.06
March	21	29	110	18.17
April	22	30	95	18.25
May	22	31	99	18.31
June	23	31	110	18.43
July	24	31	152	18.49
August	24	31	180	18.44
September	24	32	165	18.25
October	22	31	198	18.00
November	22	29	175	17.39
December	21	28	140	17.35

3 THINGS YOU MUST DO...

1 ST KITTS SCENIC RAILWAY

Take a three hour, 48 km (30 miles), train trip (tel: +1 869 465 7263) passing through sugar cane fields, around Mount Liamuiga, past beaches with views of Nevis, St Barts and Saba, through Saddlers Village then transfer to buses to see Brimstone Hill Fortress. When: Nov–Apr.

2 BRIMSTONE HILL FORTRESS

Brimstone Hill Fortress National Park is a World Heritage Site. Known as the 'Gibraltar of the West Indies', the fort (tel: +1 869 465 2609) was central in British battles with the French, who seized it in 1782. When: Sun–Sat 09.30–17.30. Price: US$8. To get there: minibus from Basseterre to Sunny Point.

3 HORATIO NELSON MUSEUM

The museum (Charlestown, tel: +1 869 469 0408) houses the biggest collection of Nelson artefacts in the Americas. Nelson married in Nevis when he was based in Antigua in the late 18th century. When: Mon–Fri 09.00–16.00, Sat 9.00–12.00. Price: US$13. To get there: taxi or bus to Government House.

WARNER PARK

MATTER OF FACT
Ground: Warner Park
Capacity: 8,000
Located: St Kitts
Address: Victoria Road, Basseterre, St Kitts
E-mail: dnicholas@windiescricket.com
To get there: a short walk from Independence Square
Stands: Southern, Carib Party Mound

Made by Taiwan

Largely funded by the Taiwanese government, Warner Park, in Basseterre, the historic capital of St Kitts, is a sporting complex that contains a cricket arena, football stadium, a cricket academy, athletics track, netball and volleyball facilities and Carnival City, a savannah that hosts carnival events.

The cricket ground, was the first of the new stadiums to open ahead of the 2007 Cricket World Cup, staging its first one-day international in May 2006 and its first Test, both matches against India, shortly afterwards. A public holiday was declared on the island on the occasion of its first Test match.

Warner Park hosted the group involving Australia, South Africa, the Netherlands and Scotland during the World Cup and was disappointingly barely half-full, despite a capacity of just 10,000 for the tournament, for all of the matches barring the game between the two heavyweights in the pool.

The east side of the ground has no stands, a deliberate effort to utilise the cooling properties of the prevailing easterly winds. Found near the heart of Basseterre, the ground has views of the harbour and the mountains of St Kitts and excellent facilities for spectators.

Some of the facilities at the ground are named after citizens of St Kitts & Nevis. The pavilion commemorates the life of Calvin Wilkin, a former St Kitts, Leeward Islands and Combined Islands player, while the media centre is named in honour of CA Paul Southwell, the late cricket commentator.

CA PAUL SOUTHWELL MEDIA CENTRE END

LOZACK ROAD END

First Test: West Indies v India 22-26 June 2006
First ODI: West Indies v India 23 May 2006
First Twenty20: West Indies v Bangladesh 2 August 2009

Tests played: 1
West Indies: Won 0, lost 0, drawn 1
Highest team total: 581 (WI v Ind 2006)
Lowest team total: 362 (Ind v WI 2006)
Highest individual total: 135 D Ganga (for WI v Ind 2006)
Highest partnership: 203 (D Ganga & RR Sarwan, 2nd wicket for WI v Ind 2006)
Best bowling: 5-147 Harbhajan Singh (for Ind v WI 2006)

ODIs played: 10
West Indies: Won 1, lost 3, (neutral games 6)
Highest team total: 377-6 (Aus v SA 2007)
Lowest team total: 129 (Ned v Aus 2007)
Highest individual total: 128 not out JH Kallis (for SA v Ned 2007)
Highest partnership: 204 (MJ Clarke & BJ Hodge, 4th wicket for Aus v Ned 2007)
Best bowling: 5-29 MG Johnson (for Aus v WI 2008)

Below: Floyd Reifer was captain in 2009 during the first-choice players' boycott. He made 40 at Warner Park.

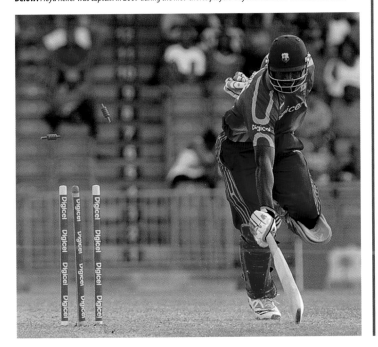

SAINT VINCENT & THE GRENADINES

Black sand and strong rum

St Vincent & The Grenadines are part of the Windward Islands and lie south of St Lucia. The Grenadines are actually a group of small islands including Battowia and Mustique – the haunt of the rich and famous.

Many of the beaches in the area are not the golden ones mostly associated with the Caribbean as St Vincent & The Grenadines are volcanic and many of the resorts have both black and yellow and sand. On St Vincent snorkeling and boat trips are popular whilst those who are feeling fit can hike up to the summit of the La Soufriere volcano. The Grenadines are famous for having some of the best sailing waters in the world.

Kingstown, the capital of St Vincent, has a bustling harbour area, many picturesque 19-century churches and cathedrals, the Botanical Gardens and the impressive Fort Charlotte which overlooks the harbour from a height of 200 metres (656 feet).

The volcanic soil on the island is, according to the locals, extremely fertile and they pride themselves on their local produce such as breadfruit and cassava. The food can be spicy with hot stews and curries popular, which gives an excuse to wash them down with a Hairoun, the local beer, or a Sunset Rum which is distilled on the island. Beware: there are a variety of Sunset Rums with the strongest 84.5 per cent by volume.

Above: *A good float before lunch.* **Below:** *...and then lunch.*

WEATHER	LOW (°C)	HIGH (°C)	RAIN (MM)	SUNSET
January	17	29	125	17.50
February	17	29	100	18.06
March	18	30	100	18.15
April	19	32	81	18.17
May	21	32	102	18.21
June	21	32	223	18.29
July	21	32	225	18.36
August	21	32	275	18.33
September	21	32	251	18.15
October	21	32	225	17.54
November	20	31	225	17.38
December	18	30	203	17.36

3 THINGS YOU MUST DO...

1 LA SOUFRIERE
Take a hike and eat your lunch 1,234 metres (4,048 feet) above St Vincent at the top of La Soufriere volcano (tel: Haze Eco Tours, +1 784 457-8634). Participants must be in good health to take the trip. Not for the faint-hearted.

2 BOTANICAL GARDENS
The National Botanical Gardens (tel: +1 809 457 1003) in Kingstown contain the descendant of one of Captain Bligh's original breadfruit trees. Visitors can also spy the St Vincent Parrot, the national bird of the island.

3 BLACK POINT TUNNEL
Take a trip back in time through this tunnel constructed by slaves in 1815. The tunnel, 110 metres (360 feet) in length, was made to aid sugar transport from the Grand Sable Estate to Byreau. To get there: an hour's drive from Kingstown.

PLAYING FIELDS

Home of the Windward Islands

The Arnos Vale Ground, built in 1996 and commonly known as the Playing Fields, is a multi-purpose stadium used for cricket and football that staged its first Test in 1997 when Sri Lanka and the West Indies played out a draw. Sri Lanka, who finished just 26 runs short of their target, were unlucky with the weather as their run chase was disrupted by rain.

Home of the Windward Islands Cricket Board, which has its offices in the complex, the ground was upgraded ahead of the 2007 World Cup when it hosted warm-up matches featuring England, Bermuda, Zimbabwe and Australia ahead of the tournament.

Arnos Vale underwent extensive renovations, mostly to the east with a double-decker stand for 5,000 spectators being added and a four-tier media centre. The western side of the ground was only altered slightly with minor improvements to the Frank Thomas Pavilion, the Michael Findlay Pavilion and the Sir Philip Viera Pavilion.

Situated next to the Caribbean Sea, this picturesque ground hit the headlines before the World Cup when a plane crashed nearby as the Australia team were practising. The pilot was attempting to land at the ET Joshua Airport, at the north end of the stadium, when the plane went down. Thankfully everyone aboard escaped major injury. The ground also hosts netball, concerts and carnival events.

Below: Nikita Miller, here in one-day action, made his Test debut at The Playing Fields but failed to take a wicket.

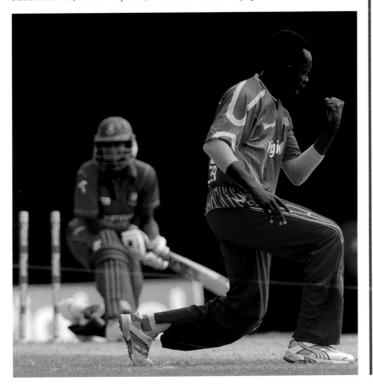

MATTER OF FACT
Ground: Arnos Vale Ground
Capacity: 12,000
Located: Saint Vincent
Address: PO Box 1719, Kingstown, St Vincent
Telephone: +1 784 456 2567
E-mail: dnicholas@windiescricket.com
To get there: buses loop the island
Stands: Michael Findlay Pavilion, FG Thomas Pavilion, Sir Philip Veira Pavilion

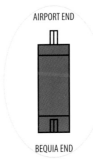

AIRPORT END

BEQUIA END

First Test: West Indies v Sri Lanka 20-24 June 1997
First ODI: West Indies v England 4 February 1981
First Twenty20: N/A

Tests played: 2
West Indies: Won 0, lost 1, drawn 1
Highest team total: 345 (Ban v WI 2009)
Lowest team total: 147 (WI v SL 1997)
Highest individual total: 128 Tamim Iqbal (for Ban v WI 2009)
Highest partnership: 146 (Tamim Iqbal & Junaid Siddique, 2nd wicket for Ban v WI 2009)
Best bowling: 5-26 CL Hooper (for WI v SL 1997)

ODIs played: 17
West Indies: Won 14, lost 3
Highest team total: 313-6 (WI v Eng 1994)
Lowest team total: 117 (Pak v WI 2000)
Highest individual total: 104 BC Lara (for WI v NZ 1996)
Highest partnership: 186 (BC Lara & PV Simmons, 3rd wicket for WI v NZ 1996)
Best bowling: 6-15 CEH Croft (for WI v Eng 1981)

TRINIDAD & TOBAGO

Above: Once a Spanish Colony, Trinidad & Tobago gained Independence from the British in 1962.

Calypso island

Trinidad, the home of calypso, and Tobago are two islands lying just off the east coast of Venezuela, separated from the mainland by the Gulf of Paria. The islands were united politically in 1888 and gained independence in 1962.

Port of Spain, the capital of Trinidad, is a bustling seaport and tourists can get a fairly hostile reception if they venture into the docks. At the centre of the city is Queen's Park Savannah, a large sports field, which is surrounded by the main tourist hotels on the island (such as the Hilton and the Kapok), the Botanical Gardens and several landmarks, including the residences of the President and Prime Minister and the National Museum and Art Gallery.

Cricket lovers will not need any clues as to why Brian Lara Promenade is so named. The street joins with Independence Square and forms one of the most popular places for Trinidadians to grab a beer and lime, as they say, or simply hang out and relax with friends. Many sightseeing tours can also be booked from a number of operators who work out of the area.

To the east of the square is the Cathedral of the Immaculate Conception, while to the west is the Cipriani Statue, a memorial to Arthur Cipriani, a war hero and former Mayor of the city.

There are some top-quality restaurants, many of which have live music, which many locals use as drinking places or they while away the evenings in rum shops or hold impromptu parties in the street whilst listening to steel bands.

Tobago is rated as one of the top places for a beach break in the Caribbean with the best bays found in the north of the island. It is a 25-minute plane journey from Trinidad and a stark contrast to the hustle and bustle of downtown Port of Spain.

3 THINGS YOU MUST DO...

1 MARACAS BAY
Head through the Northern Range Mountains to Maracas Bay, Trinidad's most popular beach. Busy at weekends because of its excellent waves, the area is filled with huts selling food, such as the local favourite, Shark and Bake. To get there: 30-min taxi from Port of Spain (agree price before leaving).

2 ROTI
Rotis are thin flatbreads filled with curried meat and vegetables and have been perfected by the descendants of Indian immigrants on the island. There are hundreds of roti shops in Trinidad. Try Dobson's Roti Shop (Maraval Road, tel: +1 868 628 6141). To get there: near the US Embassy.

3 THE CRICKET WICKET AND THE PELICAN BAR
The Cricket Wicket (149 Tragarete Road, tel: +1 868 628 6766) is a lively bar close to the Queen's Park Oval. The Pelican Bar (2-4 Coblentz Ave, St Ann's, tel +1 868 624 7486) is an English-type pub close to the major tourist hotels, quiet in the week but busy at weekends. When: 11.00–02.00.

Above: The Trinidad and Tobago Carnival is an annual two-day event held before Ash Wednesday.

WEATHER	LOW (°C)	HIGH (°C)	RAIN (MM)	SUNSET
January	20	31	42	17.55
February	20	31	36	18.10
March	21	32	15	18.17
April	22	33	28	18.18
May	23	32	67	18.19
June	23	31	149	18.25
July	24	32	193	18.33
August	24	32	246	18.30
September	23	32	187	18.15
October	23	32	141	17.57
November	22	32	209	17.42
December	21	31	73	17.42

QUEEN'S PARK OVAL

Where cricket history is made

Queen's Park Oval is found just north of Woodbrook, a suburb of Port of Spain in Trinidad, and has the Northern Hills as a stunning backdrop. The stadium is dripping with history having hosted its first Test in 1930, when Patsy Hendren made 205 not out to help England to a win by 167 runs. In 1976 India made a then world record 406 in the fourth innings to beat the mighty West Indies.

England have less pleasant memories of the match played in 1994 when chasing 194 to win they were blown away for 46, their second lowest score of all time, with Curtly Ambrose taking 6-24 in the second innings and only one England batsman, Alec Stewart, reaching double figures.

In 1974 England's Tony Greig inflamed the locals by running out Alvin Kallicharran when most fans thought the day's play had ended. Kallicharran was given out, but re-instated the next day after spectators had laid siege to the pavilion demonstrate at Greig's unsporting conduct. In 1998, after the Jamaica Test was abandoned because of an unfit pitch

Queen's Park Oval stepped in and hosted back-to-back matches against Mike Atherton's England tourists.

For spectators, a day at the Queen's Park Oval is one of the great cricket-watching experiences. Peanut sellers, pie men and children with buckets full of Carib beers roam the terraces, the crowd is full of vocal local fans, blowing conchs and screaming advice to the players of both sides. After play spectators retire to the Cricket Wicket pub over the road to mull over the day's play.

Home of the Queen's Park Cricket Club the playing area is surrounded by a cycle track and has staged carnival contests, boxing, soccer and even appearances by the Harlem Globetrotters.

The ground also boasts the Queen's Park Cricket Heritage Museum, which opened in 2009 and showcases West Indies cricket history. It has the bats Brian Lara made his record scores of 375, 400 and 501 with on display.

Below: West Indian cricketers are famous for their flamboyant cricketing strokes. This one remains unnamed as yet.

MATTER OF FACT

Ground: Queen's Park Oval
Capacity: 25,000
Located: Port of Spain, Trinidad
Address: 94 Tragerete Road, Port of Spain, Trinidad
Telephone: +1 868 622 4325 or +1 868 622 2295
E-mail: ttcricketboard@mail.tt
To get there: Five-min taxi from Port of Spain
Stands: Trini Posse, Jeffrey Stollmeyer, Learie Constantine, Dos Santos

BRIAN LARA PAVILION END

MEDIA CENTRE END

First Test: West Indies v England 1-6 February 1930
First ODI: West Indies v India 9 March 1983
First Twenty20: West Indies v England 15 March 2009

Tests played: 56
West Indies: Won 18, lost 17, drawn 21
Highest team total: 681-8 dec (WI v Eng 1954)
Lowest team total: 46 (Eng v WI 1994)
Highest individual total: 220 SM Gavaskar (for India v WI 1971)
Highest partnership: 338 (EDC Weekes & FMM Worrell, 3rd wicket for WI v Eng 1954)
Best bowling: 9-95 JM Noriega (for WI v Ind 1971)

ODIs played: 59
West Indies: Won 28, lost 17, no result 4, (neutral games 10)
Highest team total: 413-5 (Ind v Ber 2007)
Lowest team total: 75 (Can v Zim 2006)
Highest individual total: 146 not out BC Lara (for WI v NZ 1996)
Highest partnership: 202 (SC Ganguly & V Sehwag, 2nd wicket for Ind v Ber 2007)
Best bowling: 6-25 SC Styris (for NZ v WI 2002)

Above: Grenada was one of the host venues for the 2007 World Cup.

CRICKET NET

Brian Lara, born in 1969, in Santa Cruz, is known as the 'Prince of Trinidad' and is virtually royalty on the island. He made a world record 375 against England in 1994 and when that was beaten he reclaimed it with 400, also against England in 2004. In 1994 he made 501 not out for Warwickshire against Durham.

ZIMBABWE

THE
3
**MINUTE
GUIDE**

Capital: *Harare.* **Languages:** *Shona, Ndebele, English.* **Beers:** *Zambezi, Lion.* **Food:** *Biltong (dried, spiced meat), sadza (porridge) kapenta (fish).* **National Anthem:** *Blessed be the Land of Zimbabwe.* **Population:** *12.5 million.* **Time zone:** *GMT +2.* **Emergency number:** *999.* **Did you know?** *In 1993 more than 500 elephants were moved 250 km (156 miles) in family groups across Zimbabwe. It's the largest elephant relocation ever.* **Cricket body:** *28 Malden Drive, Highlands, PO Box 2739, Harare, Zimbabwe. Tel: +263 4 788 092/3/5. E-mail: info@zimcricket.org. Web: www.zimcricket.org.*

Below: Victoria Falls remains one of the great world sights even at low water.

Dogged by controversy

Since playing its first Test match, against India in 1992, Zimbabwean cricket has been dogged by controversy yet still produced players like Andy Flower, who went from the world's number one batsman to England coach and Heath Streak, who took over 400 international wickets. The country also gave us Duncan Fletcher, who masterminded England's Ashes win in 2005 and led Zimbabwe to a shock win over Australia in the 1983 World Cup and Dave Houghton who hit 266 against Sri Lanka in 1994.

But the development of cricket in the country was handicapped by the ongoing political situation and the reluctance of teams to visit Zimbabwe.

During a 2003 World Cup match against Namibia, Flower and bowler Henry Olonga wore black armbands to protest against the Zimbabwean President Robert Mugabe and mourning 'the death of democracy in Zimbabwe'. Flower and Olonga then retired from international cricket and fled the country. In 2004 captain Streak was sacked and a self-imposed one-year suspension from Test cricket followed after Zimbabwe were forced into fielding weakened teams but when they came back they were even weaker. They played their last Test in 2005, although continue to play one-day internationals with limited success. By 2009 they were pushing for reinstatement into the five-day game. In 2007 the Australian government blocked their team's tour of the country following the lead of other countries who refused to travel to Zimbabwe because of the political situation.

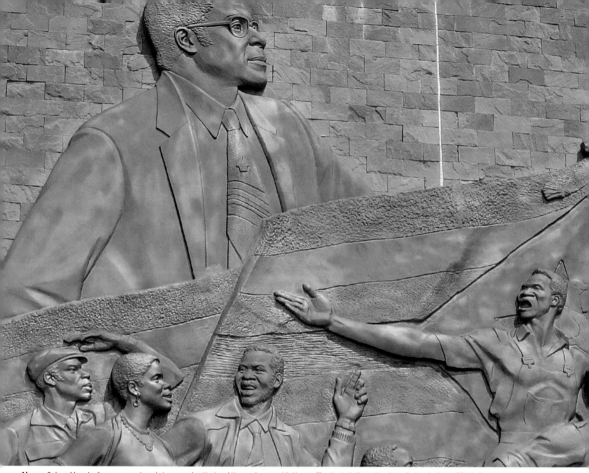

Above: Robert Mugabe features prominently in a mural at National Heroes Acre outside Harare. The site is dedicated to those declared a hero of Zimbabwe.

TEST RECORD

Versus	First Test	Matches	Won	Lost	Drawn
Australia	Oct 1999	3	0	3	0
Bangladesh	Apr 2001	8	4	1	3
England	Dec 1996	6	0	3	3
India	Oct 1992	11	2	7	2
New Zealand	Nov 1992	13	0	7	6
Pakistan	Dec 1993	14	2	8	4
South Africa	Oct 1995	7	0	6	1
Sri Lanka	Oct 1994	15	0	10	5
West Indies	Mar 2000	6	0	4	2

Most runs: A Flower (1992-2002) 4,794 runs, 63 Tests, average 51.55
Most wickets: HH Streak (1993-2005) 216 wickets, 65 Tests, average 28.14
Most catches: A Flower (1992-2002)151 catches, 63 Tests

WORLD CUP RECORD

Year	Venue	Finished
1975	England	Not eligible
1979	England	Not eligible
1983	England	Pool
1987	India and Pakistan	Pool
1992	Australia and N Zealand	Pool
1996	Ind, Pak and S Lanka	Pool
1999	England	5th
2003	South Africa	6th
2007	West Indies	Pool

Most ODI runs: A Flower (1992-2003) 6,786 runs, 213 matches, average 35.34
Most ODI wickets: HH Streak (1993-2005) 239 wickets, 189 matches, average 29.83
Most ODI catches: A Flower (1992-2003) 141 catches, 213 matches

HARARE

Worn but not torn

From a distance the many parks, wide streets and mid-rise buildings give Harare a vibrant, prosperous air. Look a little closer, though, and the wear and tear of years of economic problems will show clearly. For years the difficulties of living in this city have been documented – hyperinflation, lack of petrol, foreign currency and other basic goods, all followed from economic and political turmoil. In 2009 this was named the worst city to live in according to *The Economist*'s Liveability Index. It's no wonder visitor numbers dropped – and yet there are enough attractions such as restaurants, nightlife, wildlife, golf courses and, (a short plane trip away) Victoria Falls to keep some people returning.

Zimbabwe's capital city, known as Salisbury until 1982, is home to more than 1.5 million people, with many more living in the larger metropolitan area.

One of the main roads running through the downtown area is Sam Nujoma Street (formerly Second). It is along here and the roads feeding off it that you will find many of the city landmarks including the main train station, African Unity Square, the High County and Harare Gardens.

Harare Sports Club is centrally located, about 2 km (1 mile) north of the main train station.

Above: *The Harare skyline.* ***Below:*** *Zimbabwe art.*

WEATHER	LOW (°C)	HIGH (°C)	RAIN (MM)	SUNSET
January	16	26	204	18.35
February	16	26	178	18.37
March	15	26	119	18.21
April	13	25	24	17.58
May	9	23	13	17.36
June	8	21	4	17.27
July	7	20	0	17.32
August	8	23	3	17.42
September	13	26	5	17.50
October	14	29	29	17.53
November	16	27	97	18.01
December	16	26	163	18.18

3 THINGS YOU MUST DO...

1 MEIKLES HOTEL

If you're after a bit of luxury, visit one of the city's premier hotels (Jason Moyo Ave, tel: +263 4 251705) that opened in 1915. Grab a beer in the relaxed pub setting of the Explorer's Club. When: daily 10.00–22.30.

2 KEG & MAIDEN

Part of a chain that operates in South Africa offering a good pub atmosphere (Harare Sports Club, Josiah Tongogara Ave, tel: +263 4 700 037) with pub food favourites like bangers and mash and steak, egg and chips. When: daily. To get there: it's at the Sports Club.

3 ONE HUNDRED TRILLION DOLLARS

By 2009 US dollars was the de facto currency (South African Rand and Euros also accepted) of the country. The Zim dollar was put on hold as hyper-inflation took off in the mid-2000s. Try to find one of the 100 trillion dollar notes that were issued briefly at the start of 2009. Yes, it has a lot of zeros.

HARARE SPORTS CLUB

Where it all started for Zim cricket

The Harare Sports Club, found a short walk from the centre of Harare, is directly opposite the heavily-guarded Zimbabwe House, the home of president, Robert Mugabe, and next to Royal Harare Golf Club, considered one of the best courses in Africa.

This picturesque ground is surrounded by jacaranda trees and became the first Test venue in the country when India visited in 1992. The game ended in a draw but only after Dave Houghton had become Zimbabwe's first Test centurion after making 121.

In 1995 it was the scene of Zimbabwe's first Test win when Pakistan were beaten by an innings and 64 runs and the Flower brothers, Grant and Andy, scored 201 and 156 respectively.

Home to the Zimbabwe Cricket Union, the stadium was due to host three matches during the 2003 Cricket World Cup, but only staged two as England refused to travel to Harare and forfeited their match against Zimbabwe, citing security concerns.

The ground's capacity can be increased by the use of temporary stands and the main gathering point is the Pavilion, a Dutch-gabled structure, whilst the other end is home to Castle Corner, the liveliest part of Harare Sports Club. In common with many grounds in southern Africa, the barbecues are constantly being fired up, with steak sandwiches the local speciality. The Keg & Maiden pub that forms part of the Sports Club, which serves simple bar meals, is a popular gathering place and is filled with memorabilia commemorating games played at the ground.

Below: Harare Sports Club, scene of Zimbabwe's first Test match in 1992.

MATTER OF FACT
Ground: Harare Sports Club
Capacity: 10,000
Located: Harare, Zimbabwe
Address: Josiah Tongogara Avenue, Harare, Zimbabwe
Telephone: +263 4 704 616
E-mail: hsc@zol.co.zw or lovemoreb@zimcricket.org
To get there: Five-minute taxi from city centre
Stands: Castle Corner, Pavilion

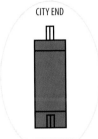

First Test: Zimbabwe v India 18–22 October 1992
First ODI: Zimbabwe v India 25 October 1992
First Twenty20: N/A

Tests played: 26
Zimbabwe: Won 5, lost 13, drawn 8
Highest team total: 600-3 dec (SA v Zim 2001)
Lowest team total: 59 (Zim v NZ 2005)
Highest individual total: 220 G Kirsten (for SA v Zim 2001)
Highest partnership: 281 (MS Atapattu & ST Jayasuriya, 1st wicket for SL v Zim 2004)
Best bowling: 8-71 AA Donald (for SA v Zim 1995)

ODIs played: 88
Zimbabwe: Won 24, lost 58, tied 1, no result 1, (neutral games 4)
Highest team total: 340-2 (Zim v Nam 2003)
Lowest team total: 35 (Zim v SL 2004)
Highest individual total: 178 not out H Masakadza (for Zim v Ken 2009)
Highest partnership: 186 (JA Morkel & AB de Villiers, 3rd wicket for SA v Zim 2007)
Best bowling: 6-22 FH Edwards (for WI v Zim 2003)

BULAWAYO

Home of the Matabele

Bulawayo is Zimbabwe's second city and the heartbeat of Matabeleland. It has wide roads lined with trees and enjoys a much more relaxed atmosphere than the capital Harare. It has traditionally been the base for opposition to Robert Mugabe's rule over the years and some argue that because of that it has suffered from a lack of government support and investment in recent years.

The downtown area is small and easily navigable, with landmarks such as City Hall, the High Court, the Museum of Natural History and the Bulawayo Centre (for shopping) all close together. To the southeast is a large parkland area and next to this the city suburbs (called, wait for it, The Suburbs).

Bulawayo was originally established as the capital of the Ndebele people by King Mzilikazi, a leader who originally fought with Skaka, but after a falling out he trekked north from Zululand. Although Mzilikazi is generally regarded a great leader, he was also ruthless and the name Bulawayo comes from a word which means 'the place of slaughter'.

Above: *The Zambezi River offers great water rafting.* **Below:** *Zimbabwe is renowned for its sculpture.*

WEATHER	LOW (°C)	HIGH (°C)	RAIN (MM)	SUNSET
January	17	27	142	18.49
February	16	27	103	18.47
March	15	26	85	18.32
April	13	26	18	18.06
May	9	23	12	17.44
June	6	20	3	17.33
July	7	21	0	17.38
August	9	23	0	17.50
September	13	27	5	17.57
October	15	29	23	18.04
November	16	29	81	18.16
December	16	28	122	18.32

3 THINGS YOU MUST DO...

1 MATOBO NATIONAL PARK
Amazing rock formations and rock paintings, a good chance to see leopards, plus at World's View the grave of Sir John Cecil Rhodes. Price: US$10. To get there: 52 km (32 miles) to the south of Bulawayo.

2 VICTORIA FALLS
Quite simply one of the modern wonders of the world. Go white water rafting (Shearwater, tel: +263 13 44471/2/3) scream and get wet. Price: US$110 full day. To get there: 400 km (250 miles) to the northwest of Bulawayo.

3 MUSEUM OF NATURAL HISTORY
An excellent museum (Cnr Takawira and Park Rds) with good information, especially on the country's animals. When: daily 09.00-17.00. Price: US$2. To get there: it's by Centenary Park.

QUEEN'S SPORTS CLUB

Runs, records and runs

The Queen's Sports Club, established in 1894, is close to the city centre of Bulawayo, and staged its first Test in 1994, becoming cricket's 73rd venue with the visit of Sri Lanka. Test cricket at the stadium had looked unlikely as no first-class games had been played there since 1984 as the arena slipped into disrepair and big games were staged at Bulawayo Athletic Club. However, the Matabele Cricket Association realized that the Sports Club had potential to be a better international venue and instigated a programme of renovations to bring the ground up to standard.

The ground is one of two to host home matches for the Matabeleland cricket team which was captained by Heath Streak, who took 37 Test wickets there.

Dave Houghton made 266 for Zimbabwe in the inaugural Test match which was drawn and in 1996 the ground staged a thrilling match involving England, which finished with the scores level after Nick Knight was run out off the final ball going for the third run which would have won the game. That day is famous for the Zimbabwean bowlers, legitimately, bowling wide and the touring coach David Lloyd claiming 'we murdered them'.

In 2009, Charles Coventry equalled the world record for runs in a one-day international by scoring 194 not out for Zimbabwe. It was still not enough as Bangladesh overhauled the hosts score of 312 with 13 balls to spare.

The Sports Club, which hosted three games in the 2003 Cricket World Cup, is surrounded by grassy embankments with trees providing welcome shelter from the sun.

Below: Grant Flower played in 62 Test matches and 219 one-day internationals for Zimbabwe.

MATTER OF FACT
Ground: Queen's Sports Club
Capacity: 9,000
Located: Bulawayo, Zimbabwe
Address: Corner 1st Avenue and George Silundika Road, Bulawayo
Telephone: +263 9 880 453
E-mail: lovemoreb@zimcricket.org
To get there: Five-min taxi from city centre

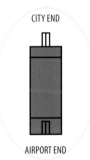

First Test: Zimbabwe v Sri Lanka 20-24 October 1994
First ODI: Zimbabwe v England 15 December 1996
First Twenty20: N/A

Tests played: 17
Zimbabwe: Won 1, lost 9, drawn 7
Highest team total: 713-3 dec (SL v Zim 2004)
Lowest team total: 104 (Zim v WI 2003)
Highest individual total: 270 KC Sangakkara (for SL v Zim 2004)
Highest partnership: 438 (KC Sangakkara & MS Atapattu, 2nd wicket for SL v Zim 2004)
Best bowling: 8-109 PA Strang (for Zim v NZ 2000)

ODIs played: 42
Zimbabwe: Won 10, lost 27, tied 1, no result 2, (neutral games 2)
Highest team total: 397-5 (NZ v Zim 2005)
Lowest team total: 125 (WI v Zim 2003)
Highest individual total: 194 not out CK Coventry (for Zim v Ban 2009)
Highest partnership: 204 (SP Fleming & L Vincent, 1st wicket for NZ v Zim 2005)
Best bowling: 6-19 SE Bond (for NZ v Ind 2005)

CANADA

Cricket's longest rivalry

Below: Hiral Patel (left) and Zain Mahmood of Canada during the 2010 U19 World Cup.

Canada may not be in the top-flight of cricket but they boast the longest rivalry in the sport at international level having played the game against their neighbours, the United States, since 1844. The two teams now play for the KA Auty trophy, named after one of the driving forces of American cricket.

The Canadian side has traditionally relied on descendants of Asian and West Indian immigrants for their playing base. A Division One associate member of the International Cricket Council, Canada qualified for the 2011 Cricket World Cup, only the third time they had made it to the tournament – and are regarded as one of the best non-Test playing countries in the world.

Recent stars of Canadian cricket include John Davison, who made the fastest century in World Cup history when he decimated the West Indian bowling, hitting 111 in 76 balls, including six sixes at Centurion Park in South Africa, and wicket-keeper/batsman Ashish Bagai, born in India, who played for the Canada Under-19 side at the age of 15.

Canada has also hosted many one-day matches between India and Pakistan in Toronto, including one in 1997 when the Pakistani batsman Inzamam-ul-Haq attacked a spectator for calling him a 'fat potato'. Canada is pushing to be used as a neutral venue for matches between other nations.

WORLD CUP RECORD

Year	Venue	Finished
1975	England	Not eligible
1979	England	1st round
1983	England	Did not qualify
1987	India and Pakistan	Did not qualify
1992	Australia and N Zealand	Did not qualify
1996	Ind, Pak and S Lanka	Did not qualify
1999	England	Did not qualify
2003	South Africa	Pool
2007	West Indies	Pool

MATTER OF FACT
Governing body: Cricket Canada
Address: 3 Concorde Gate, Suite 301, Toronto, ON M3C 3N7
Telephone: +1 416 426 7209
E-mail: cricketcanada@gmail.com

International Grounds
Toronto Cricket, Skating and Curling Club
First ODI: India v Pakistan 16 September 1996

Maple Leaf North-West Ground, King City
First ODI: Canada v Bermuda 28 June 2008
First Twenty20: Sri Lanka v Zimbabwe 10 October 2008

One-day records
Most runs: A Bagai (2003-)
1,197 runs, 43 matches, average 32.35
Most wickets: S Dhaniram (2003-)
41 wickets, 38 matches, average 26.90
Most catches: A Bagai (2003-)
45 catches, 43 matches

ICC Trophy best finish
Runners-up 1979

IRELAND

Pushing for a step up

Below: Ireland playing against Essex at Castle Avenue in Dublin.

When a largely part-time Ireland team qualified for the World Cup for the first time in 2007, no-one expected them to last beyond the first stage. But a St Patrick's Day win over Pakistan, inspired by the bat of Niall O'Brien, who scored 72 not out, sent Bob Woolmer's men home and Ireland into the Super 8s. Prior to that success, the most famous day in Irish cricket came on 2 July 1969 when they beat the touring West Indies by nine wickets after bowling a side including Clive Lloyd and Basil Butcher out for 25.

Cricket has been played in Ireland since the early 1800s, and Ireland was included in the Gillette Cup in 1980 and the Benson & Hedges Cup in 1994. A win in the ICC Trophy followed in 2005 and their first one-day international, against England, in 2006.

The Irish national side has struggled to keep hold of its better players such as Ed Joyce and Eoin Morgan, who threw in their lot with England, but after their success in the 2007 World Cup they were pushing for Test status which would enable them to retain their stars.

WORLD CUP RECORD

Year	Venue	Finished
1975	England	Not eligible
1979	England	Not eligible
1983	England	Not eligible
1987	India and Pakistan	Not eligible
1992	Australia and N Zealand	Not eligible
1996	Ind, Pak and S Lanka	Did not qualify
1999	England	Did not qualify
2003	South Africa	Did not qualify
2007	West Indies	8th

MATTER OF FACT
Governing body: Cricket Ireland
Address: Unit 22, Grattan Business Park, Clonshaugh, Dublin 17
Telephone: +353 1 894 7914
E-mail: info@irshcricket.org

International Grounds
Civil Service Cricket Club, Belfast
First ODI: Ireland v England 13 June 2006
First Twenty20: Kenya v Netherlands 2 August 2008

Castle Avenue, Dublin
First ODI: Bangladesh v West Indies 21 May 1999

One-day Records
Most runs: WTS Porterfield (2006–)
1,150 runs, 37 matches, average 33.82
Most wickets: WK McCallan (2006–)
39 wickets, 39 matches, average 30.97
Most catches: NJ O'Brien (2006–)
24 catches, 34 matches

ICC Trophy (ICC WC Qualifier) Best Finish
Winners 2009

KENYA

World Cup surprises

Colonial settlers took cricket to Kenya with a three-day match between Officials and Settlers starting in 1910, the MCC toured in 1957-58, led by Freddie Brown, and some Kenyan players played in the 1975 World Cup as part of the East Africa side. Don Pringle, the father of Derek, who played Test cricket for England, was also part of that side.

In 1996 Kenya beat the West Indies during the World Cup but did not make it out of their pool. In 2003 they stunned the cricket world by reaching the semi-finals in South Africa. In that tournament they managed wins over Canada, Sri Lanka and Bangladesh whilst New Zealand forfeited their game over security concerns. A win over Zimbabwe in the Super Six stage saw them through but they were well beaten by India in the semi-final.

Disputes between the board and players led to strikes but the rows left Kenya without sponsors and floundering and they were stripped of their one-day international status in 2005. The rebuilding started with the formation of a new governing body, Cricket Kenya, but that was hit by controversy when chief executive Tom Tikolo resigned after allegedly misappropriating funds.

Along the way Kenya have produced players such as Collins Obuya, a batsman-spinner who played for Warwickshire and starred in the 2003 World Cup and Steve Tikolo, probably their best batsman.

Below: Medium-fast bowler Elijah Otieno made his international debut v Canada in 2007.

WORLD CUP RECORD

Year	Venue	Finished
1975	England	1st round*
1979	England	Did not qualify*
1983	England	Did not qualify
1987	India and Pakistan	Did not qualify
1992	Australia and N Zealand	Did not qualify
1996	Ind, Pak and S Lanka	Pool
1999	England	Pool
2003	South Africa	Semi-final
2007	West Indies	Pool

* As part of East Africa

MATTER OF FACT
Governing body: Cricket Kenya
Address: Ruaraka Sports Club, Utalii Lane, off Thika Road, PO Box 16962, Nairobi, Kenya
Telephone: +254 2 675 2895/2899/2958
E-mail: inamdar@africaonline.co.ke

International Grounds
Mombasa Sports Club Ground
First ODI: Kenya v Bermuda 11 Nov 2006

Jaffery Sports Club Ground, Nairobi
First ODI: Kenya v Bermuda 29 Jan 2007

Gymkhana Club Ground, Nairobi
First ODI: Kenya v Sri Lanka 28 Sept 1996

Ruaraka Sports Club Ground, Nairobi
First ODI: Canada v Netherlands 30 Jan 2007

One-day records
Most runs: SO Tikolo (1996-)
3,304 runs, 126 matches, average 29.76
Most wickets: TM Odoyo (1996-)
120 wickets, 115 matches, average 30.72
Most catches: KO Otieno (1996-)
43 catches, 90 matches

ICC Trophy (ICC WC Qualifier) Best Finish
Semi-finals 1990, 2009

NETHERLANDS

A country on the fringe

Below: Roland Lefebvre (left), just one of the Dutch players who have impressed in England.

One of the most popular sports in the Netherlands in the mid-1800s, cricket has been overtaken by soccer, cycling, tennis and the like but there are still over 6,000 players in the country.

The Dutch beat an England team, including future England captains Nasser Hussain and Alec Stewart, in 1989 and in 2009 caused a major shock in the World Twenty20 by beating the hosts, Paul Collingwood's England, by four wickets at Lord's. In 1964 an Australian team, including Bill Lawry, were beaten by three wickets at The Hague.

An associate member of the ICC since 1966, the Netherlands won the ICC Trophy in 2001, were runners-up in 1986 and 1990 and have played in the English domestic one-day competition. They were excluded from this in 2005 but invited back by the England and Wales Cricket Board for the 2010 season. In 2009 the Dutch finished third in the qualifying tournament to make it to the sub-continent for the 2011 World Cup with Edgar Schiferli being named player of the tournament after taking 24 wickets.

Several Dutchmen have made an impact on the English county scene, with the likes of Dirk Nannes, Roland Lefebvre and Ryan ten Doeschate all impressing on the English County Cricket circuit.

WORLD CUP RECORD

Year	Venue	Finished
1975	England	Not eligible
1979	England	Did not qualify
1983	England	Did not qualify
1987	India and Pakistan	Did not qualify
1992	Australia and N Zealand	Did not qualify
1996	Ind, Pak and S Lanka	Pool
1999	England	Did not qualify
2003	South Africa	Pool
2007	West Indies	Pool

MATTER OF FACT

Governing body: Royal Dutch Cricket Association/Koninklijke Nederlandse Cricket Bond
Address: Wattbaan 31-49, 3439 ML Nieuwegein, The Netherlands
Telephone: +31 30 7513 780
E-mail: cricket@kncb.nl

International Grounds
VRA Cricket Ground, Amstelveen
First ODI: Kenya v South Africa 26 May 1999

Hazelaarweg, Rotterdam
First ODI: Netherlands v Bermuda 18 August 2007

One-day records
Most runs: RN ten Doeschate (2006-) 1,026 runs, 24 matches, average 64.12
Most wickets: RN ten Doeschate (2006-) 44 wickets, 24 matches, average 20.86
Most catches: J Smits (2003-) 41 catches, 38 matches

ICC Trophy best finish
Winners 2001

SCOTLAND

A long history of cricket

Scotland has produced several fine cricketers who have represented England such as Douglas Jardine, captain during the 'Bodyline' Series of 1932-33, Mike Denness, Dougie Brown and Gavin Hamilton. Scotland played their first full match, against Surrey, in 1865, beat Australia in 1882 and competed in English domestic one-day cricket from 1980. The first recorded match in Scotland actually took place in 1785 so it predates football in the country as an organized sport.

In 1994 Scotland gained associate membership of the ICC and won the 2005 ICC Trophy, beating Ireland in the final and competed in the 1999 and 2007 Cricket World Cups.

In December 2008 Cricket Scotland gave their first full-time central contracts to captain Ryan Watson and bowlers Dewald Nel and Gordon Goudie. In 2010 the ICC confirmed that the qualifying tournament for the 2015 Cricket World Cup would be held in Scotland in 2013.

Grange Cricket Club in Edinburgh hosted Scotland's first home one-day international in the 1999 World Cup against Bangladesh in 1999 and is one of the most picturesque grounds in the country. The club was founded in 1832 and hosted the touring Australians in 2009.

Below: Dewald Nel is one of the Scotland players who was awarded a central contract in 2008.

WORLD CUP RECORD

Year	Venue	Finished
1975	England	Not eligible
1979	England	Not eligible
1983	England	Not eligible
1987	India and Pakistan	Not eligible
1992	Australia and N Zealand	Not eligible
1996	Ind, Pak and S Lanka	Not eligible
1999	England	Not eligible
2003	South Africa	Did not qualify
2007	West Indies	Pool

MATTER OF FACT
Governing body: Cricket Scotland
Address: MES Sports Centre, Ravelston, Edinburgh EH4 3NT
Telephone: +44 131 313 7420
E-mail: benfox@cricketscotland.com

International Grounds
Titwood, Glasgow
First ODI: India v Pakistan 3 July 2007

Mannofield Park, Aberdeen
First ODI: Ireland v New Zealand 1 July 2008

Grange Cricket Club, Edinburgh
First ODI: Scotland v Bang 24 May 1999

Cambusdoon New Ground
First ODI: Scotland v Ireland 5 August 2006

One-day records
Most runs: GM Hamilton (1999-)
1,150 runs, 35 matches, average 35.93
Most wickets: JAR Blain (1999-)
41 wickets, 33 matches, average 28.60
Most catches: CJO Smith (2006-)
22 catches, 27 matches

ICC Trophy (ICC WC Qualifier) Best Finish
Winners 2005

UAE

ICC headquarters

Below: Abu Dhabi's Sheikh Zayed Stadium.

The United Arab Emirates cricket team are one of Asia's strongest non-Test teams, won the ACC Trophy four times between 2000 and 2006, the ICC Trophy in 1994 and took part in the 1996 Cricket World Cup.

The area has become known for staging neutral matches in some high-quality stadiums. The Sharjah Cricket Association Stadium hosted the region's first Test match, between Pakistan and the West Indies in 2002 and one-day internationals from 1984. However since the opening of the Sheikh Zayed Stadium in Abu Dhabi it has been overtaken as the area's foremost international venue.

The Sheikh Zayed Stadium cost over US$22 million to build and was nominated by the MCC to replace Lord's as the venue for English cricket's season opener between the champion county, Durham, and the MCC in 2010. The location of the UAE makes it an ideal place to stage neutral matches and in 2009 Pakistan and Australia played a one-day series there and several English counties have played pre-season matches in the area.

The International Cricket Council moved their offices from Lord's to Dubai in 2005 for tax reasons.

WORLD CUP RECORD

Year	Venue	Finished
1975	England	Not eligible
1979	England	Not eligible
1983	England	Not eligible
1987	India and Pakistan	Not eligible
1992	Australia and N Zealand	Did not enter
1996	Ind, Pak and S Lanka	Pool
1999	England	Did not qualify
2003	South Africa	Did not qualify
2007	West Indies	Did not qualify

MATTER OF FACT
Governing body: Emirates Cricket Board
Address: Zayed Cricket Stadium, PO Box 31523, Abu Dhabi UAE
Telephone: +971 255 81331
E-mail: dmani@eim.ae

International Grounds
Sheikh Zayed Stadium, Abu Dhabi
First ODI: India v Pakistan 18 April 2006

Sharjah Cricket Association Stadium
First Test: Pakistan v West Indies 31 January–4 February 2002
First ODI: Pakistan v Sri Lanka 6 April 1984

Dubai International Cricket Stadium
First ODI: Australia v Pakistan 22 April 2009

One-day records
Most runs: Mazhar Hussain (1994-96)
179 runs, 7 matches, average 25.57
Most wickets: Khurram Khan (2004-08)
7 wickets, 4 matches, average 30.42
Most catches: Imtiaz Abbasi (1994-96)
4 catches, 7 matches

ICC Trophy (ICC WC Qualifier) Best Finish
Winners 1994

OTHER CRICKET COUNTRIES

AFGHANISTAN
Address: *National Youth Cricket Stadium, Kabul Nandari, Kabul, Afghanistan*
Telephone: *+93 786 487 885*
Email: *ceo@afghancricket.af*
Web: *www.afgcric.com (under construction)*

ARGENTINA
Address: *Paraguay 1270 PB B Capital Federal, 1057 Buenos Aires, Argentina*
Telephone: *+54 11 4816 4783*
Email: *admin@cricketargentina.com*
Web: *www.cricketargentina.com*

BERMUDA
Address: *PO Box HM 992, Hamilton, HM DX*
Telephone: *+1 441 292 8958*
Fax: *+1 441 292 8959*
Email: *info@cricket.bm*
Web: *www.bermudacricketboard.com*

BAHAMAS
Address: *PO Box N10101, Nassau, Bahamas*
Telephone: *+1 242 328 3019*
Email: *firstslip@hotmail.com*

CAYMAN ISLANDS
Address: *PO Box 1201, Grand Cayman KY1, 1108, Cayman Islands*
Telephone: *+1 345 945 6447*
Email: *cicaadmin@candw.ky*

DENMARK
Address: *Idraettens Hus DK 2605 Broendby, Denmark, DK 2605*
Telephone: *+45 43 262 160*
Email: *dcf@cricket.dk*
Web: *www.cricket.dk*

GIBRALTAR
Address: *23 Merlot House, The Vineyards, Gibraltar*
Telephone: *+350 735 82*
Fax: *+ 350 735 82*
Email: *Use contact form on website*
Web: *www.cricketeurope.net/GIBRALTAR/index.shtml*

HONG KONG
Address: *1019 Olympic House 1 Stadium Path, So Kon Po Causeway Bay, Hong Kong*
Telephone: *+852 2504 8101/2*
Email: *hkca@hkabc.net*
Web: *www.hkca.cricket.org*

ISRAEL
Address: *PO Box 65085 Tel Aviv 61650*
Telephone: *+972 3 642 5529*
Email: *sperlman@internet-zahav.net*
Web: *www.israel.cricket.org*

JAPAN
Address: *1-1-18 Toyama, Shinjuku-ku Tokyo 162-0052, Japan*
Telephone: *+ 81 3 6801 7721*
Email: *s-tomita@cricket.or.jp or n-miyaji@cricket.or.jp*
Web: *www.cricket.or.jp/eng/*

MALAYSIA
Address: *Lot 105866-1, Jalan, BK 5A/1, Bandar Kinrara 47100 Puchong Selangor, Malaysia*
Telephone: *+60 3 8070 8079 or +60 3 8070 8075*
Email: *crikmal@tm.net.my*
Web: *www.malaysiacricket.com*

NAMIBIA
Address: *9 Love Street, Windhoek, Namibia*
Telephone: *+264 81 122 5551*
Email: *cricket@iway.na*
Web: *www.cricketnamibia.com*

NEPAL
Address: *GPO Box 20291, Anarghar, Krishnadhara Marg Panipokhar, Kathmandu, Nepal*
Telephone: *+977 1 441 5122 or +977 1 442 0925*
Email: *tpaneru@gmail.com*
Web: *www.cricketnepal.org/*

SINGAPORE
Address: *31 Stadium Crescent, Singapore 397639*
Telephone: *+65 6348 6566*
Email: *cricket@singnet.com.sg*
Web: *www.cricket.org.sg*

UGANDA
Address: *c/o National Council of Sports Headquarters, Lugogo Stadium, PO Box 8346 Kampala, Uganda*
Telephone: *+256 312 264 916*
Email: *ugandacricket@utlonline.co.ug or mpekam@yahoo.com*

USA
Address: *429 Lenox Avenue, Suite P405 Miami Beach, FL 33139 USA*
Telephone: *+1 305 537 3764*
Email: *dlockerbie@usaca.org*
Web: *www.usaca.org*